WHY SHOULD WHITE GUYS HAVE ALL THE WEALTH?

WHY SHOULD WHITE GUYS HAVE ALL THE WEALTH?

How You Can Become a Millionaire Starting From the Bottom

CEDRIC NASH

HOUNDSTOOTH
PRESS

Why Should White Guys Have All the Wealth?

How to Become a Millionaire (And Beyond) Starting from the Bottom

ISBN   978-1-5445-3649-1 *Hardcover*

        978-1-5445-3650-7 *Paperback*

        978-1-5445-3651-4 *Ebook*

        978-1-5445-3652-1 *Audiobook*

To John L. Nash and the late Rosa A. Nash,
it was miraculous to be born your son.
Your love and guidance have made all the difference in my life.

To my kids Taylor, Tyler, Johnathon, and Bryana,
you will forever be my muse. I hope I've made you proud.

To the late Reginald Lewis (and his family),
whose timeless book, Why Should White Guys Have All the Fun,
is the inspiration for my book title and showed Black people
what's possible to achieve in business.

I hope this book shows us what's possible in building wealth

CONTENTS

INTRODUCTION

"It doesn't matter how much money you make.
If you can't manage a little bit of money,
you won't be able to manage
a lot of money."

—ROSA A. NASH

The overwhelming majority of wealth in this country (84 percent) is in the hands of White households. Black households, on the other hand, own an estimated 4 percent of that enormous wealth pie. So, I ask you: why should White guys have all the wealth? There's no doubt White folks had a huge head start over us. They've benefited enormously from four hundred-plus years of free labor through slavery, and now they control the majority of the capital and income-producing assets. Meanwhile, Black folks have been and continue to be discriminated against in employment, housing, education, income, banking, access to capital, and throughout the criminal justice system.

But this book isn't about calling out and reminding us what "they" did or continue to do. It's about providing you with a road map for what you can do to build wealth *in spite of the odds.* My mission is to show you how to get yours—concretely—by creating your wealth journey, even if you're starting from the bottom. I and countless other Black folks have learned how to build real wealth using a systematic and specific approach that is short on empty promises and long on techniques that can work for anyone. I'll show you how to take what you have, earn considerably more, build up your investment capital, and make what I call Millionaire Money Moves (M$M) to accumulate appreciating assets that generate income and wealth. It won't happen quickly, but it will happen most assuredly. Although it will take time to build significant wealth, the lessons you patiently learn in these pages will not only bear fruit in the long term, but they will also serve as the foundation for genuine generational wealth that you and your loved ones can continue building upon for years to come.

There are far too many so-called prosperity experts out there who prey on the Black community, promising us fast, effortless riches if we'll only invest in ourselves by, of all things, signing up for their seminars and conferences. Yet, after we've plopped down their hefty entrance fees, in hopes of learning the secrets to creating vast riches, we inevitably wind up more broke than before, having learned that there *is* no secret to building wealth. There's only effort and sacrifice. Sadly, these scam artists target our community time and again in a cynical attempt to leverage the by-products of systemic racism and discrimination—namely, our pain and discord.

I'm here to keep it real with you. My wealth-building system and approach ain't easy, it ain't fast, and it sure as hell ain't free. Matter of fact, it's difficult, slow, and frequently frustrating. But what makes this method so different from the others is that, if it's done consistently over time, it will work for you no matter who you are, what you look like, where you live, where you're starting from, how much money you have or make, or what you think the government may someday do. Your race, faith, age, education, family background, or current level of income are unimportant. I'm not saying they don't matter; I'm just saying that your financial fate will be in your hands and yours alone. If that sounds like a reasonable trade-off, then please read on.

My method is based on what I call Value and Behavior Transformation. It's a completely different lens through which to look at wealth building, based on prioritizing and practicing the value system that goes along with becoming and remaining a millionaire. What you learn about those values along the way may surprise you. Wealth building is like a muscle; it takes time to develop, and it develops incrementally rather than all at once. The same is true of the values that go along with wealth building. Traits like frugality, restraint, investment, and deferred gratification are hard to learn, master, and enjoy. Change is never fast or easy, and when it comes to money, which is so deeply connected to our emotions and the people with whom we surround ourselves, change is tougher still.

I believe our financial situation as a community, and in many cases as individuals, is a result not only of our money values and behaviors but something more. While we must continue to do everything possible to eradicate the impacts of slavery, discrimination, and oppression, our overall financial position continues to lag dramatically. Changing what we do with what we have, on the other hand, is well within our control and can have an immediate impact on our financial fate. Our money behaviors are the shadow, if you will, of our money values (priorities). Change those values and the behaviors will obediently follow suit. The process is honestly that simple. This book is intended to help you with the execution of that process because, let's face it, our money values have been baked in by what we've seen all our lives in our immediate families, among our relatives, in our neighborhoods, and in our places of worship. They're reinforced daily by the various media we consume, be it movies, television, music, social media, and so on. Even the people we choose to marry affect our money values.

Changing your money values and behaviors will allow you to regularly make Millionaire Money Moves. When done consistently over time, they will turn you into a millionaire in name, deed, and best of all, bottom line. Mindset development is required too; without it, you won't be able to complete the Value and Behavior Transformation process nor make Millionaire Money Moves long enough for them to be effective. More on that in Chapter 5.

My wealth-building system is based on three central components:

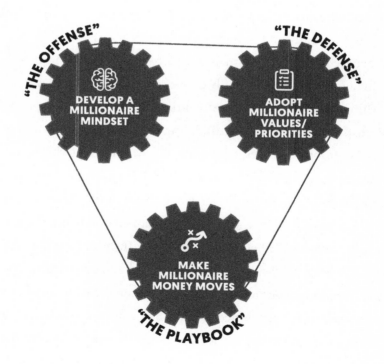

MILLIONAIRE MONEY MOVES
Wealth Building System

"THE OFFENSE"

"THE DEFENSE"

DEVELOP A
MILLIONAIRE
MINDSET

ADOPT
MILLIONAIRE
VALUES/
PRIORITIES

MAKE
MILLIONAIRE
MONEY MOVES

"THE PLAYBOOK"

1. Developing a Millionaire Mindset
2. Adopting Millionaire Values and Behaviors
3. Making Millionaire Money Moves

Change in your financial life can happen. The payoff in making that change is the freedom to live your life on your own terms, using money as a tool instead of allowing money to control or stress you out. What's central to my method is a process for building wealth that works hand in hand with a process for refining your money values in order to stay the course. You will learn the critical role that mentorship can play in your financial growth and not only how to find the right mentors but how to prepare yourself to be mentored once you find them. Whatever you gain from using my methods—money, knowledge, or experience—I will show you how to use it to continuously further your financial goals.

What do I mean by financial goals? I'm glad you asked, though that's one of the many aspects of wealth building we'll cover later on, such as how to identify a goal (as opposed to a wish) and how to follow it through to completion. Let's first take a quick overall look at change, courtesy of journalist, Benjamin P. Hardy:[1]

When it comes to achieving goals, commitment involves:

- Investing up front
- Making it public
- Setting a timeline
- Installing several forms of feedback/accountability

---

[1] Benjamin Hardy, "A Practical Guide to Achieving Any Goal and Living Beyond Fear," *Inc.*, September 18, 2017, https://www.inc.com/benjamin-p-hardy/trust-yourself-a-practical-guide-to-achieve-any-go.html.

- Removing or altering everything in your environment that opposes your commitment

If you're committed to running a marathon, you're going to put everything in place to make sure it happens. You're not going to leave it up to chance.

You're going to start by signing up for a race (investment). You're going to make it public (phase one of accountability). You're going to get a running partner who holds you accountable. You're going to track your progress (feedback) and recount your progress to your accountability partner. Last, you're going to remove things in your life that keep you from running.

Commitment means you build external defense systems around your goals. Your internal resolve, naked to an undefended and opposing environment, is not commitment.

Hardy's words, to me, are wise ones, and what's best is that they are systemic in nature. Simply saying, "I got this," or "I'm grinding" over and over isn't going to work. Change is a process and, truthfully, a slow one, though the good part about it is that it's available to anyone willing to give it a shot.

Throughout this book you'll find me, like Hardy, asking you to continually reassess and adjust your environment to align it with your financial goals. Willpower alone isn't enough. You have to work in harmony with yourself, and that means making the right choices for who you are and what you ultimately want. Put another way, if you need to quit drinking, don't go hanging out in bars or with other alcoholics. By the same token, if you need to quit overspending, stop walking into stores, logging on to Amazon.com, or hanging out with shopaholics.

Each chapter in this book is a building block designed to transform you into an active and consistent investor because that is how wealth is created—through investments. When you reach Chapter 7, you'll see I've divided it into a series of subchapters devoted to each specific step in my Millionaire Money Moves system. (Sub) Chapter 7.6 on Investing is both an introduction to investing and a bridge to the four supplemental chapters contained in my *Millionaire Money Moves Supplemental Investment Guide* that accompanies this book. In the Supplemental Investment Guide, I go into greater detail on investing in securities, real estate, entrepreneurship, and alternative investments. When you're ready to begin investing, dive into the supplemental chapters. These supplemental chapters are not intended to be read from top to bottom; they're intended as a resource guide for each of the four investment pillars.

Before I get too far ahead of myself, let me give you a little background on who I am and where I came from. I was not born rich. I worked hard, but as you'll see, hard work alone doesn't make you rich (ask any coal miner). I was fortunate to have two wonderful parents. They were God-fearing and forever supportive of me. My mom, Rosa Nash, was raised in Danville, Virginia. She only had an eighth-grade education because, where she grew up and when she grew up, many folks considered it better to quit school and go to work to support their families. She and my dad married in their early twenties and stayed together until my mom passed thirty-one years later. Dad liked to dabble in the stock market, and he especially liked to buy land and build houses. He was entrepreneurial even though he was a little risk-averse because he'd grown up extremely poor. Mom was a big saver, a trait she passed on to me. She loved to save coins, which likely explains why, to this day, I still have a five-gallon jug full of pennies in my house. Yep, you read that correctly. I also have a jug filled with nickels, dimes, and quarters.

Truth be told, the probable source of our savings gene was none other than my maternal grandmother. She earned a mere $200 a month working in a dry cleaner business, yet she managed to stash away enough money over time to buy a house in the Bronx for $25,000. I kid you not. I've seen the deed to that house, and as of today, it's worth somewhere north of $750,000. By the time she died in 1983, my grandmother had that house fully paid for plus another $43,000 in savings. Of those savings, $13,000 went toward her funeral with $30,000 bequeathed to her three grandkids. As my tribute to my grandmother's savings genius, I took my $10,000 legacy from her and eventually turned it into millions. It resides in the same Charles Schwab investment account where it's been ever since her passing. As you'll soon see, saving and learning to use savings is a big part of what this book is all about.

My dad didn't grow up regular poor; his people were *country* poor. His dad worked as a sharecropper in North Carolina, and they lived in a speck of a town called Pellum, where he and my grandfather worked a piece of land for a White fellow who owned it. They were paid pennies for the work they did. They grew everything they ate, from corn to vegetables, and they raised chickens and pigs. Picture a pair of good ol' country farmers, and you'll be looking at a portrait of my dad and grandpa.

One of the houses Dad grew up in was painted white with a pair of small rooms and an even smaller room in the attic. It was modest but reasonable. At least I *thought* that was the house my dad grew up in.

One day, I went down to a family reunion and said, "Hey, Dad, take me to the house where you were raised."

I assumed we were headed to the white one I just described. Instead, we drove down a few country roads until we reached a dirt road with barely a tire mark in sight. The surrounding trees were overgrown to the point of obscuring the road itself. We headed a bit further down that dirt road, and the next thing I knew, he was pointing out a tiny red house perched atop a bunch of rocks.

"It's that one there," he said. "That's the house I was raised in. And this here's the land we worked."

Well, that house, the *real* house my dad grew up in, had only two bedrooms where he and his four brothers all slept—in the same bed. Four big ol' boys who each grew to six feet and taller, if you can imagine it. I'm talking about a seriously tight squeeze. There was no running water and no type of indoor plumbing at all. They heated the house with firewood and drew fresh water from a nearby spring.

Clearly, neither of my parents was rich or wealthy. My dad grew up old school, through and through. He was born in 1932 in the midst of the Great Depression. After being drafted and serving in the Army, Pops settled in the oceanfront town of Seaside, California. Seaside was a tight-knit predominantly Black military town where everyone knew and supported one another. I mention this for one simple reason: I want you to see that I subtitled my book, *How You Can Become a Millionaire (Starting from the Bottom)* because, economically speaking, that's where my family and I came from and that may be where you're starting from too. My journey to Destination Millionaire is an authentic one. I got there by the time I turned thirty-two, seven years after I finished college. I didn't get any startup capital from angel or venture capitalist investors, nor did I receive bank loans to fund my journey. I worked long and hard and made the same sacrifices that anyone else can. However, and of equal importance, I found two Black millionaires who mentored me, Robert Taylor and Alfred Glover. Later on, I'll explain why mentorship is so important to the wealth-building process and how you can find the kind of mentors who can guide you to the top. My mentors were different from each other. Mr. Glover was more hands-on while Robert was an exceedingly private man. Both of them were men of few words, which imbued the rare words they did use with great power. I was and still am a person who asks a lot of questions until I fully understand something, and Mr. Glover and Robert would graciously answer every last one of my queries. I learned from watching them and from hearing my dad talk about their Millionaire Money Moves.

It's in that same spirit of giving that I aim to share my personal stories, experiences, and lessons learned in order to teach you how to become a millionaire. Having millionaire mentors has meant everything to me and has profoundly impacted my ability to understand and implement what I learned. My hope is that this book will be to you what Mr. Glover and Robert were to me. Of course, I'm only one person, though hopefully I'll be able to inspire you enough to go out and write your own success story as an investor.

My experience has shown me that anyone, regardless of race, age, educational background, or starting point can become a millionaire and beyond. My goal is to get you to begin investing right away, regardless of your income or debt level. You heard right; I want you to start investing *now*. It takes time for your investments to compound and grow. It also takes time for you to build momentum to the point where you experience what I call an "investor's high," that state of mind where you're investing like a madman or madwoman and experiencing excitement rather than that feeling of sacrifice. Once that happens and you become more enthusiastic about saving and investing than you are about spending and consuming, the wait will have been richly worth it. Pun intended. So, let's get started with a mental picture.

I want you to try to visualize your future comfort and prosperity because:

- Visualization gives you hope
- Hope gives you faith
- Faith gives you confidence
- Confidence gives you courage
- Courage leads to actions
- Actions yield results!

CHAPTER 1

WHY I'M WRITING THIS BOOK

"Start where you are. Use what you have.
Do what you can."

—Former tennis great, ARTHUR ASHE

This is no ordinary book on personal finance, as you'll soon see. That's because there are countless books on the subject available that can give you a hundred great investment or saving ideas and still do nothing to help you actually build wealth. That's the truth. Technique is critical, but technique without the desire and will to execute that technique is nothing more than unrealized potential. I'm sure some great wealth builders were born always wanting to become rich and willing to do what's necessary to get rich, but the rest of us need to develop those desires to do so. The good news is that we can, and this book will show you how. My M$M system is designed to meet you where you are now—wherever that may be—and get you focused on making the necessary adjustments in yourself and in your wallet or pocketbook to build wealth willingly and effectively. If you stick to it over time, you are guaranteed to build wealth and become a millionaire.

Many people's objective is to have enough money to be "comfortable." My emphasis on getting to millions is not about greed or having bragging rights; it's far more urgent. Becoming a millionaire is no longer a question of desire; it's become one of necessity. Here's why: many experts believe you need twenty-five times your annual income by age sixty-five to have enough money to retire. I agree with them, especially if you use the 4 percent rule for making account withdrawals in retirement. That rule states that you can comfortably withdraw 4 percent of your savings in your first year of retirement and adjust that amount for inflation for every subsequent year without risking running out of money for at least twenty-five to thirty years. Using the 4 percent rule, if you had $1 million in your Freedom Fund by retirement age, you could withdraw $40,000 annually. But when you factor in annual inflation, the value of $40,000 in thirty to forty years will be dramatically less. Look back at the price of things thirty years ago, and you'll see what I mean. That's why getting to Destination Millionaire and beyond is necessary. You will someday grow tired of working or be unable to work and need money to live on for the rest of your life. Without *several* million dollars in assets to generate income, you'll end up broke a lot sooner than you think. Remember, there's only so much change in the world you can bring about with your gifts and talents if you're struggling to keep the lights on at home. Building wealth is not hard; it's just slow and sometimes difficult to stay on course, but I'm supremely confident I can get you there because I, and countless others, have done it, starting from the bottom.

Ever since I first began reading personal finance books, I've felt there was a vital missing element to all of them. Didn't these financial authors and gurus understand that I was broke and didn't have startup capital, nor a rich parent or uncle to invest in my ideas? Did any of these so-called financial authorities start from the bottom or even know what it's like when you're living in what feels like an endless cycle of paycheck to paycheck? How was I or anyone else gonna pull myself up by the bootstraps when at times I could barely afford a pair of boots? There is plenty of advice out there about what to do with your money, but not much about how to get that money in the first place.

The purpose of this book and my motivation for writing it are one and the same. I'm here to show you where the rubber meets the road when it comes to building wealth. That's the missing component I intend to fill in for you, not just what to do and how to prepare yourself for the task at hand, but how to do it—now—using what you have, no matter how much or how little that is. I don't come from what you'd call "money." When I was twenty-three and working as a summer intern in Los Angeles, I began seeing wealth all around me, and I told myself, *I want that. I want to have the nice things those people have and enjoy the security and comfort that they seem to have from being wealthy.* Know whom I didn't see? Black people like me. Not a whole lot of them anyway. I saw plenty of Black folks driving fancy cars and wearing expensive jewelry, but I recognized what they had was the appearance of wealth, not the genuine article. Big difference. I decided I would come up with a plan to become a millionaire as quickly as I could, and then later on, when I finally did reach that plateau, hopefully at a point in my life when I could dedicate the time and effort to do so, I would teach what I'd learned on the way up to other Black people who desired to become millionaires. I'd seen firsthand that an

African American person like me, through no special ability and possessing no extraordinary athletic, musical, or literary prowess, could become wealthy despite having to work with the stacked deck known as institutional racism.

The racial wealth gap is widening, with some experts predicting[2] that Blacks will have a net worth of *zero* by 2053 if the trajectory does not change soon. (Later on, I'll show you how to calculate your net worth, though for now, suffice it to say that zero net wealth for *any* community is a terrifying number.) I want to use my knowledge and experience to change that trajectory, one emerging millionaire at a time, starting with you. The most reliable indicators of African American wealth place us at the bottom in nearly every category. Fewer than half (42 percent) of Black families own their homes, compared to almost three-quarters (73 percent) of White families. Black children are three times as likely to live in poverty compared to White children. The average Black household earns a fraction (59 percent) of comparable White households. According to the Federal Reserve Bank, only 44 percent of Black Americans have retirement savings accounts, with a typical balance of around $20,000, compared to 65 percent of White Americans, who have an average balance of $50,000. And only 34 percent of African Americans own any stocks or mutual funds, as opposed to more than half of White people.[3] We are at or near the bottom in land ownership, business ownership, and employment. We pay the highest rates and fees for home and business

---

[2] Jamiles Lartey, "Median Wealth of Black Americans 'Will Fall to Zero by 2053,' Warns New Report," *The Guardian*, September 13, 2017, https://www.theguardian.com/inequality/2017/sep/13/median-wealth-of-black-americans-will-fall-to-zero-by-2053-warns-new-report.

[3] Rodney Brooks, "The Retirement Crisis Facing Black Americans," *US News*, December 11, 2020, https://money.usnews.com/money/retirement/aging/articles/the-retirement-crisis-facing-black-americans.

loans and have to struggle more than everyone else to get them.[4]

We're in a bad way as a community, and we didn't get here by accident. No sir. Many have been the plans put into place to keep the wealth, real estate, and material riches of this country in the hands of its White "founders" and out of ours. As Malcolm X famously said, "We didn't land on Plymouth Rock. Plymouth Rock landed on us." That's why I think it's time we stop hoping for—or worse—relying on some sudden change of heart on the part of the White financial majority to bring us up to where they are. I say this as a person who has loads of White business partners, employees, friends, and mentors who support equality. It ain't about that. We need to continue to fight the good fight for racial equality together, but in the meantime, we Black people need to focus our attention and efforts on building wealth so as not to further undermine the very thing we're fighting for. We also have to separate what we can change in our lifetime from what we are never going to change in our lifetime, so we make sure to fix the things we can as part of a generations-long effort. In other words, let's control the things we can, such as how we spend our time, effort, and earnings, while we continue to chip away at the things we cannot easily control like racism, discrimination, and oppression. Otherwise, we risk diluting or forever obscuring the tremendous contributions made by our ancestors to this country and to the world.

I get particularly frustrated whenever I bring up financial matters like saving and investing—the key ingredients of wealth building—at the barbershop. I don't know where you get your hair cut, but where I go, the conversation inevitably devolves into a passionate debate about

---

[4] "The Economic State of Black America in 2020," Joint Economic Committee: Congressman Don Beyer, Vice Chair, accessed June 14, 2022, https://www.jec.senate.gov/public/_cache/files /ccf4dbe2-810a-44f8-b3e7-14f7e5143ba6/economic-state-of-black-america-2020.pdf.

the misdeeds of White folks: slavery, Jim Crow, redlining, blackballing, mass incarceration, and so on...all the indisputable, valid, and painful reasons why we are so far behind our fellow Americans who "happen to be White." Yet, at the end of each of these arguments, I can't help feeling a certain hollowness, like all we've managed to do is announce the score again instead of figuring out how to make a comeback. That's why I'm here on these pages alongside you. I'm going to put the ball in your hands and teach you exactly the money moves to make to set that comeback into motion.

I remember reading *Black Wealth: Mastering Money by Understanding the Past, Correcting the Present & Realizing the Future* by J.R. Gibson, where he wrote, "If Black people's incomes rose with the same rate (the rate with which they rose between the period 1967 to 2005), it would take another 537 years for Blacks to reach...per capita income parity with White Americans." When I used to reflect upon that kind of shocking statistic, it was hard not to reach the conclusion that—economically speaking—it's the year 2021 for White folks while, here in Black America, it's 1484! How are we ever gonna catch up?

Nowadays, I try to look at the issue in a different light. Yes, we are way behind. Yes, the deck is stacked against us. I don't believe that any group holding as large of an economic lead as Whites do over Blacks is going to work too hard to diminish that lead either. Honestly, would you? That's not the way human history has ever worked. Professor Steven Rogers[5] correctly points out that an enormous part of the initial wealth accumulated by White America was...drum roll...us! Like the Pharaohs of ancient

---

[5] Steven S. Rogers, *A Letter to My White Friends and Colleagues: What You Can Do Right Now to Help the Black Community* (Hoboken: Wiley, 2021).

Egypt, White slave owners amassed the fruits of our lifelong labor for over four hundred years while we collectively earned zero. We weren't merely workers either; we were wealth itself. As slaves, we represented financial equity that a slave owner could take to a bank and get a loan against. Think about how a home equity loan works today and imagine that in the place of that home, there was a living, breathing human being who could be bought, sold, traded, or mortgaged. Is it any wonder that the cumulative dollar value of all that free labor, compounded over centuries of investment, dwarfs a number like the amount of money we got...zero? Add to that the massive financial head start that even non-slaveholders enjoyed simply because they were paid for their work and could later invest and grow their income freely. That too contributed to today's racial wealth gap. Even good people on the right side of the slavery question—morally speaking—benefited from the "strange fruit" of our enslavement.

I'm writing this book to help you change the things you focus on when it comes to your personal finances and wealth building. Did you happen to notice, in the passage I cited above, the word "rate?" Racism takes generations to undo. There's no question about that, but rates are much more susceptible to the forces of human effort. As we look at the state of Black wealth in present-day America, instead of looking at the long road ahead, I want us to begin focusing on increasing the speed at which we move—the rate of our progress *as well as* the distance. Our goal is to change the engine of Black wealth from labor to capital, which is just a fancy way of saying that we need to stop using our sweat to make money and start using the power of asset creation and appreciation to do the work for us. Ol' John Henry's time has come and gone. We need to modernize our strategy and create an economic locomotive to power us—hyper-speed—into the future.

As a community, we have been waiting too long for the government—or, in some cases, Jesus—to fix America's sins of slavery, racism, discrimination, and oppression. The truth is that we're not going to get our forty acres and a mule; race and wealth do not matter to Jesus. Jesus cares about our spiritual salvation and our deeds toward others, not our situation as Black people in America. It's time to take matters into our own hands, be the change we seek, and become self-reliant to the extent that we can. All this time that we've been waiting for the White man to make the game fair, or for Jesus to "fix it," our collective losses have been accumulating. While we've been waiting, they've been taking: all the land, our culture, opportunities, and our chances for a better future. If we wait any longer, the task will only get harder as the wealth gap continues to widen.

So, given how far we're behind, what can we do to fix it? We can immediately change what we do with what we have—in other words, our money behaviors (which I'll delve into in Chapter 6)—and begin to base our overall approach to wealth building on the accumulation of appreciating assets that generate income. When we combine that approach with the enormous potential of our $1.2 trillion-plus of Black purchasing power,[6] then we can rapidly and decisively affect the rate at which our wealth increases and—equally important—extend that growth across generations. For us, and not for others. That's a plain fact. This type of capital-driven accelerator can work as a time machine for us as individuals and as a community.

I'm also writing this book because I believe we need to understand the financial impacts of all we've been through as a community in order to

---

[6] "Audience Is Everything," Nielsen, February 15, 2018, https://www.nielsen.com/us/en/insights/article/2018/black-impact-consumer-categories-where-african-americans-move-markets/.

know what got us here and what sorts of actions we must take to distance ourselves from the pitfalls of the past. As I said earlier, some things aren't going to change in your lifetime or mine. Take a quick look at history, and you'll see what I mean.

You know all the talk lately (and once again) about reparations for African Americans to rectify a historical wrong and bridge the gap in Black and White wealth? Why should we expect or wait for reparations to come about now when the first effort at reparations for slavery began failing way back in 1865, at the end of the Civil War? Long before you and I were born, this country acted like it was headed down the path of meaningful retribution for our suffering. But it was not to be. We African Americans never got a homeland or billions of dollars in reparations like the Jewish victims of the Holocaust rightly received. In fact, our reparations never even made it out of the starting gate.

After the war, President Lincoln signed Special Field Order 15, which would have given us our forty acres and a mule, but he was assassinated shortly thereafter. His successor, Andrew Johnson, quickly reversed the order through executive action. The Southern Homestead Act of 1866 opened up millions of acres of land for freed former slaves and Union soldiers, yet ten years later—wouldn't you know it—only 5 percent of Black families owned land in the South.[7] Even the farmland we were given was largely taken away, usually through physical violence or through the subtle art of "stealing with a pen" as was done to the Native Americans before us. Between 1910 and 1997, African Americans lost about 90 percent of

---

[7] Lizzie Presser, "Kicked Off the Land," *The New Yorker*, July 15, 2019, https://www.newyorker.com/magazine/2019/07/22/kicked-off-the-land.

their farmland.[8] According to Ray Winbush of the Institute for Urban Research at Morgan State University, "There is this idea that most Blacks were lynched because they did something untoward to a young woman. That's not true. Most Black men were lynched between 1890 and 1920 because Whites wanted their land."[9]

In post-Civil War America, the horrific brutality of slavery gave way to economic slavery, leaving the entire Black population landless and dependent on White folks to make a living and survive. What followed in almost every form you can imagine is more of the same pattern. Ghettoization. Redlining, which began in the 1930s when the Federal Housing Authority issued a manual to lenders with red lines drawn around the areas where we lived to discourage them from offering us mortgages. The list goes on and on. Housing values in Black neighborhoods have been suppressed for generations, up to and including the present day. Given that home equity is typically two-thirds of a family's net worth, you can see how this phenomenon has been and continues to be a major contributing factor to the ever-increasing wealth gap. One hundred years after the end of slavery, as the following chart indicates, White America's massive financial head start had snowballed into an avalanche.

---

[8] Ibid.

[9] Ibid.

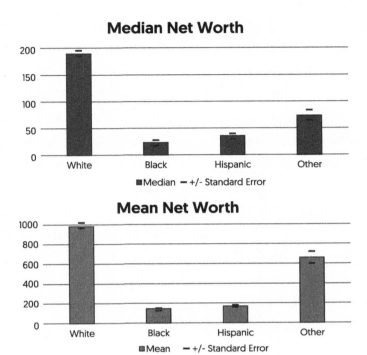

Median Net Worth

200		
150		
100		
50		
0		
	White	Black	Hispanic	Other

■Median — +/- Standard Error

Mean Net Worth

1000		
800		
600		
400		
200		
0		
	White	Black	Hispanic	Other

■Mean — +/- Standard Error

Source: Federal Reserve Board, 2019 Survey of Consumer Finances. Figures display median (top panel) and mean (bottom panel) wealth by race and ethnicity, expressed in thousands of 2019 dollars.

Fast forward to a few short years ago, and according to the Federal Reserve's survey of 2019 consumer finances, the median net worth of the White population was $188,200, while ours was $24,100, or about one-eighth the net worth of our fellow Americans.[10]

---

[10] Neil Bhutta, Andrew C. Chang, Lisa J. Dettling, and Joanne W. Hsu, "Disparities in Wealth by Race and Ethnicity in the 2019 Survey of Consumer Finances," Board of Governors of the Federal Reserve System, September 28, 2020, https://www.federalreserve.gov/econres/notes /feds-notes/disparities-in-wealth-by-race-and-ethnicity-in-the-2019-survey-of-consumer -finances-20200928.htm.

This book is here to change that equation by showing you how to create wealth and specifically how you can grow your own net worth to contribute to the closing of the racial wealth gap and to reach millionaire status and beyond. Wealth building is all about relationships. Let's face it: our network is more limited than that of others who've been in the wealth game longer. Anecdotal and statistical evidence suggest that it's singularly difficult for African Americans to get home-buying loans, equity loans, business loans, and even venture capitalist funding from the big guys in Silicon Valley or on Wall Street. (Imagine the impact this has had on—among other things—Black business ownership.) Even when we are seen as creditworthy, we all too often end up with the short end of the stick. The Center for Responsible Lending reports that at the onset of the Great Recession of 2008, Blacks had been 150 percent more likely to have been given high-cost loans.[11] Even those Black folks with similar income and credit scores to their White counterparts were 30 percent more likely to be steered to more expensive, subprime mortgages. Clearly, there is not a level playing field. The only reliable antidotes we have to this kind of racially based poison are financial knowledge and empowerment. Our society and our government have demonstrated that they will—at best—drag their feet toward equality. In the meantime, our increasing financial know-how and power can and will lead us to financial salvation. I hope this book will empower you to the point that the banks and venture capitalists will have to compete with each other to lend you money or invest in your business ideas at the best rates, for the lowest fees, and for the best repayment or equity terms.

---

[11] JR Gibson, *Black Wealth: Mastering Money by Understanding the Past, Correcting the Present & Realizing the Future* (2014) 207.

I want to inspire you—in the words of Rick Ross, one of my favorite rappers—to "buy back the block" you shop on in your community by reversing the abysmal pattern of dollar flight out of our communities. We need to redirect funds into Black-owned commercial properties and businesses, so we can in turn fund jobs, youth programs, scholarships and influence the political scene and local business opportunities for Black entrepreneurs (much more on that in Chapter 7). Years ago, the NAACP did a study[12] on how long a dollar circulates in various ethnic communities. Their research showed that a dollar's life cycle lasted thirty days in the Asian community, twenty days in the Jewish community, and seventeen days in the overall White community. Now in all fairness, that study is somewhat controversial because it's a very difficult thing to actually prove, but can you guess how long the study showed a dollar circulating in the Black community?

Six hours.

That's not a typo. You might wonder, as I did, *How can that be? How is it that our money flies out of the community before it's had the slightest chance to do any good?* It's a shocking disparity.

We can make our dollars circulate in our communities longer, so we can in turn support more Black businesses. As we create more Black businesses, we can create more Black wealth and more Black millionaires. As we create more millionaires in our own community, we can create more social initiatives because those businesses and those millionaires are giving back to programs in our community, such as Little League, the Urban League, after-school programs, and so on. All the while, our circulating dollars

---

[12] Gary A. Johnson, "How Do Black People Spend Their Money?—The Racial Wealth Gap," *Black Men in America*, September 2, 2021, https://blackmeninamerica.com/updated-how -do-black-people-spend-their-money-3/.

could be employing people in our community because Black businesses are far more likely to hire Black people who live in the community, at higher wages.[13] These gains extend to a macro level as Black millionaire business owners become empowered to demand better services from politicians in their own communities in exchange for both political *and* financial support. Like it or not, politicians need money to run and win their campaigns, and as a result, their decisions in office are largely guided by the needs of their biggest donors. In this fashion, issues like sensitive nonviolent police leadership evolve from a wisp of hope into concrete action. It's all part of our own snowball effect, only this snowball will be made of our African American dollars.

Another pain point we'll address together in the pages that follow is what I like to call the four-letter words of finance, or as they're more commonly known: fast, easy, and free. Sound familiar? In the past, it's been far too simple for us to be separated from our money, so much so that I think it's eaten into our collective courage. At times, it seems all anyone has to do is tell us that we can make money fast, with little-to-no effort or entry fee, and we're willing to hand over our last $1,000 in the hope of making a quick fortune. But if you look at the richest people in America, you'll see that no one made it fast, no one did it easily, and no one did it for free. It took Facebook founder Mark Zuckerberg, the second youngest self-made billionaire, over four years in business, several years of relentless dorm-room coding, and $12.7 million of venture capital to get to that mountaintop. It took Jay-Z twenty-four years from the time he founded Roc-A-Fella Records until he too became a billionaire. Nonetheless, the

---

[13] Andre M. Perry and Carl Romer, "To Expand the Economy, Invest in Black Businesses," Brookings, December 31, 2020, https://www.brookings.edu/essay/to-expand-the-economy-invest-in-black-businesses/.

lure of pyramid schemes, late-night "I'm going to teach you how to flip houses with no money down" salesmen, and other slippery folks promising to show us how to make fast, easy money with no money down continues to enchant and entrap us.

Put simply, it is imperative that our community tackle the challenge of wealth building head-on. No one is coming to save us but us. We have what it takes to do it, if we focus our efforts on consistently putting the building blocks of wealth in place one brick at a time. Let's accept that we're starting from the bottom. Let's no longer allow the reality that we're starting from behind to keep us from getting started in the first place. That's how all great comebacks begin. Where we find ourselves is not entirely our fault, but it *is* our responsibility to fix it. Now is the time for us to lace up, strap in, and begin to save, invest, team up, and patiently build momentum and wealth. If we fail to start, we risk starting to fail all over again.

Fortunately, none of us has to do it alone. You'll hear me talking a lot about mentoring and being mentored in this book because your journey to Destination Millionaire is going to require some help like mine did. I'm here to pay it forward for all the guidance and support I received and continue to receive from my many mentors—Black, White, Jewish, Latino, and others—who always impressed upon me that I must pay it forward as a way to repay them for their generosity in time and wisdom.

I'll show you how to find the right people to guide you on your journey as well as how to set yourself up to be properly guided by your mentors. I've been lucky to have had gifted mentors throughout my life. Yet, in spite of all that wisdom, I've made plenty of mistakes too. You'll soon discover my share of foolishness that's gone along with the things I've done correctly. Fortunately, I had the strong shoulders of my mentors to help me course-correct. That may be why I've never considered mentorship to be "optional," nor should you. In many respects, your experiences with your mentors may turn out to be the most rewarding of all aspects of wealth building. I know mine were and continue to be.

Here's how that debt of gratitude began to take shape for me...

CHAPTER 2

HOW I BECAME A MILLIONAIRE BY AGE THIRTY-TWO

---

*"Children have never been very good at listening
to their elders, but they have never failed to imitate them.
They must, they have no other models."*

—JAMES BALDWIN, *Nobody Knows My Name,*
"Fifth Avenue, Uptown: A Letter from Harlem"

They say the road to hell is paved with good intentions. While that may be true, no matter where you are headed in life, you are guaranteed to get nowhere at all if you haven't got a decent road map to point you to your objective. Nowhere is this more evident than in the quest to reach a place I call "Destination Millionaire."

My own journey truly began when I found my first mentor (besides my mom and dad). His name was Gus Martin. Gus was a White electrical engineer who worked for the richest man I knew at the time—a guy by the name of John Walton who'd inherited a lot of Texas oil money. I became acquainted with him through my dad's best friend, who we respectfully called Uncle AJ (though he wasn't really our uncle). Uncle AJ grew up with John in Texas. John took over his family's fortune and thanks to a love for music, he decided to go into the radio business, with Uncle AJ working as his de facto Chief Operating Officer (COO). Eventually, John moved to Pebble Beach, California, where he began buying and operating radio stations.

Uncle AJ and his family moved to California from El Paso, Texas, as well, and our two families quickly became the best of friends. Gus Martin would come to service the radio station towers for John, and he'd often stay with Uncle AJ. They'd have dinner parties—Christian parties, that is, where drinking alcohol was not allowed. It was in those settings I began to get a sense of Gus. I knew he was an electrical engineer, and when I heard that Gus was making $1,000 a day consulting for John's radio stations, my ears pricked up like bean sprouts. He made $1,000 a day? That is nearly $3,000 in today's dollars. Not only that, Gus would fly roundtrip between Texas and California on John's private plane and get paid portal to portal—from the time he stepped on the plane in Texas until the time he returned home and stepped off the plane again.

It wasn't long before I decided that I too wanted to be an electrical engineer like Gus. As fate would have it, I was already taking an electronics drafting class at my high school and greatly enjoying it. So, I figured, why not? Unfortunately, I ended up designing one of the stupidest things that a kid could ever design in that class, and what's worse, I thought it was pretty smart! The year was 1980, and we were studying solar energy. I created a solar energy panel that (this is embarrassing to write) was connected to a series of electric heating lamps which in turn...oh never mind. It was about as useful as a cocktail umbrella in a thunderstorm. And naturally, I couldn't wait to show it to Gus!

In hindsight, I assume he immediately saw how lame it was even though he told me he thought it was "amazing." I think he knew my youthful confidence was blossoming at the time, and it wasn't worth destroying it at such a tender age. Eventually, I would come to my senses. What mattered most about Gus's reaction to my project was that he made me believe I was brilliant, and that belief fueled me for decades (though, thankfully, I build high-functioning businesses now in place of useless contraptions). That's what a mentor can do for you. Mentoring is not only about helping you make the right investments. It's also about teaching you how to believe in yourself. The legacy of Gus's mentoring is that now I carry a message forward to every young person I encounter. The message is: "You can dream big dreams. You can let yourself believe that you can do whatever you dream to do. You too are brilliant in your own way. And you're going to fail sometimes. It's all part of the journey."

The mentoring work I currently do isn't anything extraordinary or amazing, and I'm not a person of any great renown. However, I do think that when viewed through the lens of where I came from and the kids who were around me growing up, the success I've had as an adult is still remarkable. It's all because Gus Martin made an eleventh grader believe he was a bright kid. Gus's example made me decide that I wanted to become a consultant as well. I wanted to be a person who got paid for their expertise. Owing to Gus's influence, I began studying electrical engineering, and after taking one computer class at Monterey Peninsula College, I was hooked. I transferred to Cal Poly San Luis Obispo where I chose to study computer science, even though, at that time, I was one of only about four African Americans to ever do so at my school. Plenty of kids were studying engineering, but no one wanted to touch this newfangled "computer thing." Whereas for me, computer programming didn't feel like work at all. I relished a chance to get paid to play with computers all day.

I was as practical and meticulous as the day was long. In other words, I was the kind of person who could dream of becoming a consultant or a computer expert. But I needed someone like Gus Martin to demonstrate that this was not only possible, but as worthwhile as any other aspiration. Otherwise, I may never have known how to believe in my unconventional dreams.

Years later, when I was about twenty-four years old, I was introduced to a Black gentleman by the name of Gilbert D. Bruce. Mr. Bruce, as I've always called him, lived in San Luis Obispo, California, where I attended college. My school, Cal Poly San Luis Obispo, was a predominantly White university, though I met Mr. Bruce through our African American dean of students, Carl Wallace. Cal Poly specialized in engineering, architecture, and agriculture. There were other majors too, but those were its most renowned areas of study.

Dean Wallace and I took a liking to each other right away.

He knew I was entrepreneurial, and he said, "You've got to meet Gilbert D. Bruce."

Mr. Bruce owned a grocery market that was locally famous for their homemade sandwiches. He also owned this old rundown motel that looked—I hate to say it—extremely run down. But he owned it, he lived there, and he was a self-made millionaire. I was astonished to learn that he'd previously had a day job as a janitor at a correctional facility, until he suffered a back injury on the job and ended up on disability. At that point, Mr. Bruce changed gears and became an avid investor and consistent saver. He made a number of sacrifices to eventually become a millionaire. Before I go on, I want to be sure you caught that trajectory because it sure got my attention back then: he started as a janitor with an injured back and ended up a millionaire. That's quite a distance to cover.

There was nothing lavish about Mr. Bruce's lifestyle. He looked like he wore the same clothes every day (though naturally he didn't wear the same *items* every day). Mrs. Bruce was completely supportive of him and his spartan lifestyle choices. She would cook for them every night, and during the day, she'd clean the rental apartments he'd bought over time. Why do I point this out? Because a lot of people mistakenly believe that you have to spend a lot of money and look extremely wealthy to build or "attract" wealth. That's simply untrue. Wearing Gucci will never be the reason someone takes a meeting with you. Of course, you *can* look rich and be rich, but to do so, you have to be willing to first look poor while you're becoming rich. That's the toughest part of the deal to accept—because who wants to make sacrifices, right? Sacrificing is difficult and often painful, and like trying to lose weight, it means you're going to have to resist temptation. That doesn't sound like much of a party.

One day, Mr. Bruce and I arranged to get together in San Luis Obispo. By that time, Mr. Bruce had sold the Roach, err...I mean, old motel of his. Lord only knows what kind of crimes and misdemeanors went on at that motel back in the day! Nonetheless, with some of the sale proceeds, he bought a thirteen-unit apartment building in nearby Arroyo Grande plus another lovely, private home with a finished and unoccupied lower-level basement.

By coincidence, my college roommate Randy was about to graduate, and one of my fraternity brothers, Paul, wanted to rent Randy's room and live with me. I was going into my last year of school and was focused on finishing my studies. I knew that if Paul and I lived together, we would be up to who-knows-what kind of shenanigans, and I'd probably never finish school. So, I had a conversation with Mr. Bruce about living in his basement, and he graciously agreed to let me stay there. It turned out to be one of the best decisions of my life.

Here's a glimpse of what daily life was like with Mr. Bruce. In the mornings, you'd find him in bed with a cigarette in one hand and a *Wall Street Journal* in the other. At the same time, he'd be watching some investment show on TV while a financial news show was blaring away in the background on the radio. I mean, Mr. Bruce was *all in* when it came to investing, and his enthusiasm was so infectious (not to mention ubiquitous) that the simple act of living with Mr. Bruce inspired me—as if through osmosis—to begin reading books about investing. In short order, I was picking up *The Wall Street Journal*, or reading *How to Be Your Own Stockbroker* by Charles Schwab, or blazing through Donald Trump's *The Art of the Deal*. (I don't agree with Trump-the-politician at all, though his book was undeniably inspirational.) I started reading anything about finance I could get my hands on, all while hammering away at my last year of computer science in school. I devoured these and other books, such as *The Magic of Thinking Big* by David J. Schwartz, highlighting their texts until they glowed fluorescent yellow. Even today, I can quote entire sections of them, chapter and verse, so profound was their impression upon me. Every night, including weekends, I'd be downstairs reading investing books while growing increasingly motivated to become a *playa* and elevate myself to the point where I could invest in the kind of deals I was reading about.

It was Mr. Bruce's mentorship and example that propelled me into reading these books and hungering to understand, "How do you build wealth? How do you start with your everyday job and turn yourself into a person of wealth? How do you get access to capital when you're starting from the bottom up?"

One morning, two days before my graduation, I woke up and essentially wrote myself a plan to do just that. I still have that plan and refer to it even today.

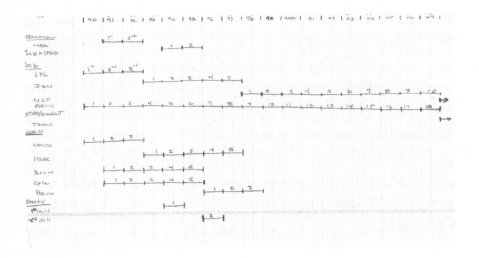

As you can see, I wanted to get my master's degree and potentially even a PhD, so I could someday teach. In my time doing military reserve, I wanted to start my own consulting firm, have my first child, then a second kid, then buy my first BMW (more on my car obsession later on in our story), buy an IBM personal computer (back then, IBM PCs cost a whopping $6,000 or so), and so on. My plan was seriously granular and kinda crazy for a college kid, right?

Maybe, though let's set the debate about my nuttiness aside for a moment and look at the key issue which underlies a plan like mine—namely, how important it is to set your goals early on. Writing a plan does more than just lay out the steps of your journey. It conditions your behavior. The sheer act of writing the plan, and then adhering to it, programs your subconscious for years to come. In this very manner, your commitments to saving, investing, and by extension, wealth building eventually become second nature.

A couple of decades after I wrote and began my plan, I took it out again and realized that I'd accomplished nearly every one of my goals. Not only that, I'd done it within the time frame I'd set out as well. Now, clearly, I'm not some clairvoyant genius who can magically see into the future, nor am I a pillar of efficiency. I'm a regular guy who mapped his future out and then trained himself in the art of following a map, even when that map demanded that I make sacrifices I'd have gladly not made along the way.

What I believe this all illustrates is the combined power of strong planning, good influencers, and supportive surroundings. I believe these are some of the key components missing from so many young African American lives, in particular. Given our disparity of investment vis-à-vis White folks, their higher rate of engagement in investing theoretically means that their children have greater exposure to learning about investing from their parents. Does every White family take advantage of it or invest? Of course not. There's no *everyone* to any of what I'll be talking about in this book. But there's little doubt that White children in America are more likely to be exposed to their mothers', fathers', and grandparents' investing than most Black children are to theirs.

This type of environment matters because, for the privileged, it means their parents don't have to explicitly teach them to save or put money in a 401(k). They simply mentor by example. I see this with my own sons, who didn't live with me all their lives but have been around me enough—during the summer, Christmas breaks, and so on—to see how I operate financially. As a result, since they've graduated from college, they've already begun to imitate that mindset of wanting to invest and wanting to save for the future.

Let me be clear. My African American mentors, such as Mr. Bruce, never said, "Cedric, buy this stock," or "Cedric, save this amount." They mentored through example and by being available to me to answer any questions I had. They were not very hands-on, and in retrospect, it's clear they didn't need to be. Simply allowing me to see what they were doing and being able to ask questions about it made all the difference in the world to me, my future, and now my children's futures.

GETTING TO DESTINATION MILLIONAIRE

Once my plan was in place, it was only a matter of time before an opportunity would arise to take it to the next step. It came in the form of a plastic surgeon named Dr. Tsao. While I was in college, Dr. Tsao approached the minority engineering department at Cal Poly and asked our department head, David Cantu, for a student to set up a computer system in his medical office. David's wife worked as a nurse in Dr. Tsao's office. I was one of a tiny handful of minority computer science majors enrolled in the program, so I figured I had a decent shot at getting the gig. I wrote a proposal, implementation plan, and timeline for completing the work. I told Dr. Tsao I could do his work for $25 an hour. I was already intensely determined to become a consultant, and I recognized this was my first chance to do it. Luckily, Dr. Tsao accepted my offer.

Equally lucky, before this opportunity arose, I'd worked a six-month co-op assignment at a computer manufacturing company in Sunnyvale where I'd met a couple of guys who were into writing computer programs on personal computers. They hipped me to some other fellows in the town of Fremont who were building PC clones in their homes. I bought one of their machines for myself, then built a relationship with the guys. This enabled me to go back to college and start selling computers to fellow students at a profit of over a thousand dollars per computer! Yes, sir. It was the dawn of the PC clone, a generic, far less-expensive option than the IBM PCs costing in the thousands of dollars.

I quickly extended that sales model into reselling a couple of computers to Dr. Tsao. I implemented his network by hiring my fraternity brother, Paul, who was an electrical engineering major and skilled in electronics. He helped me run the cables while I focused on installing the network. I honestly knew nothing about computer networking at the time, but I quickly learned Novell Network software on the job, meaning while I was getting paid $25 an hour.

By the time I graduated from college, I'd saved $7,000. I took that $7,000, put a down payment on a $115,000–condo, and moved out straight into my own condo rather than renting an apartment like everyone else. Naturally, there was a reason that condo only cost $115,000; it was in Pacoima, California, right around the corner from where Rodney King got beaten by the cops. So, while the price was nice, the neighborhood was definitely on the dicey side.

A couple years later while visiting one of my fraternity brothers, Gerald Watson, in nearby Pasadena, I noticed there was an African American woman who lived next door to him in his mostly White neighborhood. She worked at the Jet Propulsion Laboratory (where I too had found a job), and she was having a hard time trying to sell her house because it needed some work. I talked to her about it and came up with a plan to buy her house for $285,000, with her financing 15 percent of the sale price herself as part of a loan strategy called "carrying equity." This is when the buyer doesn't have the full 10 percent or 20 percent down payment needed to purchase the property, so the seller agrees to provide a portion of the needed down payment in exchange for equity, which allows the bank to finance the property at the required loan-to-value ratio. Wondering how I knew I could do all this at the tender age of twenty-eight years old? All of that reading I did living with Mr. Bruce, that's how.

Eventually, I refinanced the larger mortgage with the bank and paid her off, which left me with only one loan on the house. I continued living in the house for several years before I sold it for a $25,000–profit. That was the most money I'd ever made on an investment to that point.

(That house today is worth upward of $1.33 million, a clear sign of how much real estate has appreciated over time.)

Meantime, my career was on an upward trajectory as well. My first job out of college was the one I mentioned at the Jet Propulsion Laboratory, a NASA contractor, making $36,400 a year to start. I stayed at that job for three years while working on my MBA at Pepperdine University. What I'd always wanted to do was be a consultant in the vein of my mentor Gus Martin, so I eventually sought and found a job in consulting at Deloitte & Touche. In no time, I was earning $65,000 a year, and while I was happy, I still had a strong hankering to write code left over from my time as a computer science major.

Deloitte offered me an opportunity to work on a new Enterprise Resource Planning (ERP) software product called SAP (Systems,

Applications, and Products). It was developed in Germany, and I'd never heard of it before. Back then, nobody in the firm wanted to specialize in SAP, so they hired three minorities to take it on: me, an Asian guy named Victor Hou, and an Indian guy named Kumar Chitani.

After SAP training in Philadelphia, we returned to the office and sat around waiting for Deloitte to win new work. Then, all of a sudden, SAP became the next "it" thing and demand for people with SAP skills and training went straight through the roof. Lucky for me, right? Especially if you believe that old adage about luck being when opportunity meets preparation.

Included in my plan for myself was a swift promotion to manager. I was young, ambitious, and in a hurry to succeed. So, after only eighteen months on the job, I reached out to the leadership team and asked them to read the tea leaves about a promotion for me. They talked among themselves, and when it emerged that I was—to my astonished disappointment—unlikely to make manager, I beat a hasty retreat to a competing consulting firm, Ernst & Young (EY), where a guy with my SAP skillset was evidently in far greater demand. EY made me a manager and offered me an $88,000 salary, plus a $5,000 signing bonus to boot.

I spent the next eighteen months at EY honing my SAP skills while the market for those skills grew ever hotter. Soon, I had a handful of intriguing growth options awaiting me. I could stay at Ernst & Young and accept a new raise to $110,000 a year. I could go to one of the other rival consulting firms—PriceWaterhouseCoopers (now known as PwC) or Andersen Consulting (now known as Accenture) for $100,000 a year. Another option was I could take a real chance by working for and hopefully becoming a partner in a German startup company through a couple of guys I'd met on an EY project.

I did what I thought was the smartest thing; namely, I talked it over with my dad. He said something profound, which helped me tap into the more courageous part of myself.

He said, "Son, you're young. You have time to recover if things go wrong. Why not go for it?"

I learned then that much of risk-taking is simply the recognition that things can and do go wrong, even terribly wrong, and yet the world does not end as a result. I didn't have kids at the time, and so, even though this career move meant leaving my home and friends in Southern California for the Bay Area, where the US office was located, I set my sights on joining the Germans and threw caution to the wind.

For many African Americans like me, entrepreneurship is a struggle because so many of us are raised to go to school, get a good education, and then find a good job. End of story. Entrepreneurship is seen as an unnecessary risk. Sometimes I wonder what I would've done if my father had said, "No, no! You have a good job. Those folks have been good to you; you shouldn't take the risk." I might never have started my own business. Hopefully, this is changing somewhat today, although I still believe we have a long way to go to catch up to the traditions you'll find in many other ethnic cultures.

My good fortune was that my dad felt his own lucky break was being drafted into the Army, and even that slight interruption in the school-to-job pipeline had been enough to give him a differing perspective. The Army was a job too, but it nonetheless exposed him to other ways of thinking than what he might have encountered going to work for Sears, General Electric, or any other traditional company like that. Hence, all those years later, rather than advising me that my German opportunity was "too risky," my dad helped me mine the requisite gumption to give it a try.

My eventual partners, Wolfgang and Gerhardt, were themselves partners in a German firm called Consulting and Resources Distribution (CaRD). I met Wolfgang in 1995 on an SAP project for EY in which I was the technical consulting manager. I recognized early on that Wolfgang possessed a deeper technical ability in SAP than most others, and over time, my other colleagues and I would learn a great deal from him. When Wolfgang and I would go to lunch or dinner, we'd talk about how this amazing new SAP technology was creating new business opportunities. As I learned more about CaRD, my mental gears began to spin about how I might help their company grow and, at the same time, leverage the opportunity for my own benefit. How could I help them while helping myself? Using the skills I'd acquired in business school, I came up with a business plan to grow their business, with me as an equity partner. That way, if the business did indeed grow, so would my share of the proceeds. Wolfgang and Gerhardt were on board with my idea, but their other partners in Germany would need to sign on as well. So, I refined the business plan and presentation and scheduled a meeting in Germany to present it all to the remaining CaRD partners.

I took that Wednesday off at EY, worked all day on the presentation, flew out on a Delta red-eye to Atlanta, and then I worked all the next day in Atlanta until my evening red-eye to Frankfurt. I arrived in Germany early Friday morning, took a nap, said a prayer, and presented my plan at 10:00 a.m. The next morning, I flew back home to Los Angeles. In case you're wondering, the German word for exhausted is *erschoepft*, and let me tell you, I was hella *erschoepft* after that trip!

But it paid off; the presentation went well, and the remaining partners were deeply impressed. A few weeks later, Wolfgang informed me that one of his other clients, Hewlett Packard (HP), had given him a request-for-proposal (RFP) to handle all of the technical work for a new SAP implementation they had. He didn't know how to respond, though I did because I had three years of professional consulting under my belt by then. I reviewed the RFP and proposed seven consultants for an entire year to the tune of $1.5 million.

Wolfgang said, "Cedric, are you crazy? There's no way they would pay that much."

Happily for us all, Wolfgang's hunch was incorrect, and the client accepted our proposal. Now it was showtime. I resigned from Ernst & Young and moved to the San Francisco/Oakland Bay Area. My consulting skills immediately came in handy at CaRD. I knew things about starting and running a project that Wolfgang and Gerhardt knew little to nothing about. We had the kick-off meeting with HP, and it went swimmingly. They were so wowed that they even asked us to bring on *more* staff to support their other business areas. By the time I was done adding resources, we had a total of fifteen consultants working on the assignment. Our revenue grew from $1.5 million annually to $7 million.

My first year at CaRD I took home $321,000. In the first six months of the following year, I made $299,000. As you might imagine, I was working my ass off—thirteen-hour days at the office, and then back down south to see my family in Pasadena over the weekends. I also couldn't help noticing that my German partners weren't working nearly as hard as I was. They were going home at 6:00 p.m. every night while I stayed behind toiling away in the office. They were chilling and enjoying their families while I was working till late in the night. I knew this would eventually become a problem.

On the other hand, I learned so much from them by watching how they managed their money. I managed my dollars respectably enough, but these guys were money-managing beasts. They paid everything off. Everything! Their cars, condos, houses...you name it. They didn't buy fancy clothes or pricey jewelry. They had nice German cars—Mercedes-Benzes and Audis—and they took great vacations, but other than that, they stayed debt-free and cash-rich. Soon after we joined forces, I began changing the way I managed my own money. I saved more. I paid off both my cars and my remaining debt from graduate school. I put 37 percent down on a residential lot in Oakland Hills to build a house. Normally, banks only require 10–20 percent for a down payment, but I was beginning to look at and understand debt as a tool rather than as a well to drink from endlessly.

It took CaRD a while to negotiate the partnership agreement with me. As in, a very, very long while. When I finally received a copy of the agreement and had my attorney review it, he pointed out that the Germans wanted to give me diluted shares that were subordinate to theirs. I was shocked and disappointed, to put it mildly, but I was so glad I'd listened to the advice of another of my mentors, Chuck James III, who told me I always needed to have an attorney review all of my agreements before I signed them. (Spoiler alert: I will be hammering this point home with you in the pages to come.) I expressed my disappointment with the agreement and refused to sign it until my shares were made equivalent. After all, I was the force behind the growth of the company. We were at a stalemate, but we continued to work and make money while trying to come to an acceptable agreement overall.

Nearly two years later, I received a letter from CaRD America informing me that the partners had voted to withdraw my shares because I had never signed my agreement and paid into the partnership. Just like that. They took it away, and now I would be nothing more than an employee at the company I'd been instrumental in building up. I was crushed, but by this time, I knew the business inside and out, and I was confident that I could do it on my own. The timing wasn't exactly right given that my then-wife was home raising twin baby boys, we had another child on the way, and we were in the middle of expensive construction on a custom home. Nevertheless, I resigned and started my company, Oakland Consulting Group, in 1997. I was scared, alone at work, and angry...but more than anything, I was fired up and determined to succeed!

I worked out a deal to continue getting paid for the CaRD projects I'd been working on and in the meantime, I became a machine—Robo-Consultant—racing to complete all my paperwork while calling potential clients for my new business nonstop. I wish I could say I was brimming with faith, but honestly, I felt haunted by doubt and fear all through the process of getting my first contract. What if I couldn't make it on my own?

At last, I came across a deal with IBM in Texas and was able to hire my first consultant under my new Oakland Consulting Group brand. He was a South African guy named David Ducray. You should have seen me the day I hired him. As I drove my car home from a client meeting that afternoon, I had a full-on Jerry McGuire moment. Tom Petty's anthem "Free Fallin'" came on the radio, and I started singing, err...I mean, screaming along, "I'm Free...!!!" It was true. I was finally free to pursue my dream of financial independence (and perhaps get some singing lessons along the way).

My dad had been right: I took a chance, it didn't pan out the way I wanted it to, and I recovered. And every experience you have like that is another lesson not only in how to build wealth but also self-confidence. A short time prior to starting my business in 1997, I was looking at houses in Oakland, California.

My dad, who'd built all the houses I was raised in, suggested I build myself a house, but I told him, "Nah. I don't want to go through that process. It takes too long."

I rejected that idea, although—as with many things my dad or other mentors have told me—I never completely got the idea out of my mind. The more I looked at houses, the more I came to realize I didn't want to pay the asking prices for the type of houses that interested me. So, I decided to build my own. Back then, you could end up with something really nice if you were willing to put up with the time and headache of overseeing its construction. I found a nice piece of land for $242,500, which I bought from a gentleman whose house on the plot had burned down in the notorious Oakland fire.

I persuaded my dad to come supervise the construction because the builder I'd selected had tried to convince me to take out a loan for a (whopping!) million dollars to build the house. I quickly rejected that idea while my dad called some of his buddies who'd built our church. It so happened that his longtime friend George, George's son, George's grandson, and a helper from Oregon were available to help. My prayers had been answered. I bought George a trailer house for them to live in while building my home, and we were all off to the races.

In the end, it cost $622,000 to build that 4,800-plus square foot custom house, which is a long way shy of the million dollars my original contractor quoted. I moved in roughly a year later just as, coincidentally, the housing market in the Bay Area began to rise like mad. In no time, that same house was worth north of $2 million (today Zillow.com estimates that house to be worth $3.8 million). When I combined my equity in the house ($1.3 million), my condo in the San Fernando 'hood ($200,000), and the value of my business ($500,000), my net worth added up to well over a million dollars. In other words, I was officially a millionaire.

At this point, you might think, *Mission accomplished.* I was a millionaire who could relax, live out my life, settle in my business, and play golf whenever the spirit moved me. But I was still a long way from my goal of becoming financially independent, to where my income and wealth would be sizable enough to last through my lifetime. I had plenty more work to do. The leisurely life of golf, champagne, caviar, and crumpets was gonna have to wait.

CHAPTER 3

DEFINING AND UNDERSTANDING WEALTH

The racial wealth gap refers to the difference in wealth between Whites, Blacks, and other ethnicities in the United States. Ironically, even though we're not told to build wealth, we are still being measured as if, the moment we were born, a "wealth doctor" informed us that we'd be evaluated on the basis of how much wealth we created over our lifetime, and then handed us an instruction manual on how to create and maintain wealth. I don't remember much about my birth, but I know for sure that never happened. I think this is a strong contributing factor to the widening of the wealth gap. Most of us don't even know we're in the game, yet we're constantly being told that we're losing the game.

On top of that, we African Americans typically make the mistake of measuring wealth in terms of how much we earn (income), instead of what we keep (net worth). Net worth is the measure of your wealth level, and it is one of the most important concepts to understand in your personal financial life, especially when it comes to building wealth. Once you understand what affects net worth, you can take concrete steps to increase it on your own. Your net worth is not a measure of your value as an individual; it is simply a clear, mathematical indicator of your individual financial state and level of wealth.

Here's why I want you to have a high net worth:

- It can provide you with financial security during economic downturns, such as the one caused by COVID-19.
- It can minimize stress if you ever lose your job or key source(s) of income.
- It can provide you with solid options for how you choose to live your life.
- It can allow you to create generational wealth that can be passed down to your children and grandchildren.

Above all, a high net worth will allow you to create income without you having to physically work for that income. Your money does the work for you, and believe me, like a well-oiled machine, it can work a helluva lot harder and generate more income than you can.

If you take a look at the following template, you'll see what goes into calculating your net worth. One thing you won't see illustrated and which is of paramount importance to this process is the need to be completely honest with yourself in calculating your net worth. This is no time for wishful thinking or lying to yourself. If you've got any unpaid high-interest credit debt somewhere you'd rather forget, well, don't forget it for now; work it into the calculations I'm about to show you.

Determining Your
Net Worth

Assets	Values	Liabilities	Values
Cash		**Student Loan**	
Checking Account	$1,000	Sallie Mae	$37,000
Savings Account	$60,000		
Accounts/Notes Receivables From Others		**Accounts/Notes Debts [Debts to Others]**	
Loan to a Family Member	$2,000	Not Applicable	$0
Retirement Accounts		**Credit Card Debt**	
401[k]	$22,000	Visa Credit Card	$10,000
IRA	$0	American Express	$1,000
		Macy's Credit Card	$2,000
Securities			
Stock [Value]	$0	**Tax Liens/Debts**	
Bond [Value]	$0	Federal Government	$1,000
		State Government	$1,000
Life Insurance Cash Value	$0	**Life Insurance Loans**	$0
Real Estate Values		**Real Estate Liability**	
Primary Residence [Value]	$200,000	Primary Residence Loan Balance	$180,000
Rental Property 1 [Value]	$0	Rental Property 1 Loan Balance	$0
Rental Property 2 [Value]	$0	Rental Property 2 Loan Balance	$0
Business Value/Equity		**Business Debt**	
My Business Name, LLC [Value]	$0	My Business Name, LLC [Debt]	$0
Automobile[s] Value		**Automobile[s] Liabilities**	
BMW [Kelly Blue Book Value]	$40,000	BMW	$30,000
Other Personal Assets		**Other Personal Liabilities**	
Jewelry [Value]	$3,000	Jewelry Debt	$1,000
Furniture Re-sale [Value]	$5,000	Furniture Debt	$3,000
Total Assets	$333,000	**Total Liabilities**	$266,000

Your Net Worth is: **$67,000**

Your net worth is equal to the sum of your assets minus the sum of your liabilities. When news articles report that the racial wealth gap is widening, that Whites have eight times more wealth than Blacks do, and that African Americans have a median net worth of approximately $19,000 (meaning half of us have a net worth above $19,000 and half below), this is the yardstick they are referring to.

Each of you has either a positive net worth (assets greater than liabilities), a negative net worth (liabilities greater than assets), or a zero or neutral net worth. The two columns to focus on in this template are Assets and Liabilities. Assets are anything you own of material financial value. If something has a resale or cash value, it is an asset. For example, your home, if you own it, is an asset (though any mortgages and/or liens against it are liabilities, which we'll get to in a moment). Any rental properties or commercial properties you own are assets. Your cars, jewelry, signature tennis shoes, art, furniture, and handbags are assets too, though more speculative ones. Many assets are speculative because their value depends on how much a buyer is willing to pay for them, and not many people are into buying old furniture, shoes, handbags, and jewelry unless they are considered rare or antiques. If goods are not seen by potential buyers as rare or antique, then their value can drop to as low as $0. Your baseball card or coin collection is an asset. The equity/cash-in value of your life insurance policy is an asset (and an example of a nonspeculative asset). Any sort of royalties you receive on intellectual property, such as an invention, a song you've written, or a book you've published are assets. The value of your business is an asset. Anything that maintains value or generates income for you is an asset.

Assets are classified as either appreciating or depreciating. Appreciating means they tend to go up in value over time. A few common appreciating assets are houses, apartment buildings, commercial offices, retail spaces, land, jewelry, precious metals and gems, rare art, collector coins, specialized furniture, business ventures, and last but not least, stocks and bonds. There's an important distinction to make here: simply because assets are considered appreciating doesn't necessarily mean they *will* appreciate in value. They are always subject to the whims of the marketplace. Also, not all assets generate income. You can generate income with an apartment you rent out, for example, though you'd have a much tougher time trying to generate income by renting out assets like your jewelry, your Jordans, or your Chanel handbags.

Depreciating assets are the opposite of appreciating ones. They tend to go down in value over time. New cars, furniture, and boats are good examples of depreciating assets. They are unlikely to appreciate in value, except for, say, a rare or vintage car. When an asset depreciates over time, as mentioned, its value can depreciate all the way to zero. What matters is not what you paid for it originally or what you think its resale price should be; what matters is how much you can actually sell it for now. When I remodeled my house in Florida and needed to sell my old furniture to make room for the new furniture I'd purchased, I got next to nothing for the old furniture. I'd paid thousands for it but only got hundreds at resale. Fortunately, I'd paid for it all in cash. Imagine how bad that would have been had I initially borrowed those thousands to pay for the old furniture and was still making principal and interest payments, only to receive even less than what I owed on it when I had to sell it.

When you calculate your net worth, the value of your assets goes into the Asset or "plus" column. The Liability or "minus" column is where your debts belong. Your liabilities are the balance owed on the items for which—you guessed it—you are liable. They are the loans, recurring payments, and debts you have to pay off over time, such as your mortgage, your credit card debt, your pay-to-own appliance or furniture payments, any loans you have from family or friends, your student loan payments, and so on; these are the items that counterbalance your assets in determining your net worth.

It might surprise you to learn that not all liabilities are bad. Here's the difference. Good liabilities are those that are anchored to your assets like your mortgage payments (tied to the home you own), student loans (tied to skills that will get you a higher-paying job), or business loans and lines of credit (tied to expansion, new facilities, increased hiring, etc.). I consider a liability good if the debt was acquired to grow your net worth or your income—and, thereby, your wealth. It's also a good liability if someone, say a tenant or your business, is paying it off instead of you.

Bad liabilities, on the other hand, are untethered to assets or anything else that can increase your wealth or income. Bad liabilities are also debts paid for you, by you, and not by anyone else like a tenant or business of yours. Common types of bad liabilities include high-interest car loans, credit card debt, furniture debt, jewelry and pricey wardrobe debt, personal loans, and tax liens. Your goal should be to eliminate them as quickly as possible.

Chances are your net worth is less than what you thought it would be, am I right? If so, no problem. It only means you're human like the rest of us. Throughout our lives, we imagine what our lifestyle will look like at a certain age, but if we haven't set specific financial goals and followed a specific plan to achieve them, then our imagination usually bumps up against financial reality. If you intend to get to Destination Millionaire or beyond, as I hope you do, it's essential that you know your starting point. To be classified as a millionaire, your assets minus your liabilities must be equal to or greater than $1 million. It doesn't matter if you're starting out in the red (negative) or the black (positive), or if you already think you're a millionaire. Do the math and figure out where your road to the top begins. To this day, I keep an up-to-date Excel spreadsheet of my net worth and constantly refer to it in order to track my progress year over year. Your net worth is your scorecard, *not* your income (only when your income reaches and remains in your bank account does it become part of your net worth). When it comes to the game of finance, you always need to know the score and how well you're doing.

Let's begin your voyage to Destination Millionaire by clearly identifying your starting point. List all of your assets and their corresponding values. Use a spreadsheet, an app like Personal Capital, or a plain ol' piece of paper (or feel free to use my template). It doesn't have to be 100 percent accurate for now; 90 percent will do just fine. If the asset is real estate, jot down what Zillow.com or Realtor.com thinks your property is worth. It's only an estimate, so it won't be completely accurate, but it's a scientific calculation based on the price of similar properties in your area. For your 401(k), savings, and stock investment accounts, go online and jot down the value of your accounts today. Add them all up to determine your total assets on your net worth statement or personal balance sheet. (Get it? "Balance," as in the scale that weighs your net worth.)

On the other half of the page, I want you to list and add up all your liabilities. Simply list the amounts you still owe as of right now: your mortgage(s), your car(s), your credit cards, any rent-to-own furniture or appliances, tax liens, judgments, or personal loans you've taken out. Sum these up to determine your total liabilities.

Now subtract the value of your total liabilities from the value of your total assets, and you will know your net worth. That's your starting point.

Congratulations on knowing your current level of wealth! Now you have something to work with, and we can begin to focus our efforts and explore ways of making your net worth and wealth go up, as well as implement strategies to prevent it from going down.

THE MECHANICS OF WEALTH

Let's break down some of the factors that affect net worth. Some financial decisions you make will cause your net worth to go up; others will cause it to go down, and still others will have no impact on your net worth at all. All of them can be learned in order to increase your odds of success.

There are four ways to make your net worth go up:

1. Adding to your assets, which can be as simple as putting money in your savings, retirement, or investment account or as complicated as buying stocks and bonds, a house, a building, land, or a business. Because cash, real estate, business equity, stocks, and bonds live on the asset side of your net worth sheet, if and when any of their values increases, your net worth increases along with them.

2. Decreasing your liabilities or debt makes your net worth go up. Any payments you make on mortgages, car payments, credit card payments, tax liens, and so forth lower your total liabilities and thus elevate your net worth.

3. Purchasing or selling an asset that is worth more than you paid for it makes your net worth go up. If you buy a house for $100,000 and it appraises for $125,000 (meaning a bank or professional appraiser determines it is worth 25 percent more than

what you paid for it), then your net worth has just increased by 25 percent, or $25,000. This is true as long as you didn't simultaneously increase your liabilities elsewhere by taking out a second loan or a credit line against that $25,000 in equity. If you purchased stock for $100 a share and then sold it for $125 a share, you'd increase your net worth by $25 per share as long as you avoid the temptation to spend that profit on an item that's not an asset (travel, new wardrobe, etc.).

4. Asset appreciation is the final way to increase your net worth. Remember earlier how we determined that some assets appreciate while others depreciate? Because of that, any assets you purchase which appreciate over time increase your net worth. Even if you borrowed money to acquire an asset such as real estate, the equity (meaning the asset's value minus any debt owed on it) increases through appreciation, while the liability decreases as you pay it off over time. In short, your asset goes up in value at the same time that your liability on it goes down, thereby increasing your net worth in two ways. This is how millionaires and billionaires are created. They use their income to buy appreciating assets; then, they sell those assets over time to buy even more valuable assets that can generate greater income until their net worth/wealth reaches several million or billions of dollars. This is precisely what I'm trying to teach you to do so that you too can achieve Destination Millionaire and beyond.

Let's now look at what makes your net worth go down.

1. Any increase in liability or debt not associated with a higher-valued asset makes your net worth go down. In the previous

example, if your asset's value were to go down, or if you took on more debt associated with it and spent it (such as a home equity loan), your net worth would automatically decrease. By the same token, if you go on a shopping spree and spend $5,000 on your credit card, which increases your liabilities, you'll have just lowered your net worth as well. Spending on things that don't appreciate in value diminishes your wealth.

2. Another way net worth decreases is when you overpay for an asset or sell it for less than you paid for it. For example, if you'd paid $100,000 in cash for a house and then decided to sell it in a buyer's market for $80,000, your net worth would decrease by $20,000, plus the closing costs.

3. Investing in and owning assets that depreciate also lowers your net worth. Assets that typically decrease in value over time are cars, jewelry, handbags, and furniture. When you purchase them brand-new, they are at their highest value. Over time, their value depreciates as newer items become more desirable. Each year the expensive cars, jewelry, handbags, and furniture you own decrease in value. Their value will eventually drop to zero or thereabouts. Some assets (like my old furniture) will even cost you money to get rid of.

Using your hard-earned money to purchase depreciating assets will never result in building your wealth. I will show you how to acquire assets that appreciate over time as well as how to simultaneously lower your liabilities and thereby increase your net worth—and, therefore, your wealth. That's how we can do our part to begin reversing the racial wealth gap. Let's look at these concepts in everyday life.

WEALTH VERSUS INCOME

Remember earlier how I said that your salary isn't an asset until it stays permanently in your bank account? That's because income and wealth are entirely different from each other. It's an important distinction to understand because a lot of folks earn large incomes but never grow their wealth because they don't put that income to work. Instead, they spend it on things that depreciate outright, or they neglect to invest it in assets that can maintain or increase in value and also create more income. Your income is the money you earn, whereas your wealth is the money or value you keep. Income can be generated either from your labor or, as it is for countless millionaires and billionaires, from your assets (cash, real estate, stocks, and businesses).

Too many people make the mistake of assuming the income from their job or jobs will make them rich. But even a major sports figure like LeBron James, who earns $39.22 million a year playing basketball for the LA Lakers, may only add 25 percent of that income to his wealth/net worth. Why? Because he has to pay the government something like 40 percent of his income in taxes, his agent is owed another 5–10 percent, his accountants and lawyers need to be paid, he has to pay his living expenses just like you and I do, his entourage needs to be paid (personal assistant, extended family, stylist, house manager, homeboys, etc.), and he has to pay off any liabilities or debts he may have. So, yes, LeBron has a gigantic income but his net worth, like yours, depends not only on his salary but on how much of his remaining salary he saves and uses to purchase assets that will appreciate and provide him with additional investment income. If you think that's just splitting hairs, let me remind you that the 2020 basketball season was nearly canceled due to COVID-19, a circumstance no one foresaw. If LeBron thought he was going to make $39.22 million and had created a *playa's* lifestyle to go along with it, he'd have been hard-pressed to cope with a massive salary cut *unless* he had a high net worth, generating income to fall back upon. Several athletes did suffer during the early stages of the pandemic because they made baller-level money but hadn't invested enough in income-generating assets to cover their ballerific lifestyles. That's why you must never confuse income with wealth, and it's also why in these pages you will learn how to use your income to purchase and invest in assets that grow in value and generate income.

HOW WEALTH IS MAINTAINED

Wealth is maintained through the seemingly simple act of not allowing it to be depleted. But don't let that simplicity fool you. Your wealth must always grow faster than the rate of inflation, and it cannot be spent without being further replenished. Try to think of your wealth as a muscle; if ignored or left to depreciate, it will atrophy and eventually die. Wealth must be consistently reinvested, grown, and carefully managed to be sustained and expanded. There is a lot of talk among Black folks about the need and desire to create generational wealth. We use the words so often and in so many ways that I think it's essential we clarify and understand what generational wealth is and isn't and, more importantly, how it is sustained. Generational wealth is not merely about an estate worth billions of dollars that can be passed on from generation to generation. Even billion-dollar fortunes have been lost before. One of the biggest mistakes people make is assuming that they can't possibly lose their fortune because it is too large, which is like thinking you can never run out of gas. After all, your tank is full today. Sometimes all it takes to destroy wealth is a stock market crash (of which there were at least three in the last century), the right kind of thief (remember Bernie Madoff?), or—more commonly—bad money behaviors (Nicholas Cage, Mike Tyson, Evander Holyfield; the list goes on among the famous and the less-than-famous). Whether fortunes vanish in an instant or die progressively over time, both large and modest ones are more easily extinguished than you'd think. Many famous families such as the Rockefellers built massive fortunes, though not all of them have succeeded in creating generational wealth. The Rockefeller's wealth has extended seven generations with as many as 170 heirs.[14] That's more than a hundred years after John D. Rockefeller became America's first billionaire after founding Standard Oil Company in the late nineteenth century. They cited four main components as the keys to the success in maintaining generational wealth. Through regular family meetings and maintaining family history, the family changed its purpose from business to charity, and they focused on maintaining certain core values around giving.

To create generational wealth, you need two essential components. First, there has to be enough wealth created in one generation to last more than another generation. Otherwise, a legacy has only one shot at being passed on any further. Second, the receiving generation must possess the values, principles, practices, and skills to maintain and build wealth that can be passed on to the next subsequent generation. These same values, principles, practices, and skills must be taught, learned, and developed over time. They don't come automatically with money or legacy. They need to be taught by the previous generations and established over time. The Rockefellers, for example, have maintained and extended their wealth for seven

---

[14] Robert Frank, "4 Secrets to Raising Wealthy Kids, According to the Billionaire Rockefeller Family," *CNBC*, March 26, 2018, https://www.cnbc.com/2018/03/26/david-rockefeller-jr-shares-4-secrets-to-wealth-and-family.html.

generations by holding regular family meetings, paying close attention to maintaining the family's history, focusing on philanthropy (rather than a business, which can easily create tension across an extended family), and maintaining giving as a core value of the family.[15]

LEVELS OF WEALTH

Your net worth provides you with a clear picture of where you stand financially. Are you a millionaire? Are you financially independent? Let's look further at what those terms exactly mean.

To achieve Destination Millionaire and beyond, the total value of your Assets column...

- Your house
- Your cash
- Your real estate
- Your ownership interest in any business(es)
- Your private equity deals, stocks, or bonds
- Your valuable artwork, rare collections (books, coins, etc.), or jewelry that's been recently appraised

Minus the total value of your Liabilities column...

- Property debt
- Mortgages against your house
- Credit card debts
- Car debt
- Outstanding student loans

---

[15] Ibid.

...must sum up to $1 million or more. That means your net worth is above $1 million, and you are in fact and name a millionaire. However, as desirable as that may sound, you may still not be financially independent even when you become a millionaire. I'm not saying you shouldn't congratulate yourself on reaching such an important milestone. It's a fantastic achievement. It just shouldn't be confused with financial independence.

Financial independence is when your assets (which include pensions and social security income) are producing enough income to cover your lifestyle. Dividends, stock appreciation, real estate income, and other forms of self-generating, passive income can pay for everything your heart needs or desires. When that happens, you will officially be financially independent. It means your money is working *for you*, and you now have the means to choose to stop working for money if you choose to. You don't have to retire of course, and you sure can't stop the work of carefully managing your assets, but there can and hopefully will come a point in your financial life when all the money to meet your needs is being earned by your assets themselves.

WHAT NET WORTH (LEVEL OF WEALTH) DO YOU ASPIRE TO?

Let me share with you how I see the various levels of wealth to which you can aspire. These aren't scientific observations by any means; they're simply intended to give you an idea of what the various levels you envision for yourself may require in order to reach them. I also want to give you a sense of what you can and can't do at each level. I know that not everyone feels they need to become an actual millionaire, nor is everyone willing to put in the hard work it takes to become financially independent, to say nothing of becoming a billionaire. We all have different hopes and desires. But as

I mentioned at the start of our journey together, you won't get anywhere if you don't start with a clear destination in mind.

I've narrowed down wealth aspirations to the following six levels, in rough order of ascendancy:

1. Financial Comfort
2. Financial Independence
3. Millionaire
4. Rich
5. Ultra Rich
6. Billionaire

Of these, the only hard and fast levels are Millionaire and Billionaire, which correspond to a net worth of $1 million and $1 billion, respectively. The others are more malleable depending on your own personal situation. I like to frame them like this:

- **Financial Comfort/Security**—Having near-zero debt, ownership of modest-to-large assets (one house, one to two cars, etc.), six to twelve months of savings in the bank, on track to retire comfortably at age sixty-five or later.
- **Financial Independence**—Having income from your retirement or assets (pension, social security income, cash, investments, business) that exceeds your living expenses. Zero or near-zero debt balance that can be comfortably paid for by your income.
- **Millionaire**—Having a net worth of $1 million or more, though not necessarily financially independent if the income generated by your assets don't exceed your living expenses.

- **Rich**—Having a net worth greater than $5 million, liquid cash in your investment account greater than $1 million, financially independent (see above), and zero personal debt (credit cards, personal loans, car loans, etc.). Rich can range from the lower end of $5 million in net worth to anywhere under Ultra Rich at $100 million.
- **Ultra Rich**—Having a net worth greater than $100 million and liquid cash in your investment account greater than $25 million.
- **Billionaire**—Having a net worth of $1 billion or more.

These levels are merely intended to give you some idea of where you may choose to go, not to box you into one aspiration or another. For instance, can you consider yourself rich if your net worth is only $4 million? I suppose so, depending on the cost of living in your area and your lifestyle choices. What matters is that you use the framework outlined in this book to align with a definitive, achievable goal.

I've known a lot of positive net worth people who mistakenly believe they're rich, and I don't want you to make that same mistake. Let me break it down a bit more colloquially, based again on some of my own observations, and let's see how these definitions often look in real life...

High in income, low in assets? *Nah, you're not rich.*

Bottle service at the club? *Sorry, you're not rich.*

Red bottoms, Gucci down to the socks? *That's flossin'...that ain't rich.*

One house or no house and only one income stream? *Un-unh. Not rich.*

Big Body Benz, nowadays a Rolls-Royce "Phantom." *Face it, playa... that don't mean you're rich.*

Exotic vacation, no stocks and bonds? *Nope. You're not rich.*

Closet full of top designers, empty 401(k)? *Seriously? No comment...*

Business owner, zero in the owner's equity column of your balance sheet. *You said, "Zero," right? Sorry, son, you're not rich.*

Living rich, acting rich, spending like you're rich? *That ain't rich. That's just actin' a fool.*

I'm not trying to be mean or cynical, though truth be told, I do hope some of my hard-edged observations make you a little uncomfortable. If you felt something, that means you care enough to change. The immortal Harriet Tubman once said, "I could've freed a thousand more slaves if they had knew (sic) they were slaves." Black people, we have every justifiable reason for blaming White America for our financial situation, but it's time we evaluate our own behaviors and decisions, so we can finally control our own destiny.

In all likelihood, to achieve your purpose and live out your dreams, you will need to try to achieve financial independence and Destination Millionaire. My goal with this book is to remove the mystery and myths about becoming a millionaire by providing you with the steps and process to get you there. The process is not hard; it's just slow, and it's difficult to stay the course. I'm confident I can get you there because I, and countless others, have done it too, starting from the bottom.

Let's stop acting, playing, living, and spending like we're rich. Instead, let me show you how to get rich for real!

CHAPTER 4

FINDING YOUR WEALTH-BUILDING PURPOSE

Here's an essential question to ask yourself as you begin this journey: What is your endgame? What is your true wealth aspiration? Let's explore why you want to be wealthy, and then let's pick an endgame that will help lead you to it. You'll experience a lot of unexpected changes and circumstances as you make your way to your endgame. For now, let's start by imagining your dream in its purest form. I define the endgame as the point in your journey where you can either continue to build wealth and income for life or divert your efforts to the items on your bucket list. You can make this choice because you are financially independent and have achieved the financial goals that you have set out for yourself. When the buzzer sounds and you look up at the scoreboard and see you've reached your goals, what should that moment look and feel like to you? Author Dan Sullivan asked a similar question when he wrote,[16] "If you and I were to meet three years from today, what would you want to have happened for you personally and professionally, in order to consider those years a success?" I think this is an excellent way to set yourself up not only for the near term but the long term as well. Where do you want to be ten, twenty, or thirty years from now?

Building wealth is about using your income to invest in assets and thereby putting your money to work for you instead of you working endlessly for your money. That's why several years ago my own endgame looked something like this: a minimum of $12.5 million in cash, which in turn would earn me $500,000 in income per year. I planned to invest all $12.5 million of my cash in the stock market, assuming (conservatively) an average annual yield of 6 percent. I could withdraw 4 percent a year, or $500,000 as income, and allow the remaining 2 percent to cover inflation. I also wanted to own enough rental properties to earn another $500,000 per year which, based on a 10 percent annual return, meant I would need an additional $5 million invested in real estate. Together, with the income I'm making off the cash reserves, that would have me earning a total of $1 million per year. But I wasn't finished drawing my endgame yet because that was only a picture of my income, not my entire net worth. I wanted and still want to maintain zero personal debt on my personal properties, credit cards, automobiles, etc. I want to live a debt-free life and maintain a lifestyle that supports that dream. In short, I'm determined that my living expenses will never exceed my income. Once I accomplished that, I'd set my sights on my bucket list items.

That's only one example of an endgame and admittedly, it's an ambitious one. Your endgame could be as simple as wanting to have $50,000 a

---

[16] Dan Sullivan, *The Dan Sullivan Question* (Illinois: The Strategic Coach, Inc, 2009), 16.

year (roughly $4,200 a month) to draw from your 401(k) for your retirement, plus $2,000 per month from your IRA. We're all different, and it's important to understand that *your* endgame is the only one that matters. What kind of life do *you* want to have? You might work forty hours a week now and have an endgame of only having to work twenty hours a week by the time you're sixty. If so, more power to you. I like that endgame because it's specific, measurable, and achievable, so long as you also ask yourself where you're going to derive other income in order to compensate for the time you won't be working at your full-time job.

Perhaps you want to travel in retirement, ride your Harley, play golf or tennis, or pursue another passion four times a week. Maybe you'd like to set up an endowment in your name at the local college. All of these pursuits are components of an endgame. In Chapter 2, I showed you how I wrote my plan when I finished my undergraduate studies and how it enabled me to reach Destination Millionaire by the time I was thirty-two. In Chapter 7, I'll show you a template I've created to help you write your own plan. When I first looked back and realized how closely I'd hewn to my plan and how much of it had worked out as outlined, I was astonished. I wasn't expecting those kinds of results, although with the benefit of hindsight, I see that I became my own proof of concept. Planning works. I can officially report *based on actual experience* that writing a good plan can believably lead to Destination Millionaire. And as you'll see, it doesn't take a genius to do it. Heck, I'm living proof of that!

To begin laying out your endgame, write down the exact month and year at which you want to achieve it. Don't be shy; in order to get where you're going, you need to pick a deadline now and start working toward it. How much sustainable income (income that you don't have to work for) do you want to have by that date? How much income will you be obtaining from each of your various income sources (Social Security, pension, 401(k), IRA, rental properties, stock and bond withdrawals, dividend income, alternative investment income, businesses, etc.) at your endgame date? How much personal debt do you plan on having at that point? What are the levels of wealth and net worth goals you want to have achieved by then?

The Book of Proverbs says, "Where there is no vision, the people perish. But happy is he that keepest the law." For our purposes, that "law" is your financial plan, and that plan has to come from a meaningful place in your heart and mind because, if it ain't worth it to you in the right way, then trust me, it ain't worth diddly. Wealth building is a task that must be imbued with personal meaning; otherwise, you'll struggle to find the courage to persist when life's inevitable hurdles come up against you and, by extension, your portfolio.

I've found that the best way to find your purpose for wealth is to ask yourself questions like these: How do you want to live your life in your thirties? How about your forties, fifties, sixties, seventies, and beyond? What kind of interactions do you want to have with your family and friends? How should the days and weeks of your future life unfold? Do you want to retire? Keep working your day job? Try something you've never done before? How much time do you want to spend working each week? How will you generate sufficient income for any of these scenarios at each milestone—your fortieth birthday, your fiftieth, and so on? Suppose your purpose is to give back. What type of philanthropic activities would you want to be involved in? It's important to understand that money can't necessarily make your life happy; it can only make it easier. Happiness, I believe, comes from a sense of purpose.

Once you know what those targets and time frames are, you can begin to work backward and figure out how to turn them into reality. Choose your destination and then find the best path to get there. In my case, I've decided that between fifty-five and sixty-five years of age I want to live my life as a wealth evangelist, educator, and investor. I want the choice to wear shorts, T-shirts, or flip-flops whenever I'm "at work." I don't want to attend daily meetings, constantly be on conference calls, or have to return emails. Been there, done that. I want to spend time with my friends and family. I want to enjoy watching my kids and eventually my grandkids grow up. I want to be able to do whatever I do either from my home in the US, or on a boat I own, or from my place in the Caribbean where the temperature likes to hover in the eighties. I want to be untethered from any sort of grind, and in order to achieve that ideal, I know I'll have to create enough income to support my desired way of life. That's why my plan is so financially ambitious. I was lucky enough (opportunity plus preparation equals luck) and wise enough (thanks to guidance from my many mentors) to begin putting the building blocks in place early in order to have the right income at the right time frame in my life. But as I said earlier, don't assume that now is not too late for you. Now is always right on time.

I believe you have to vividly define how you want to live at specific periods of your life because, if you don't document it, if you don't actually write it down, you'll be left with a vision that is blurry at best. You wouldn't drive your car with a dirty windshield, so why settle for a vague perspective on some of the biggest questions you will ever face? You can always be flexible and make changes, but you have to build and commit to a core idea first. You may feel a sense of regret at not having started earlier, though believe me, it's not too late; it only means you've got to be that much more intense and focused about developing and executing your plan going forward.

Let me ask you this: do you want to live your life serving your purpose or someone else's? That was a big either/or for me. I once had the opportunity to ask this question of actual executives of major Fortune 500 companies whose conference I was invited to speak at in the Bahamas. When I completed my presentation, entitled "One Life to Live: Living Life on Your Terms," the room was so quiet, you could have heard a coconut fall outside. Either I'd completely bombed my presentation or else the audience was seriously deep in thought. Fortunately, it turned out to be the latter. One of the executives from Johnson & Johnson (J&J) came up to me immediately afterward and confessed that perhaps the path he was on wasn't genuinely aligned with his purpose. Most of the execs had never even considered posing that sort of "whose purpose" question to themselves. Perhaps they were too distracted by their world of generous salaries, big houses, and children in private school to allow themselves a question so challenging yet so fundamental. Yet, no matter how you slice it, the folks who work at a big company like J&J are serving the purpose of their company's largest shareholders (Vanguard Investments, as of this writing), even if they also have a small stake in the company. That doesn't make J&J or any other large corporation a bad place to work or invest, though it does raise the question as to who's serving whose purpose. Mind you, there's nothing wrong with that way of life; in fact, there's a great deal to envy, so long as it's grounded in *your* purpose and *your* plan. Otherwise, it can quickly lead to unhappiness. There are many awful things to die of, so do yourself a favor and make sure that regret isn't one of them. A failure to plan is truly a plan to fail. Using my various "whys" for desiring wealth as an example, I want you to start putting pen to paper, or fingers to keyboard, and come up with your own.

Any sincere inquiry into purpose begins with the question why? Why do I want this? What do I hope to get from it, not in dollar terms, but in the spiritual sense? I think it's as important to know why you aspire to something as it is to know what you aspire to. I'm grateful to author Tony Robbins, who in his book, *Money: Master the Game*, identifies several universal needs for wealth, though I see the topic slightly differently, more as desires we all share rather than absolute needs. I call my version "The Whys of Wealth Building":

1. Comfort—The dream of Financial Peace in which you no longer have to worry about money.
2. Freedom and Independence—The ability to do whatever you want, whenever you want.
3. Significance—The desire to feel like you matter or are important for what you do. The hunger to obtain greater standing among your peers.
4. Contribution—The urge to give back to or make an impact on your community and/or the larger world. Spending to make a difference.
5. Love and Connection—The need to be wanted and loved and to draw people to you.
6. Power and Control—Using wealth to achieve dominion, control territories and/or others, and influence personal outcomes.
7. Legacy—The ability to pass wealth down to future generations of your family. To make a name for yourself and family who will be known by others and will last for years.

Knowing your "why" or "whys" can point you in the direction of the wealth level which corresponds to your aspirations. They may require you to be ultra wealthy in order to make the level of contribution you desire.

For instance, billionaire Michael Jordan recently pledged $100 million over the next ten years to fight racial injustice by opening a clinic in Charlotte, North Carolina, to help those without healthcare. To contribute at that level, you must aspire to be—like Mike—a billionaire. Alternatively, you can make a significant contribution by donating your time, provided you aspire to and attain a wealth level of financial independence. It all depends on how you plan on contributing.

If your "why for wealth" is legacy, you'll need to amass enough wealth to pass down several generations like the Rockefellers. Given that one generation lasts about twenty to thirty years, the Rockefeller's seven generations of legacy wealth adds up to 100 to 150 years total. You'll need to reach an ultra-rich-to-billionaire range of wealth to accomplish that.

If your "why for wealth" is significance, then you only need enough money to pay for the things that make folks notice you. Bottle Service in the club, if that's your thing, runs $3,000–5,000 a night in most places. Or you can lease a big house in the LA hills or buy enough flashy cars to get you an episode of MTV Cribs. Significance doesn't require wealth at all. It simply requires enough income to make the monthly payments on your fabulous lifestyle so that everyone can see you and see how important you are on YouTube and Instagram.

I've narrowed my own "whys" and motivations down to these five:

1. Freedom/Independence—I've always been afraid to entrust my destiny to anyone else. My thing has been "if I can make my own money, then no one can mess with me." I have an abiding fear that someone—a boss, a company, or someone else—could take everything I've worked so hard for away from me without notice. My motivation isn't rooted in greed; I fear dependency

on something outside of my control. When it comes to money, I want to be the boss of me.

2. Comfort/Security—It's a big beautiful world out there, and I want to be able to live my life, travel around in peace, and experience it without having to worry about money.

3. Contribution—My parents always respected the struggle of their fellow man. We kids grew up watching my parents help others, like when they would shelter entire families by having them live with us for various periods of time. My dad had a halfway house for former inmates to help them transition back to normal life. My sister and brother would give the shirts off their backs to help others as well. I want to be the kind of example to others that they have been to me.

4. Significance—You've probably already noticed that I like flashy things that draw attention to me. And I've got a feeling I'm not alone, am I right? Look, the key to buying yourself shiny objects is balance. That and never mistaking the glitter for an appreciating asset. In Chapter 7, we'll talk about managing the need for significance by creating a responsible reward system that allows you to ball hard along the road to wealth building.

5. Legacy—My gramps was a sharecropper. My dad worked for the US Army and the State of California. I want to take my family to a higher level financially and create generational wealth. I'm the first entrepreneur in our family, and I'm challenging my children to take us up to a level above what I am able to accomplish. I want to leave behind a legacy that can endure and be built upon.

What I see happening with most young people when they start making money is they immediately go on a buying spree. They see other people with nice stuff, and they either don't know or don't accept that their money should have a greater purpose beyond material accumulation. The same thing generally happens to people who hit the Lotto. The money comes surging in before a purpose for the money has been established, which explains how that brand of multimillionaires so often end up penniless (more on that later).

My reasons for desiring wealth changed over time and grew largely out of my observations of others. At first, all I wanted was simple comfort. My ultimate goal was Chillax-ation with a capital "C," even though I was willing to work extremely hard to reach that goal, or from time to time, if I wanted something particular that cost a lot of money.

All through high school, I worked two restaurant jobs and a job at Wells Fargo Bank while simultaneously going to class and doing my homework (not all of it of course...I'm far from perfect). My senior year, I desperately wanted to go to the prom in style, so I busted my hump in order to save up enough dough to make the scene in style. I worked at a restaurant called The Rogue on Monterey's Fisherman's Wharf, and I'll never forget my days as a busboy and juicer, working the fresh juice machine by hand for the brunch crowd. Every Sunday, it was Man versus Fruit... with Fruit usually coming out on top. Not a fun way to spend my weekends at all.

Eventually, I got promoted to being a maître d', which meant seating the guests, cleaning, and resetting tables when they finished their meals. I vividly remember the sight of all those families seated together in seeming bliss while I ducked in and out of the hellish kitchen at The Rogue. Compared to me, they were sitting in Paradise.

I remember meeting this one particular White family who came for brunch one afternoon. By then, I'd been promoted to host, and as I watched them looking from their table toward the stunning Pacific Ocean, I began imagining what their lives must be like. *He's some kind of well-paid engineer from Silicon Valley*, I thought. *Probably drives a shiny new BMW. They eat brunch like this every weekend except when they entertain guests in their beautiful hilltop home with a panoramic sweep of the coast.* Honestly, for all I knew they could have been tourists from Oklahoma, but as far as my imagination was concerned, this family was living the Dream! It was the kind of dream I thought perfectly suited me...until one fateful day, when my desire for that version of simple, bourgeois comfort unexpectedly changed forever.

It happened in nearby Palo Alto. I had stopped at a Quik Stop to pick up a snack when, lo and behold, I peeped this White dude waiting in the parking lot wearing a crisp, seriously ballerific blue suit. What's more, he was seated behind the wheel of a stunning new 7 Series BMW. I've been a lifelong car fanatic, and back then, I couldn't wait to be able to buy my first Beamer, never mind a 7 Series. My older cousin Eric Burney had a 3 Series that I was crazy about. This baller at the Quik Stop had a 7, and I determined then and there, I was going to save enough money to bag one for myself someday. Comfort and serenity would have to wait until I'd had myself a good taste of the high life.

I walked over to the baller and asked him, "Sir, what do you do for a living?"

"I'm a sales executive at IBM," he replied.

Say what? A sales executive? That wasn't the answer I expected at all. A sales guy making that kind of dough? Despite my initial skepticism, I guess, in the end, I must have believed him because that's exactly where that little entry in my first plan before the end of college—about wanting to be a sales guy at IBM selling computer stuff—came from. My ex-wife Rhonda would probably laugh at this today because she knew, back when I met her in college, all I wanted to do was become an engineer, make thirty grand a year, and kick it in a condo in Foster City where my cousin Eric and all the other yuppies lived. Period, exclamation point, end of story. To me, that was the Buppie (Black Urban Professional) lifestyle dream. That was gonna be my version of, "Hey, Cedric, now you're living!" Some people want to work their way up to the top, but I was content to scratch and fight my way up to the middle, so long as I had that BMW in the garage. But fate intervened once more when I moved to Southern California at age twenty-four and became tight with Rhonda's high school boyfriend, a twenty-two-year-old guy named Juan Walker.

At that time in my life, I thought of myself as this young, hotshot kind of Brotha who *gets stuff done*, if you know what I'm sayin'. A big fish in a medium-to-large-sized pond. Yet, the more I got to know Juan Walker and watch and compare myself to him and what he was up to, the more my pond resembled a tiny puddle. Make that a raindrop.

Juan was on fire! He was buying office buildings, running a mortgage company he owned, constructing an apartment building, and working the local political machine too. He was friends with Tom Bradley, LA's first and only Black mayor, and Roger Mosley, who played T.C. on the TV show *Magnum P.I.* I vividly remember seeing them outside of Juan's house talking for hours inside T.C.'s black 928 Porsche. This Juan cat was seriously connected. He was buying Mercedes-Benzes and Porsches to go along with the beautiful house he had no business owning at that young age, while my big dream was a BMW and—eventually, someday—a hammock on a beach somewhere.

Seeing firsthand how people like Juan and other Angelenos of his ilk lived in Los Angeles changed me. That's the honest truth. All of a sudden, I found myself thinking, *You know what? I think I want to be rich, not just comfortable.*

At the same time, I also saw Juan making deal commitments here and deal commitments there without actually knowing where he was going to get the money to do the deals. It was a bold, fascinating, risky style of investing like I'd never seen before. A sort of deal-first-find-the-money-later process. My style was, and still is, a lot more deliberative and cautious than Juan's. Way more cautious.

Still, I was blown away by the financial freedom and crazy confidence he had. There's no other way to describe it. To be able to do whatever you want when you want and how you want? It all seemed so...what's the word? Glamorous! I was totally wowed. And underneath all that gloss I saw a new purpose to the accumulation of wealth. The ability to lead my life how I wanted without ever having to worry about money. That was a revelation; beyond the superficial trappings of money, there lay something far greater and meaningful. Freedom.

Please understand: I'm not recommending any of these wealth-building motives to you. We're all different. I only hope you'll see that it's alright to explore different reasons to want to be wealthy until you find one (or more) that fits you as well as that baller's suit fits him. Without the anchor of a purpose, you will forever be adrift in your pursuit of wealth. You need to know and feel the "why" of what you do in order to muster the toughness you'll need to execute the "how."

So, take the time and ask yourself: what is your wealth aspiration and why do you want it? Those are questions for you and you alone to answer. Once you know your starting point, have your wealth destination picked out, and know your "why" for wealth. After that, the only thing left to do is select a path and timeline and set sail. When you think about the various reasons that you want to build wealth, I'd like you to add this one as well: you might unleash something wonderful in yourself that you weren't even aware of. Your purpose for building wealth often unlocks a broader, less obvious purpose that comes from within. Who knows? You may find a creative part of yourself you hadn't tapped into, or perhaps a philanthropic one, as I did.

CHAPTER 5

DEVELOPING A MILLIONAIRE MINDSET

My wealth-building system is made up of three phases. Phase One is called Develop the Millionaire Mindset. I like to think of it as "The Offense." It's where we will learn what sort of traits we'll need to accumulate income and wealth. Phase Two is called Adopt Millionaire Values. Think of it as "The Defense." That's where we develop the psychological and behavioral armor-plating you'll need to protect your gains and keep you from falling off the wealth-building wagon. Phase Three is called Make Millionaire Money Moves. That's "The Playbook." It's the nuts-and-bolts process of building a millionaire asset portfolio while sustaining and growing your wealth. All three phases must work simultaneously, and each is required to complete the journey. You will find that you cannot consistently make Millionaire Money Moves unless your mindset and values work in concert with your actions. Otherwise, your results will be dismal at best.

PHASE ONE: DEVELOPING A
MILLIONAIRE MINDSET ("THE OFFENSE")

Your mindset is the way in which you think about things. It's your mental disposition. Everyone's mindset is loaded with preconditioned ideas and beliefs based on their experiences in the world and the types of information and knowledge to which they are exposed. You can almost think about your mindset the way you do about computers. Your brain is the hardware; your mindset is the software. But developing a Millionaire Mindset isn't merely the biological equivalent of downloading a new app and learning how to use it. It's a much bigger task. It involves a whole new operating system that needs to run on a platform it's never been on (you), kind of like running Windows on a Mac, or Android on an iPhone. In developing a Millionaire Mindset, we're going to teach your brain which of your tired, preconditioned financial beliefs and practices to discard and how to embrace a new, more productive set of them. It's a forward-thinking mindset that enables wealth development instead of impeding it. I'm sure you've heard that money is power, which means that the ability to make, retain, and pass on money is the ability to empower yourself and future generations.

That process begins with possessing the correct mindset. The Millionaire Mindset is made up of the ideas and beliefs possessed by millionaires and billionaires. It is the secret sauce which fuels their practices and lies at the core of their success. Adopting the Millionaire Mindset is essential because the journey to Destination Millionaire and beyond is several years long, arduous, and seeded with obstacles and setbacks. Having the appropriate mindset is the only thing that can keep you pushing forward in spite of the impediments that life will inevitably throw your way in your struggle to succeed. People who never adopt the Millionaire Mindset never reach Destination Millionaire. They continue to believe the world owes them success, and they either give up—or worse—they pursue shortcuts and get-rich-quick schemes that lead nowhere for them and straight to the bank for the litany of hustlers and promoters who prey on their despair and gullibility.

Like most things on your new wealth-building path, making room for your new mindset will not be easy as we all have significant psychological baggage to overcome. We're taught early on about the cumulative impact of slavery to our dignity and self-esteem. Many of us believe that spending on luxury items is the right way for us to show the world that we've arrived, that we are somebody, and that somehow the residual impact of slavery has spared us its accursed wrath. This confused type of overcompensation manifests itself in many different ways. Those of us who grew up poor, in poor neighborhoods, and never had many material possessions have a tendency when we finally do get some money to immediately spend lavishly in order to feel rich and experience what we believe is the same quality of life that White people have always enjoyed. We try to feel successful by emulating what we think success looks like. Folks in our community, in turn, treat us like we're rich, and thus, we feel rich and continue buying to achieve the attention that comes with looking rich. Then, there are those of us who feel that the White man is threatened by our progress, which is why he won't allow us to progress and build wealth, so why even bother? After all, look what happened in Tulsa, Oklahoma, when Black Wall Street was destroyed by Whites in 1921 because Blacks had begun creating a strong independent economic base. Or what about those of us who've worked ten times harder than our White counterparts to become doctors, lawyers, engineers, and other highly compensated professionals? Don't we deserve to spend our money on nice clothes, nice cars, nice houses, and lavish vacations like others at our economic level? Finally, what about those raised in the church who were taught to believe that "The love of money is the root of all evil," or "It would be easier for a camel to pass through the eye of a needle than for a rich man to enter the gates of heaven?" How can you be singularly focused on building wealth when your mind vacillates between desire, entitlement, and/or guilt? This confusion impedes our focus on building wealth and thereby amplifies our racial wealth gap with respect to other ethnic groups.

It's no small feat to overcome these conflicting paradigms in our mindsets. It's especially hard for any of us to recognize flaws in our way of thinking because we've probably had at least some level of success doing things the way we always have, and at some point in our lives, they became rooted in our own sense of survival. But let's remember, even a broken clock is right twice a day. That doesn't mean it knows how to tell time. Too much of our personal and community wealth mindset has been based on the idea of faking it till we make it, acting rich until we become rich. Except that's only an acting lesson, nothing more. Has wearing Prada ever been the reason why a client selects to do business with you? What I'm going to show you is how to tell financial time all day long, twenty-four hours a day, seven days a week, for the rest of your and your benefactors' lifetimes. Why? Because it's time to change our mindset of acting rich and instead actually become rich.

True empowerment begins with this change in our mindset: we need to accept as a community that where we are on the financial scale is not our fault, though it *is* our responsibility to fix it. We must focus our efforts on the things we can control, rather than being consumed by the things we can't. No one is coming to save us, so we have to save ourselves.

Pun intended. We are capable of rebuilding our trust in one another and leveraging our $1.3 trillion in spending power to get as rich or richer than other ethnic groups in America. We have the resources, capabilities, education, and tools to end poverty in our communities by recycling our dollars and using them to build wealth, jobs, and business opportunities for ourselves.

We've all read about and seen highly successful African Americans like Tyler Perry, Tiger Woods, Robert Smith, Spike Lee, Oprah Winfrey, or Jay-Z, to name but a few. Fortunately, none of the eight elements I will outline in my system requires you to be a talented rapper, gifted storyteller, pitcher with a hundred-mile-an-hour fastball, or a six-eight guard named LeBron. That's the good news. While wealth building takes the right mindset, effort, and determination, it does not require any sort of extraordinary talent. I've got the average height and mediocre golf game to prove it.

So, let's get started...

To develop a Millionaire Mindset, we must first release the limiting beliefs we may have about how to accumulate wealth. This is extremely difficult because our beliefs and practices have been programmed and reinforced throughout our lifetime. You can't change overnight, but you can't become or stay rich overnight either, which means that fortunately, you have adequate time to change your thinking.

For our purposes, change is an action, not a noun. Change is a *decision* you make, and to change your mindset, you must make an agreement with yourself to attempt the things millionaires do—or as I call it, make Millionaire Money Moves—even if you don't yet believe that they'll work for you. This is a different type of "fake it till you make it," though it can work in your favor and help you recognize what's been standing in the way of your getting to Destination Millionaire thus far.

I believe that to be successful and achieve your financial goals you must align yourself to the Millionaire Mindset in nine specific areas, each of which is critical to wealth-success and sustainment. They are desire, faith, confidence, courage, sacrifice, emotional control, grit, consistency, and patience. Your ability to master these nine elements of your mindset will be further nurtured (or thwarted) by the people you choose to surround yourself with. So, choose your company wisely. Not only may the right circle of friends, colleagues, and mentors be exemplary in displaying these nine elements themselves, they can also provide you with the inspiration to develop each element in your own power arsenal. More on that later...

DESIRE

Success and wealth-building both begin with desire, though I prefer author Robert Kiyosaki's term "burning desire" because the degree of your hunger makes a huge difference. Everyone in their lives has had at least one thing they desired so strongly they couldn't get it out of their head for days, weeks, or months on end. Perhaps it was a toy you coveted as a child, a love interest you couldn't shake, a dream of one day going to college or sending your kids there, or a wish to be a powerful business owner or multimillionaire living in a mansion. Desire is the fuel of our human fire, and although it may often seem like a factor beyond our control, it is in reality something we exert control over every day of our lives. We tame our desires to be sure; otherwise, let's face it; life itself would be pure hedonistic chaos. So, how can we do the opposite, meaning how can we nurture desire and channel it toward a specific end like building wealth?

One important step is to write down what you want. The updated plan I wrote for myself back in 2004, which you saw in Chapter 2, is an example of what I'm talking about. Start by writing down a list of goals with a timeline and keeping it somewhere you're likely to see it over and over, be that on your refrigerator or more discreetly, on your bathroom mirror so you'll see it every morning before you start your day. A brief note from you to yourself to remember the commitment you've made with yourself and to keep the embers of desire burning brightly. Fires need fuel, so use whatever you can muster as a source of that fuel.

Then, ask yourself, "What am I passionate about? What are the things that really, truly matter to me and motivate me? How do I want my life to go? What is my true purpose?"

It's okay not to know at first. The answer for most people is initially, "I'm not sure." But the sooner you start asking yourself these deeper questions, the faster you'll eventually find the correct answer for yourself and be able to construct a pathway to your deeper goals. I asked similar questions of myself when my grandfather was on his deathbed, moments away from leaving this earth. I remember thinking, *What if I only had two weeks left to live? What would I regret not doing or accomplishing?*

It's easy to think that all you need to change is a good reason to change. If that were the case, the world would be a far better place than it is, and we'd all be much further along in our goals in life. But a good reason isn't enough. You've got to feel that the change you want to effect is so vital, so necessary, that not doing so would have a severely detrimental effect on your life. The word "should" needs to become the word "must." And the consequence of not doing what you must, the "or else" part of the equation, has to be so strong that you can't possibly accept it.

If you want to take your desire from a Level 1 to a burning desire of Level 10, I urge you to find and reach out to three millionaires. Not flashy, suspicious, self-promoting millionaires who show off their lifestyles through their cars, clothes, and jewelry. Find three millionaires who are asset rich. Men or women who own apartment buildings, commercial buildings, stocks, bonds, and private equity. Folks who own and operate successful businesses with employees. Once you have the pleasure of meeting and spending time with these millionaires, watch how your burning desire emerges. I'll show you how to find these types of millionaires later on in Chapter 9 of this book (though feel free to jump ahead and take a peek now if you like).

I want you to take some time and assess your desire for change to see if you're truly ready to do whatever it takes to reach Destination Millionaire. Do you want it badly enough? Are you willing to make the required sacrifices? Are you willing to work late nights and weekends? Are you willing to take on a side hustle to earn more cash? Are you willing to save as much as you can? Are you willing to take calculated investment risks with your money time and again? Are you ready to add to your qualifications by learning new, marketable skills? Are you willing to look poor or not far from it while you're getting rich?

If you feel you're not there yet, desire-wise, that's okay. Feel free to put this book down in a place that you can find it if and whenever you become ready. Only you know how intensely you desire to reach Destination Millionaire. But when the answer to all the questions I posed becomes "yes," then come along with me. You've got the burning desire necessary to effectively build wealth.

FAITH

I was raised in the Church where we were taught to believe that God has the power to fix everything. Over time, my beliefs evolved, particularly after watching my Mom—a truly devoted believer—die of cancer in spite of many days of prayer sessions with dynamic bishops and elders within my church. This tragic event forever altered my belief about how God works, though not my faith in God itself. I now believe that faith in God gives you the hope, strength, and/or courage for you to see and fix things on your own. The vision and tools, in other words, not the labor. Christianity was given to many of us as slaves coming over from Africa. A large number of my fellow African American brethren believe that God eventually freed us from slavery, and though I absolutely respect their opinion, my view is that rather than freeing our people, God gave us the strength and the faith to endure slavery until Abraham Lincoln and his cohort saw economic and moral opportunity in ending slavery and reuniting the North and South. Had God been our liberator, why would he have waited nearly four hundred years to answer our ancestors' cries for freedom?

I don't believe that God is going to make you or me or any of us wealthy either. What God *can* do, through faith, is give us the tenacity and hope we need to believe in a particular process and stay true to it. I'm not saying you need to be religious or believe in God. That is one of your most sacred personal choices, and it has nothing to do with me, but if that's where you draw your inspiration and the fuel that perpetuates your inner fire and desire to improve your life, then amen to that. What's important to understand is that neither God nor the government, for that matter, is going to step in and right all of America's wrongs in this lifetime. I'm sorry, but it ain't happened yet, and it ain't happening anytime soon. Thankfully, however, with the right mix of faith, know-how, grit, and tenacity, you can do it yourself.

I think there are three types of belief applicable to our wealth journey. There's the belief that you can do absolutely anything with a minimum of faith, described in the Bible as "faith as small as mustard seed." It's that deep-seated feeling that you can do all things through Christ or whomever you choose to entrust with your faith and devotion. Then, there's another type of belief that I call "belief in process." That is, you tell yourself that, if you follow a set process to achieve something, your achievement will come to fruition as a result. Otherwise, you wouldn't begin or continue with that process in the first place. The same is true when it comes to building wealth; you have to truly believe from the get-go that the process of saving and investing works; otherwise, you won't be able to fight through the rough patches you are sure to encounter along the way. There are too many folks whose mindset has them believing that saving and investing is not the key to wealth building. They believe the slow process of building up capital is futile and too slow to be effective. Their mindset keeps them chasing get-rich-quick scheme after get-rich-quick scheme, wasting their hard-earned money and going nowhere. Marketers and TV hustlers continuously take advantage of people's lack of faith in the slow process of saving and investing as a method to build wealth.

Take a moment to reflect, and you may find that beneath all the excuses or justifications you've allowed yourself in the past—the difficulty of saving, the complexity of budgeting, or even a lifelong lack of resources—beneath that pile of excuses is a person who doesn't honestly or deeply believe that saving and investing will ever lead to genuine wealth building. Somewhere deep inside your mindset, Ol' Mister or Miss Skeptical decided that making money can only be achieved if you're already rich or famous, but you're just Regular Folk, so why waste your time on something that doesn't work because, anyway, the rules are different for Black people. The starting line is further back. The finish line keeps moving. The White Man doesn't want us to be rich. And so on.

Let me be clear about something: I'm not here to judge you, nor to assist you in judging yourself. There are enough judges out there in the world without you or me chiming in with our negative thoughts. The last

WHY SHOULD WHITE GUYS HAVE ALL THE WEALTH?

person you want to pile on is yourself. I'm simply asking you to take a leap of faith in order to break free of the mindset that's keeping you where you are. Believe in the process, and in time, the process will reward you. You can't start without this belief as part of your mindset.

The last type of belief is what I call "secret belief." The only person privy to that secret is you. It's the belief that the only way for you to be happy is to do what you're setting out to do. To complete the task. To reach the goal. Next time you watch a movie or read a story, take a moment to analyze the main character's journey, and you'll see that, in spite of the odds and self-doubt, there's always something inside them, uniquely personal, which drives them to success. Thoughts like, *I always wanted to prove my dad wrong about me*, or *I'm a good man, and that woman needs to know that about me*, or *I've worked too hard not to get what I deserve*. Those are the hero's secret beliefs, the inner engines that drive him or her past the seemingly insurmountable obstacles and enable them to accomplish their goals.

I don't want you to simply say to yourself, *Yes, I can do this*. You need to believe and have faith that you *must* do it. By that, I mean wanting it so badly that your life will seem unfulfilled without achieving it. The key is to envision what you want your life to look like down the road. We often get so caught up in the here and now, we don't take the time to look up and dream about our future. What kind of house do you see yourself living in ten or fifteen years from now? What kind of car do you want to drive (or have self-drive you)? Do you want to go to a job every day, or do you want to have your own business and make your own rules?

CONFIDENCE

It's nearly impossible to do anything that you have not done without confidence. Every entrepreneur I've met is brimming with the stuff. Simply believing in oneself is one of the most powerful weapons a person has. However, only some of us are born with truckloads of self-confidence while others (or rather, most of us) have to make do with little-to-no self-confidence at all. Luckily you can improve your self-confidence with practice and over time. If nature hasn't endowed you with adequate conviction when it comes to your abilities, nurture can do the work instead.

Since you've never built wealth before, you have no reference point, meaning, you have no way of knowing if you can do it. The answer is, of course you can. In order to build your confidence successfully, start by creating a prioritized list of goals which vary in size and complexity. With each goal you surpass you can then move on to larger more complex goals, meaning goals that require you to stretch yourself and which involve significant financial resources and risks. If you find yourself struggling to hit a goal (and feeling bad about yourself), it only means you've set your sights momentarily too high and need to break things down into smaller, more easily attainable chunks. Say your goal was to save $5,000 by Christmas, but now you see you're not going to make it. Okay. Then, figure out what you can save by Halloween and do that. Afterward, figure out what you can save by Thanksgiving. Confident people don't abandon their goals; they adjust them to a level that reinforces their confidence by providing a route to repeated success. It's like that old joke about the guy who goes to his doctor, raises his arm and says: "Doctor, my arm hurts when I go like this." The doctor looks at him and says, "Well, then don't go like that."

As you achieve success along the spectrum of your goals, your confidence will increase along with it. If the plan you set out for yourself isn't working, don't stop dead in your tracks; adjust your plan so that it has a better chance of working. Whenever you run into unexpected roadblocks, start doing research and having conversations with your millionaire mentors. Your research will enhance your knowledge and preparedness and, thereby, your confidence. Seeking advice from your millionaire mentors will give you tried and tested knowledge as well as referrals to others who have accomplished what you seek to accomplish.

Remember, you're never going to know everything you need to know in any situation. But you can always figure it out by seeking advice and breaking down each hurdle to a level you feel you can get over.

COURAGE

Whether you're an employee or an entrepreneur, fear is a part of your life, be it fear of failure, fear of losing money, fear of losing your job or business, or something else. Fear is a universal human emotion, rooted in survival, and thus, we feel it most acutely in relation to the things we hold most dearly. When it comes to wealth building, however, fear assumes differing perspectives. For people who work for others and receive a paycheck, fear typically lives in the background, rearing its ugly head only when layoff rumors circulate, pink slips start to fly, or on those rare instances when you make a major mistake at your job. When those types of fear roar to life, most employees either act quickly and do something bold in order to save their jobs, or they dust off the business plan they've been hiding in their bottom drawer. Yet, once the threat subsides, the fear generally goes away with it. Crisis averted, time to get back to the day-to-day grind of the job.

For entrepreneurs, fear lives eternally in the foreground. We straddle an abyss and know exactly where the cliff's edges are at all times. We're obliged to work tirelessly to stay away from those edges, lest our businesses tumble into the valleys of bankruptcy or failure. We live with fear every day. It wakes us up in the morning and kicks us into motion. Often, it wakes us even earlier, in the middle of the night, especially when things threaten to spiral downward or take a turn for the worse.

When I first began my life as an entrepreneur, I dreaded those moments of sleepless distress. I tried everything to make them go away. Counting sheep. Thinking about fun times in college. Anything to get my mind off the work situation rattling around my insomniac brain. Eventually, I came to see how staring at the ceiling in the middle of the night like this forced me to analyze the work situation I was in rather than simply trying to avoid it. I realized that when you boiled it down, business is nothing more than problem-solving in a suit, or pajamas, as the case may be. For me, as for all the successful entrepreneurs I know, fear became a motivator and, eventually, a friend. I don't love everything about fearful feelings, but I learned to rely on them to help sharpen the edges of my thinking and focus my energy with greater intensity. I wrestled with fear for the solid seventeen of the twenty years I was in business before I was able to reach my endgame goal and a place—financially—where business failure didn't mean Cedric failure.

I believe it's important to have a healthy relationship with fear in life and business because, like it or not, it will be your companion for the rest of your life, in one manifestation or another. The mindset of "Million-Nevers," as I often call big talkers or big spenders with no assets, is paralyzed by fear, whereas the Millionaire Mindset expects and accepts fear. It confronts fear head-on and molds it from a temporary impediment into a tool for progress.

I think our reluctance usually begins with doubt and soon enough, fear gets invited to the party, which is why it's vital to understand that courage isn't the absence of fear. Courage is decisive action *in the face of fear*. Your courage has to be greater than the sum of your doubts and fears or else you will neither jump nor grow. Fear is unavoidable when risk is involved; courage is about accepting that fear but not letting it get in your way. That goes for all sorts of challenging disciplines. Probably nine out of ten Oscar-winning actors would tell you they fight butterflies every time the camera turns on, even after all their years of training and success. The same is true for superstar hedge fund managers about to buy millions of shares in a company or an asset class. It's certainly true for everyday business owners and investors. Each of these industry veterans is making a calculated risk based on research and experience, but those careful calculations can only mitigate their doubts and fears; they can't make them go away entirely. Many wouldn't have it any other way. They consider that fear to be their edge, a sort of internal adrenaline charge helping to keep them focused and disciplined.

You too will doubt yourself in this process. Everyone doubts their abilities, their hunches, and their ideas at least on occasion. That's why it's so critical to develop the Millionaire Mindset and surround yourself with millionaire mentors and other dreamers instead of haters. Haters truly want you to fail because your failure validates their lack of courage and success. They will try to talk you out of your idea and cast doubt on you and on your dream's chances of coming to fruition. Instead, dreamers and millionaire mentors are inspired by your success because it serves to validate their dreams. So, be careful who you allow into your orbit. Courage thrives in good company.

SACRIFICE

As I recounted in Chapter 2, I saved $7,000 after working for Dr. Tsao and used that money as the down payment for my first piece of property, an unfurnished condominium. As astute as that may initially sound, it was probably not such a clever investment given that the condo was smack in the middle of what was derisively called "The Barrio." But I couldn't wait to put my money to work for me. I was already married by then, and my wife and I were living on a strict budget. I was adamant when it came to keeping our debt low and our savings and investment rate high. We paid for our wedding in cash. We decided not to take a honeymoon. We furnished our home and paid for it in cash. And we set a spending limit of $100 a week each in discretionary money. Some folks call that miscellaneous cash expenses, items like gas, haircuts, lunch, movie tickets, happy hour, and so on. We were determined to follow my mantra of living frugally until we didn't have to do so anymore.

In my mind, I would divvy up my weekly allotment by telling myself that I had $40 for Monday through Thursday, and $60 for the weekend. That's hard-core, I know, but remember this was the early '90s, so things were somewhat cheaper back then (and happy hour often included free wings and finger foods). I refused to get a debit card because the minimum withdrawal was $20, and I knew if I pulled out twenty, I would spend it all that same day. I had to hold myself to ten bucks a day because, frankly, I've got impulses too.

I was working at the Jet Propulsion Laboratory in Pasadena, CA, and my work buddies and I loved to play pool during lunch at a local joint called Que's. Since I couldn't take money out at the ATM, the only alternative for me (and, by extension, them if they wanted me to play and eat lunch together) was for us to drive to the bank every day on the way to Que's, so I could withdraw my $10 inside, from a teller. Every weekday. I've considered interviewing some of them for this book, though in all likelihood, most of what they'd say about me would probably be unprintable. Let's just say that it was good I already had friends because stopping every day at the bank was no way to win friends. I'm not sure what the people who worked at the bank back then would say though it wouldn't surprise me if they'd thought I was actually casing the joint in order to one day rob it. What kind of nut goes to the bank every day who isn't a bank employee?

The answer is this kind of nut, the kind that's trying to get rich. I was sticking to a budget, and I didn't have a credit card or an ATM card because I didn't want to have to resist temptation. It wasn't until four years later, when I bought myself a Porsche as a thirtieth-birthday present, that I finally gave in to the credit union branch manager who insisted, "You can't be driving a Porsche without a credit card" when I signed the car's loan paperwork.

I wasn't trying to be annoying. I was practicing a certain type of financial discipline. I practiced it so consistently and for so long that when I eventually took the training wheels off, the discipline was still there in practice. I believe that if you're truly serious about your financial aspirations, and you honestly want a different future, these are the types of routines you need to create and follow until you're locked in on a budget and doing whatever it takes to keep yourself from succumbing to the temptation to overspend. I'm not saying you can't go to the ATM or use a credit card. That was my approach to controlling spending. You're going to have to develop your own personal set of brakes that you can rely on until they become second nature for you. Sacrifice can and must be learned on the road to wealth.

In today's hi-speed digital world, it's becoming harder and harder to control your spending when there is so much money being spent to keep you rapidly spending and too many easy ways to separate you from your money. On any given day, you can spend hundreds if not thousands of dollars with your phone or on your computer before you even are aware of it, nor aware of how much you've spent. This just means that you'll have to devise very creative ways to sacrifice and thus hold on to your money, so you can allocate your money to investing for yourself and not in the fortune of others.

The way I see it, there are two options you can choose based on your desires and your net worth:

1. You can choose to look wealthy and remain poor and, thereby, never become wealthy.
2. You can choose to look poor or modest while building your wealth.

I can tell you with supreme confidence that making financial sacrifices in order to invest as much as you can is the fastest, surest way to reach your financial goals. Fastest, not easiest. There is no easy way, and thus, the sooner you accept that reality into your mindset, the faster you'll be able to arrive at a new reality based on sacrifice, reward, and ultimately, financial success. It's a mistake to think you can earn your way out of bad spending behaviors. That's like trying to plug a leak by adding more water.

EMOTIONAL CONTROL

Change happens incrementally, though rarely in a linear way. The beginning is usually tough, and before the compulsions that have held you in your previous behaviors begin to subside, things usually get tougher, not easier. If you've ever tried to give up sugar, alcohol, or tobacco, you'll know what I mean. Day One finds you feeling good about yourself as you resist your cravings, whereas, by Day Three, you can easily find yourself standing in line at Dunkin', buying a couple of Boston Kremes and wondering how things went wrong so quickly.

While it's one thing to hear on the street or in church that "the road to hell is paved with good intentions," have you ever wondered what exactly happens to those good intentions that ends up sending them hell-ward? I think it boils down to what you allow yourself to believe about yourself. This is true whether you're kicking a smoking habit or trying to get a bad shopping or debt-incurring habit under control.

There's a good reason that every AA meeting begins with someone saying, "My name is Joe, Sam, or Desirée, and I'm an alcoholic." It's an acknowledgment that there's a problem that needs to be overcome. Mindset is about changing your values and behaviors, not changing who you are. It would be wonderful if our vulnerabilities could simply vanish into thin air, but that's not the way life works. We're all vulnerable. We all have desires and weaknesses. That's why we need to exercise emotional control to curb our worst impulses, now and forever.

As you begin saving and investing, you will start to feel your emotions go through a transition as well. It feels good to get financial "wins," even small ones, and to grow more secure and confident about your future and yourself. It's exciting to see your net worth grow. Just don't make the mistake of believing that there's a new "you" that's grown along with it. It's still the same old beautiful you, only you're doing things a different and better way. Your temptations to spend are still there and will always be there, but you will feel them less and less over time because you're replacing them with other behaviors and desires. Your mind is "set" on new values.

At times, it will be extremely tempting to return to your old money values and behaviors, such as buying expensive material items that give you pleasure. When you eventually have cash reserves, an improved credit score, and you're feeling good financially, you will almost certainly find yourself emotionally triggered because now you can afford the things you couldn't before, right? You may feel you "deserve" to spend some of your money. After all, you've been patient and sacrificing for six, twelve, or eighteen months already, right?

The issue is that our emotions tend to fluctuate in a sort of vicious circle; we save $1,000 or pay down our credit card debt, and suddenly, our desire to spend re-ignites. Then, once we blow our money on frivolous spending and our credit card debt starts rising again, our feelings of shame and fear return. We refocus on paying down our debt until desire takes over yet again, and so on. The goal of emotional control is to keep that saving/spending rollercoaster on a straight trajectory, steady and balanced, so we can continue to do the work necessary to keep debt and spending decreasing, saving and investing increasing, and preserve our gains.

You will continue to struggle with your spending trigger until your values have fully transformed. That doesn't mean you can't ever buy anything nice. You only need to wait until you get more pleasure out of investing than spending. That's when you will know you have the requisite emotional control of a millionaire, enabling you to build lasting wealth. In Chapter 7, we will discuss how to set up a reward system based on a Millionaire Mindset, so you can get that new whatever-it-is you want when the time is right. Rather than allowing you to "fall off the wagon," we'll learn how to use emotional control to keep that wagon moving and generating not only wealth, but your happiness along with it.

GRIT

Grit, also known as stick-to-it-iveness, means hard work to create the outcome that you desire. In his book *How to Win at the Sport of Business*, the author and billionaire entrepreneur Mark Cuban wrote, "Effort is not measured in how many hours and how much sweat and how hard you work. Effort is measured in the amount of work required to get the desired result." In other words, grit needs to be result-focused.

Practically speaking, the ol' nine-to-five is not going to be enough to cut it anymore. Building wealth is going to require more work than what you may be used to, not only physical work but large chunks of mental travail as well—activities like studying, reading, researching, sharpening your skills, and thinking. I remember when I first started my consulting business, I flew back and forth from California to New Jersey every single week. I'd leave on a Monday night red-eye, consult for two and a half days, then fly back and operate my business until the following Monday when I'd repeat the cycle all over again. I lived and breathed my business. I didn't go to sleep without consciously thinking about it. At three o'clock in the morning, I was thinking about it and again when I woke up to face the next day. It wasn't anxiety keeping me up back then; it was determination. Building wealth is a job you need to pour your whole self into to make it happen, much the way a top athlete trains and trains relentlessly. Not 100 percent but 110 percent.

If you're like me (and most people), you weren't born a talented entertainer, a world-class athlete, or a rich kid with a million-dollar trust fund producing income for life. That means you have to work your ass off in order to bring in enough money, so your money can subsequently earn for you. You can't increase your wealth without working harder and smarter than you currently are. You need to find ways to generate more money to invest in either a business, real estate, or stocks and bonds. Is it a side hustle like Uber? Is it weekend work assisting a small business? Is it doing hair in the evenings or on weekends? Is it selling a product in your spare time or starting a business of your own?

If you aren't willing to put the extra effort in or stick it out until you reach your goal, I won't fault you. You just need to understand that you're going to produce an amount of opportunity commensurate with the level of grit and effort that you're investing in. That's how the math works: the more seeds, the more flowers. I once had a conversation with a successful attorney friend when we were chillin' at my waterfront home in Florida. He was telling me that he couldn't see how he could reach the wealth pinnacles he truly wanted. I told him, in as friendly a tone as I could muster, "Dude, you're playing too much golf. You're not grinding. You need to grind. You need to be working some of your weekends and holidays. You need to consider having only one day of rest for the week. You need to be building other aspects of your law practice, hiring more attorneys and getting them billing."

Don't make the mistake of thinking that the same amount of revenue year after year is going to get you to Destination Millionaire. You'll have to increase your productivity or your effort level to generate more revenue, or you'll need to sacrifice more of your spending to live smaller. Ideally, you'll want to do both as each will increase your net worth. This is especially true for folks who work salaried jobs in corporate America. It takes effort and grit. Effort will increase your income while grit will aid your resilience by lifting you up each time you get knocked down or fail. And believe me, at some point you will get knocked down or fail. That's a plain fact.

It's no accident that many of the most successful tech firms like Facebook and Google have signs in their offices that read "Fail Quickly." Think about it—both of those mammoth-sized companies started in somebody's dorm room where failure was as common as late-night pizza. Failure was and is an accepted component of success, something to be embraced rather than avoided.

You've got to stay in it to win it. Dig deep, prepare for some long hours, late nights, and hard times ahead, and stay the course. Remember, fortune not only favors the bold; it rewards the diligent as well.

CONSISTENCY

Now that you've mustered the courage to invest, you're going to need consistency in order to achieve growth and build wealth. Dabbling in investment will get you nowhere whereas committing yourself to a ritual of investment is a solid way to get you to Destination Millionaire.

Every month at a minimum, you need to be investing a portion of your income. At the same time, you need to be consistent about making the sacrifices we discussed earlier in order to build up your savings. That means being consistent about living below your means (a behavior that should remain with you for the rest of your life). Think of these three activities as the essential parts of your wealth-building engine: earn, sacrifice in order to live below your means, and invest. If you are inconsistent or lackluster about any of these three activities, your engine is going to sputter instead of hum.

I think it's misguided for new investors looking to build wealth to try to "game" the marketplace. Imagine how many days, months, and years a market analyst at a major firm like Goldman Sachs or a hedge fund manager has dedicated to studying and learning how the markets work. The same way Serena Williams has spent decades perfecting her backhand, professional investors have picked apart every possible nuance of the investment game to derive any advantage they can.

So, how can amateur investors compete with that kind of know-how? The answer lies in consistency. The markets are going to cycle up and down. Over the long term, the stock and real estate markets have consistently gone upward. Over the long term. I'll say it one last time for emphasis: over the long term. If you consistently invest over time, guess what's likely to happen to your wealth over the long term? It's going to appreciate in value.

Now, some of you might think, *Why take that risk when I get a consistent return by leaving my money in a high-interest savings account at the bank.* Let's forget for a moment that interest rates are currently at historic lows and not keeping up with the rate of inflation, even though that alone should be cause for you to change your strategy. Consider this: interest rates don't historically rise over the long term. They are cyclical like the stock market, but there is no consistent pattern over the long term the way there is with the stock market. Even banks (especially banks!) consistently use the money on their balance sheets to invest in the markets in the hope of higher returns. Do you want to give them your money to invest without you reaping any of the profits? Instead, adopt the mindset of a consistent investor, and you too will build wealth over time. In Chapter 7, we'll go over Dollar Cost Averaging and other strategies to help you to consistently invest.

PATIENCE

> *"I was an overnight success all right, but 30 years is a long, long night."*
>
> —RAY KROC, founder of McDonald's

My definition of patience in wealth building is your ability to endure sacrifice for a sustained period of time until you achieve your goals. Patience is one part time and one part pain. It's about maintaining a positive mindset and attitude and putting forth consistent effort in spite of limited short-term results, your doubts, and your fears. It takes time to build wealth, time to save enough money to invest, and time for those investments to grow. All the while, you have to patiently trust the process. This is why expecting one opportunity to speed up the process and make you rich quickly is foolish. Some people are born with an abundance of patience. The rest of us have to work at it. Whichever area of the patience spectrum you occupy, remember that there's no such thing as an overnight success, only the appearance of one. Your journey as a wealth builder is going to take time, and it's going to require patience in order for you to reach your goal. Let that settle in your mind.

The very idea of overnight success is a mental trap you should avoid at all costs. It's an illusion and a damaging one at that. Do you know anyone who's gotten rich quickly other than a lottery winner (and for reference, the odds of you winning the lottery jackpot are roughly the same as being struck by lightning twice...on your birthday, no matter how many tickets you buy)? Don't take my word for it. As an exercise, research some of the people you think have made it big, and see how long they've been at it. The answers will surprise you.

The idea that many share that you can become wealthy overnight is one of the most prominent and damaging illusions out there. It dupes us into believing we're one lucky break from reaching the pinnacle of success when in reality the opposite is true. Becoming an "overnight" success takes many nights, years, and often decades. Simply because the bright spotlight shining at the mountaintop doesn't illuminate the long climb upward doesn't mean it isn't a long and arduous climb. Too often, we see the accumulation of wealth, and we mistake it for hitting the jackpot. In 99 percent of the cases, that jackpot, if it's as true as it looks, was built by adding one gold coin at a time. There's nothing wrong with that; what matters is that we understand and accept in our Millionaire Mindsets how great fortunes are truly built.

Warren Buffett, the so-called "world's greatest investor," has been at it for over sixty years. Bill Gates and Steve Jobs worked in the obscurity of their garages before hitting their strides (Jobs was even fired from Apple— the company he co-founded). Oprah worked for years in radio and local TV before she had her own show and made big money. Magic Johnson is now one of the most successful African American businessmen in the country, but he spent years after his NBA career learning the ropes and taking baby steps in business.

I stress patience so much because I've seen how long the process can be and how important it is not to go chasing waterfalls, as the old song says. It took me fifteen years from the time I became a millionaire until I achieved complete financial independence and freedom. Did I make mistakes along the way? Sure I did, so I tried to learn from each mistake as much as I could. This process taught me how to be patient and forgiving with myself, and I urge you to do the same in your own life. Aim for progress, not perfection. Be sure to reward yourself along the way as you make progress and refrain from punishing yourself when you mess up. Embrace and, most importantly, *learn* from your mistakes. Your financial moves will not always work. You have to trust and adjust your path and process, without constantly changing directions, and rely on your mentors to help keep you grounded in place whenever adverse financial winds begin to blow.

Now that we've covered "The Offense," it's time for us to look at how "The Defense" can teach you how to maintain the wealth you build. However, before we move on, I want you to begin the process of adopting the Millionaire Mindset. Write down a few specific goals that you want to achieve. Include a timeline and a list of tasks to be completed for each goal, and place it where you'll see it every day. Choose one of the following or something more suited to your desires and current circumstances:

1. Save $10,000, $50,000, or $100,000...any amount that truly challenges you.
2. Buy your first investment property: a home, a duplex, or perhaps a six-unit building
3. Open a brokerage account, and buy shares of a company's stock every month

Even if you start small, don't be afraid to think big. It's the only way you'll get to be a millionaire or billionaire. You have to think big enough to create the volume of wealth that will allow you to reach your financial goals. When you become a millionaire, you'll likely own dozens of apartment buildings and/or thousands of shares of stock. Your business will sell tens of thousands or millions of units. What's vital for you to understand at this point is that *no matter how large your portfolio of assets, the same basic principles will apply to managing them.* You can think of it in terms of education; it takes different training to get a PhD as opposed to a high school diploma, but they both require a clear study regimen, the ability to do research, and a commitment to finishing your work. That never changes. If you can do one, you can do the other.

Whichever goal you set for yourself now, write down the date you begin to pursue it and check up on it monthly (put that date in your calendar too). In addition to tracking the normal metrics you use to measure your success (did I make or lose money), I want you to evaluate your mindset using the elements we've discussed and see which of them you were successful at and which ones still need some work. Did you manage to overcome your fears?

Were you able to implement the right level of sacrifice? Did you give up? Which areas must you work on to perfect your Millionaire Mindset? Did you keep your emotions balanced, or did you begin to spend again once you saved up a particular amount of money?

This practice is not only what will guide you toward which of your weaknesses you need to address, but it will also give you the confidence to take on even bigger goals going forward. Nothing teaches or helps you to develop the right mindset like practical experience.

CHAPTER 6

ADOPTING MILLIONAIRE VALUES ("THE DEFENSE")

Now that you've begun developing the mindset of a millionaire, let's talk about how to adopt and refine the money values you will need to guide you along your journey to attaining lasting wealth. Your money values are your money priorities, the items that get the earliest and most of your money's attention. You can read this book a hundred times, and I promise you, until you've truly absorbed and implemented this section, your road to Destination Millionaire will be an endless one leading nowhere.

There are already many areas of your life where your money behaviors are being modified without you even being aware of it. Ask any marketer. Advertising and marketing messages are designed to create an emotional response inside us and trigger our spending behaviors. They attempt to direct what you see, hear, and feel in order to get you to buy into their product and service offerings by convincing you that you need what they're selling in order to improve your life or make you happy. They analyze purchasing data and leverage it to keep you spending. Marketers are keenly aware that your environment shapes your values, your values impact your behaviors, and your behaviors determine your outcomes. That's also why they use celebrities from our culture to help drive home their point.

I believe that the key to changing your money outcomes is to take a closer look at your money behaviors which are, in turn, the shadow of your money values. Fix one, and the others will change as if by default. For instance, if you're having trouble saving and investing money, it's likely a result of not having properly assessed and addressed your money values. Though our values govern our behaviors, we must be careful not to lump them into one general category. Doing so only invites us to fall into a time-honored trap of self-sabotage and failure, as in, *My values are messed up; therefore, I'm no good, so what's the point?* Not only is this unhelpful and defeatist, it fails to take into account the way values are related to each other.

We may hold completely different and even opposed values in our lives —all human beings are prone to these sorts of contradictions. Take a person with strong spiritual values. That person would likely exhibit behaviors like study, prayer, devotion, payment of tithes and offerings, and all the rest of what goes along with doing God's work diligently. However, that same person may have bad health values. Perhaps they smoke or don't eat well or fail to exercise. In order to change those destructive behaviors, the underlying values that go along with them have to change first. And adjusting your values follows the same basic methodology I've outlined previously; break it down to a manageable size, get specific, and course-correct. Therefore, once your money values transform to those of millionaires, staying on a course of frugal living, saving, and consistently investing becomes infinitely easier because your behaviors are now aligned with the things you value or consider important. The temptation not to spend irresponsibly doesn't completely go away, certainly not at first, but the intensity of it does, and that's the key to lasting and meaningful progress. It takes time for your new value system to drown out the voice of the old. This is the significant differentiator of the Millionaire Money Moves wealth-building system. While there are countless books written on the subject of improving your finances, they all follow the same approach and cover the same topics, yet every year, a handful of new books are released that are more of the same. It doesn't matter which book or how many of them you read. Until your money values (priorities) and behaviors change, your outcomes will never change. So, pay close attention to this chapter because it is the secret sauce to making everlasting Millionaire Money Moves.

You may be thinking, *If only it were that simple.* My response is that it both is and isn't. The way is clear, though the journey is a hard one. Here's a brief confession: I can't change you, and even if I could, that's not my aim with this book. I can't take the full measure of you, so it would be unfair of me to want to change you until circumstances somehow arose in which I could. That's the truth. Instead, I want to challenge you to change yourself by being more strategic, more focused, and more specific about what you're looking to change about your money values to change your money behaviors.

As I mentioned earlier the Millionaire Mindset is your offense, while Value and Behavior Transformation is your defense. Value and Behavior Transformation are difficult under any circumstances, and given our historical circumstances, the deck is stacked against us. The tragic history of racism in America has made the process of value transformation for us, as a community, something profoundly emotional and, therefore, vastly tougher to reset. It doesn't take a brilliant psychiatrist to recognize that trauma has played a large part in why we often use money as a toy rather than a weapon to defend ourselves against poverty, systemic racism, and economic warfare, or why, time and again, we manifest a need to display wealth rather than to meaningfully accumulate it. These sorts of responses to trauma are not uncommon.

For decades after their 1945 liberation from Nazi concentration camps, numerous Holocaust survivors continued to hoard food and even ate spoiled food rather than throw it away, despite being surrounded by unspoiled food in abundance. The experience of forced starvation forever colored their relationship to food and nutrition, so much so that they continued to have higher nutritional needs throughout the rest of their lives.[17] I believe there are discernible parallels between that and the post-slavery Black experience in America, especially when you consider that, unlike the Jewish community which was eventually given meaningful reparations and a country to call home, we Black folks got Jim Crow and a mirage by the name of forty acres and a mule. In many ways, our ultimate manumission in 1865 (meaning the last slave's liberation on Juneteenth of that year) didn't mark the end of our bondage so much as it harkened the beginning of a new type of slavery by other means.

I'm not a psychologist, nor is this book intended to be a disquisition on race and trauma, but I think it's instructive to understand where some

---

[17] Luke Tress, "For Many Holocaust Survivors, Effects of Wartime Starvation Still a Plague," *The Times of Israel*, May 3, 2016, https://www.timesofisrael.com/for-many-holocaust-survivors-wartime-starvation-still-a-daily-torment/.

of our money values may have come from. To my mind, these waters run deep, even though I emphatically reject the notion that we somehow can't learn to navigate these socio-psychological depths and chart a new course as individuals and as a community. As I've said many times, it won't be easy, but it can and must be done.

I believe there is truth to the idea that showing off in our community is at least in part a response to historical poverty, not to mention our prior treatment as "subhumans." I know many of my fellow African Americans would agree. Does that mean we buy all these glittering objects because we weren't allowed to have these things before, or because certain White folks think we couldn't possibly afford them now? There's definitely a piece to each of those notions. You might walk into a store and feel compelled to buy the most expensive thing they sell just to show the White sales clerk how wrong they are about you and your status. It happens every day where I live.

Still, I think what's really at the heart of these costly wealth displays (which don't actually display true wealth) is our reluctance to admit as a community that there are pride and self-esteem issues associated with our buying choices that go well beyond those of other communities because of the road we've traveled as a race. A lot of us will honestly admit that the reason we spend more on lavish goods is because we feel we deserve to be socially accepted as equals, including as consumers. But you know what? I think we may be taking the idea of "fake it till you make it" too far because our faking it is actually *preventing* us from ever making it. On any given weekend in South Beach, Miami, a place I frequent because I own a condo there, you'll see African Americans riding around in $500,000–Rolls-Royces they either own or rent. They've leveled up from the super-luxurious Mercedes and Lexuses that were the Black status symbols of yesteryear.

According to Nielsen,[18] "Blacks are 20 percent more likely than the total population to say they will 'pay extra for a product that is consistent with the image I want to convey.'"

This kind of bling over-identification continues to pass from generation to generation in the form of an insatiable hunger to purchase the most expensive things possible in order to create a perception of wealth. While I personally don't condone that type of conspicuous consumption, especially if you're trying to *build* wealth, I do understand and accept where it comes from. And I've been guilty of it myself. But to my mind, this isn't only about showing the salesman who's made it and who's not. That's damaging enough. What troubles me is this seeming need to prove this to and influence our fellow African Americans as well.

Kanye West calls this phenomenon out in his song, "It All Falls Down."

...Then I spent 400 bucks on this
Just to be like, "Nigga, you ain't up on this!"

Do we really need to show we're as successful by being a "baller, shot caller" like Diddy, Jay-Z, or Mr. Johnson down the street who thinks he's all that because he drives a fancy car and wears expensive clothes and jewelry? If not, then honestly, who is the audience for this three-bling circus? Who am I trying to convince that I'm the man—my brother or myself?

The truly sad part about all this one-upmanship is that there's nothing wrong with owning the finer things in life if—and only if—your assets instead of your labor are paying for them. Unfortunately, when you're working for money instead of your money working for you, then you're the

---

[18] "Black Impact: Consumer Categories Where African Americans Move Markets," Nielsen, February 15, 2018, https://www.nielsen.com/us/en/insights/article/2018/black-impact -consumer-categories-where-african-americans-move-markets/.

sucker who ends up paying for these luxuries and making The Man, who we often complain about, richer. This is an all-too-common issue we find among professional athletes. If you look at the statistics, 78 percent of NFL players and 60 percent of NBA players end up filing for bankruptcy two years after retirement. Not middle-class or even working poor...bankrupt![19]

Why is that? Why is it that a player like Antoine Walker, who played professional basketball for the Boston Celtics and earned over $100 million over the course of his career, ended up broke only two years after retiring? I can tell you one part of the answer: he was paying cash for bling, rather than having some of those millions in cash working for him and footing the bill. In all fairness to Walker, he is only one of dozens if not thousands of other professional athletes who either lacked or ignored the basic financial values and knowledge we're laying out here about having your money do the work for you. Walker, to his great credit, currently works as a counselor to young athletes to help them avoid the mistakes he made, telling them, "I created a very expensive lifestyle. That's how you lose your wealth real' bad at the beginning."[20]

Compare that with what happened to Shaquille O'Neal, who was also headed down the path to financial oblivion until he sought and received mentoring from Earvin "Magic" Johnson. According to a recent report in *Obvious* magazine:

When Shaq was drafted into the NBA, he spent the first million that he earned within thirty minutes. O'Neal then received a phone call from his banker, who scolded him, and told him that he would end up joining the

---

[19] Tim Parker, "Why Athletes Go Broke," Investopedia, February 22, 2022, https://www.investopedia.com/financial-edge/0312/why-athletes-go-broke.aspx.

[20] Matt Egan, "Ex-NBA Star Went from $108 Million to Bankruptcy," CNN, July 24, 2015, https://money.cnn.com/2015/07/24/investing/antoine-walker-nba-bankruptcy/.

list of former athletes who ended up broke if the current trend continued. O'Neal decided to transform his money values and behaviors by sharpening up his education about business and finance. O'Neal now lives off of 25 percent of his income and saves and invests the remaining 75 percent. He returned to college, completing his bachelor's degree, followed by his MBA, and last, his EdD... What's more, Dr. Shaq has vast holdings in retail businesses to go along with the multiple millions he earns as a corporate spokesperson and a commentator for TNT Networks.[21]

Behavior change and financial education—this is how we can reverse the raging one-way river of money going out and never coming back in. This is where the idea of significance plays its most salient role as a reason for why many want wealth in the first place. For example, look at some of our neighborhoods where the so-called "dope boys" drive fancy cars and wear enough gold and diamonds to fill a treasure chest. It's easy for young people in "Da 'Hood" to see them and reflexively think, *That's what money and success look like.* They may have no other example of wealth than what they see in their own neighborhood. Why would they aspire for a different representation of wealth if they've never seen one before? That's why the aspiration becomes, "When I get money, I want to do the same thing because I want to look, feel, and be rich. I want the type of treatment and respect the wealthy receive. I want the attention that comes from that."

However, once that idea gets rooted in our culture or any culture, it becomes increasingly difficult to disavow. What's worse, it easily branches out into countless iterations at all demographic levels, to a point where I've

---

[21] Kathleen Elkins, "Shaq Once Blew through $1 Million in Under an Hour, but Now He Saves 75% of His Income," CNBC, July 16, 2019, https://www.cnbc.com/2019/07/16/shaq-saves -and-invests-75percent-of-his-income.html.

seen college students rocking Ralph Lauren Polo and other expensive high-end brands on their way to class. College students who've barely worked a day in their lives! I understand it; I did the same thing when I was in college and not yet a millionaire. They're trying to send a message that says, *I'm successful. My family is successful. This is how good I have it.* Culturally speaking, ostentation is deeply ingrained in our collective system, and I believe this need to show off is both a self-esteem and a competition issue. We compete to be the best dressed or to get the most attention. How we're seen by others makes us feel on top, like we're somebody significant. This feeling of significance can devolve into a type of drug that gives us a high we end up chasing throughout our lives. Take it from me, the best-dressed student of 1982 at my high school.

I've known too many of my Brothas who, if given a choice between looking wealthy and being poor, or being wealthy and looking poor would say, "Oh, just give me the look. I can fake it till I make it. I'll parlay the 'look' into something real." To me, that's a serious problem. In reality, we need to strike a balance. I'm not suggesting a dull monastic life of savings and investing in which all the finer things—a nice car, a Rolex watch, a beach vacation, or any other Bling-Bling items—are off-limits. Not at all. It's okay to reward yourself for the effort you're making. In fact, it's an excellent idea to have a reward system for the sacrifices you're making to get to Destination Millionaire (and we'll get into how to set your system up in Chapter 7). But let's be sure we don't put the cart, or the Porsche as the case may be, before the horse. *Sacrifice first, and then, reward second* must always be the order in which you pursue your financial goals. It's as elementary as exchanging instant gratification for deferred gratification. First, build up your assets, then allow the income from your assets to pay for the bling. This way, you don't ball hard for a season or two; you can ball hard for a lifetime. As NBA money-managing guru Joe McLean teaches, "With great abundance comes great discipline."[22]

I want to return to the question of self-esteem for a moment. I don't believe that self-esteem can be temporarily disengaged. Confidence and self-belief are critical factors to success, and they can neither be manufactured out of thin air nor built on illusions. Everyone is different, and you will have to decide for yourself what it takes to get motivated, as well as the significance of that motive in your quest for a sound financial life. Many people discover that having a whole lot of material items is not all that fulfilling. You'll make that determination yourself; however, do yourself a favor: wait until the income from your assets, and not your sweat, is paying for your lavish goods.

What I so often see in our Black communities is seemingly rich people driving finer cars than everyone else. They wear fancier, higher-priced clothing. The rich folks in our communities, by all appearances, live a better life than us. That's what we tend to think, and based on the visual "evidence" available, it's not an unreasonable conclusion to draw. They are materially wealthier than most. We can observe a similar version of this disparity in our churches. The most blessed parishioners wear the biggest hats, finest jewelry, drive the most exotic cars, have the fanciest wardrobes, and so forth. The result of this type of material one-upmanship is that it often makes the rest of us feel inferior because we lack those same material goods or the ability to purchase them. When we do become financially able, we opt to buy material goods instead of investing and building our wealth.

---

[22] Devin Gordon, "Meet the Money Whisperer to the Super-Rich NBA Elite," *The New York Times*, June 6, 2019, https://www.nytimes.com/2019/06/06/business/nba-wealth-manager-klay-thompson-joe-mclean.html.

There are many ways we can respond to falsely derived feelings of inferiority, one of which is to furiously try to out-consume the apparently rich folks until our negative feelings about ourselves subside. The problem is that this type of reaction often turns into a debilitating slap in the face, in the form of massive credit card bills with astronomical interest rates. I'm not an uncompetitive person at all, even in this respect (forgive me, Lord, for I too have sinned), though I consider myself more of a choose-your-competitions-wisely type guy. You can't win at everything, and equally important, you have to prepare yourself to compete properly if you want to have any hope of winning at all. That comes back to the idea I expressed earlier that it's perfectly fine to want the finer things in life, as long as you don't start dressing the part before you can afford to do so comfortably. What I hope reading this book will help you to do is develop and follow a winning plan. If it also leads to financial security, or comfort, or a legacy to pass on to your children and grandchildren, then all the better. Feel free to flip this sequence on its head if you like. If the ancillary benefit of obtaining financial security, or comfort, or a legacy to pass on to your children and grandchildren turns out to be a wealth of material goods, then amen again. What matters most is that you overcome what's been hindering you from building genuine, sustainable wealth and instead set yourself up for success. That process begins by addressing and fixing core money values and behaviors both individually and within our communities.

When showy displays of wealth are met with approval, looking wealthy becomes a respected goal and value. That's human nature. It's not my place to judge whether this is a good or a bad thing; I'll let others take that on. My point is that I'm against that particular brand of positive affirmation if it's getting in the way of your wealth building. Full stop.

Think about this: have you ever seen billionaire financial titans such as Robert Smith or Warren Buffett decked out in bling? Do you know what kind of car Robert Smith or Warren Buffet owns? Don't be fooled into thinking they have small egos because you can be sure they do not. What differentiates them in the context of values is that in place of gold chains or diamond necklaces, their bling is businesses, real estate, stocks and bonds, and their rank on the Forbes Billionaires List. I call it "achievement bling." They keep the focus on their net worth, not their ride or their crib. They place supreme value on succeeding and little value in showing off their riches to others. They invest relentlessly in their own ideas and their own companies in order to make them grow. Even an entertainer like Jay-Z, whose shiny bling *is* part of his public image, makes sure he's making money off what he's wearing through paid sponsorship. He's not showing off either; he's getting paid to advertise someone's jewelry! *That's* the part our community needs to emulate. The steak, not the sizzle.

Whenever material bling rather than achievement bling defines your values, your behavior will pivot toward the accumulation of material items and not self-actualization (which in this case means wealth building). There has to be an intense desire to change and maintain those money values if you're ever going to achieve Destination Millionaire and beyond. This is where a Millionaire Mindset and millionaire values converge. If you don't address those values head-on, you risk ending up broke or in debt like the high-paid/low-net-worth athletes we discussed. Spending money with distorted values is like dumping kitchen grease on a fire. It makes a bad problem worse.

Value transformation can't be fixed overnight, which is another reason why the path to Destination Millionaire takes time, and requires consistent effort. True change comes from iterative cycles of trying, failing, and learning. A ballplayer might get two to three iterations of that cycle before their athletic careers are over for good. In most cases, the mighty river of their gargantuan annual salary eventually shrinks to a tiny trickle, at best. By that time, either they'll have invested their income into assets that work for them, or they'll have to start working for a living at some other far-lower-paying job. Given how much of their lives they've devoted to becoming elite athletes and how more and more of them are doing a "one and done" year in college, it's unlikely they'll have developed other lucrative job skills along the way, particularly something that can sustain the lifestyle they've carved out for themselves while they were kings and queens of the tennis court, baseball diamond, track, or gridiron.

Luckily for all of us, money values are by their nature malleable even when deeply ingrained. The sheer process of failing, learning, failing, and learning can be transformative and capable of upending even the most deeply rooted ideas. Nothing quite teaches like failure. Building wealth is a repetitious process that requires year after year of doing things consistently and learning from both your successes and failures. I myself learned from a big mistake I once made about the Bling Life, though it's a mistake I will always cherish because of what I learned from it.

Back in 2002, I ordered an expensive brand-new Mercedes-Benz. (I know, I know; I should have read my own book, but it hadn't been written yet.) A good friend of mine named Edsel had recently bought a brand-new Mercedes 500 with all the bells and whistles. and unfortunately, I was green with envy. Deep green. When we put his Benz on Interstate 5 one weekend on our way to LA, it drove as smooth as butter. After that, I wanted one of my own real' bad, but I had barely finished custom-building my house in Oakland, California, and I hadn't even finished buying the furniture.

I decided to put off getting the car until I could pay for that furniture, and pay it in cash.

Once that was finally out of the way, I was again feeling positive about my finances. I decided, "You know what? I'm ready to buy myself that Benz." Sticker price: $103,000. And just so I could show my good friend and our boys, "You ain't up on that!" I decided to buy a slightly fancier model than his—an S55 AMG. Diamond in the back, sunroof top, diggin' the scene with a gangsta lean...you get the picture. At that point, I had $200,000 in the bank; my company was profitable and taking in $5 million in annual revenue. When I looked in the proverbial mirror, I told myself, *I'm thirty-four, and I'm in good financial shape. I'm living in a multimillion-dollar custom-built house. I can afford a $103,000–car.* So, I took the plunge and ordered my fine new ride.

As fate would have it, the weekend before my dream car was to be delivered, I went off on a golf trip to Atlanta. I rented a modest Toyota Echelon (suggested retail price around $45,000 and change) at the airport and drove off. The make and model of the car was random; I only needed a decent sedan for a short trip. Yet, the whole way to the golf course, I found myself thinking, *Man, this car is pretty smooth. I'm really impressed. It rides like a Lexus.*

I returned to Oakland a few days later knowing that my Benz should've arrived at the dealership by then. Sure enough, the next day, the dealer called me to say that the car was in, and I could come pick it up. I'd never owned such a fancy car in my life, so you'd think I'd be as excited as a toddler at Christmas. Santa just phoned and said there's an amazing present under the tree, right?

Well, actually, wrong. I let a couple of days go by while my dream car lingered at the dealer's like a shunned orphan. Something about the decision to buy that car was eating at me, and rather than feeling ecstatic, I was agitated. I knew I could afford it, so why was I tripping? I woke up the next day convinced I was being totally ridiculous. I'd bought an awesome car that befit my lifestyle and the image I wanted to convey, yo! I said to myself, *Cedric, get your ass down to the dealership and go pick that baby up*! I called Edsel and said, "Hey man, my car's here. Come take me to pick it up!" We drove to the dealership in San Francisco together, and there it stood: my brand-new black and caramel Mercedes-Benz S55 AMG. Exactly like my friend's only—hey, now!—it was a notch above his and even slicker.

I gave the car a quick once-over and then signed all the paperwork. I hopped in my fly car, my buddy hopped in his less-fly one, and off we drove back to Oakland. That should have been the end of the story, right? Successful Brotha buys himself a smoking ride and lives happily ever after?

Wrong again. I wish this story was about that car being a lemon, or about some idiot denting one of my fenders as I drove out of the dealership, but unfortunately, the lemon and the idiot were both named Cedric Nash. Minutes after we pulled out and headed east, all I could think was, *This car is nice but it doesn't drive as smoothly as that Toyota Echelon*. Then, I remembered I hadn't told my accountant I was buying this expensive car. Even though I didn't need his approval, I felt myself dreading his reaction when he eventually found out. As hard as I tried to bury those thoughts and enjoy my new ride, my efforts were to no avail. When I reached the midpoint of the old Oakland Bay Bridge, the true source of my agitation suddenly hit me like a thunderbolt.

The ride of the car had nothing to do with my despair. Heck, I still have that car today, and it rides just fine (though it sits in my garage as a symbolic reminder). Somewhere out there—about three hundred feet above San Francisco Bay—I realized I'd made a huge mistake. Why hadn't I invested that $103,000 in some income-producing property? I was a sole breadwinner, I had three kids and a wife to support, a multimillion-dollar house to maintain and pay off, and while I had a good deal of savings in the bank, we were 100 percent dependent on the success of my business. Businesses can quickly go sour (as later proved true for me) and sometimes even collapse. Maybe if I could've rented a 5 series Mercedes while I was in Atlanta instead of that Toyota Echelon, I might have been spared all that heartache and self-recrimination. But the truth is, the Toyota rental turned out to be one of the best things that ever happened to me because it triggered a need in me to shift my money values. It was a breakthrough of my shifting values. From then on, I gave up trying to keep up with the Joneses and focused my finances on keeping the Nash's (a.k.a. my family's) financially secure. I launched myself headlong down a different path, as an investor, buying my first piece of multi-family property in October 2003 and then two more multi-family properties later that year. The following year I bought my office building. I continued driving my Mercedes S55 AMG even though it often felt like an albatross around my neck. Like most new cars, its resale value dropped by about 40 percent the instant I drove it off the lot.

The biggest change in me wasn't so much that I recognized I'd made a bad decision about the car. What changed was how I felt about the bad decision. When you make a poor financial decision and feel good about it, you're bound to repeat your poor decision-making. If instead you feel remorse, you're ready for change, and the transformation of your money values to begin.

Two years after my over-optimistic car purchase went astray, I had another sort of a personal realization. I was living in Maryland at the time of the annual Congressional Black Caucus. It's a gathering that takes place every September in nearby Washington, DC, when all the Black congressmen come together and discuss issues specifically affecting the African American community. Constituents are invited to come share their thoughts as well. As you might imagine, it's a powerful magnet for good-looking and affluent African American women and men. So, picture me, if you will, still behind the wheel of my Mercedes-Benz S55 AMG, though a couple of years removed from that car being the latest "hot" ride. I had parked in the valet area of the Renaissance Hotel, waiting for some friends, when I looked up and clocked this Brotha headed in my direction down Ninth Street. Not just your everyday Brotha, mind you; this dude was the embodiment of sartorial splendor in a brown suit, so sharp it could cut you. I mean, fashion-wise, it was off-the-hook. At that time, I was buying my own custom suits from a tailor in Los Angeles named Dion Lattimore, who was Magic Johnson's suit maker, Shaq's suit maker, and on and on. Dion was The Man when it came to getting a set of serious threads, and he never let me down. I would buy four or five of his $2,000–suits every year with all the finery too—shirts, ties, cufflinks, shoes, you name it.

That is, until this one particular day when this Fly Brotha came gliding past me, rocking a brown suit for the ages. A suit fit for an emperor. Let me tell you, folks: that was it for me. Somewhere deep inside my soul, a surrender flag started frantically waving because I realized that no matter how hard I tried and how much money I spent on my own wardrobe, I was never, ever going to be the sharpest dressed cat on the scene. Done and done. There was no longer any point in my trying to compete with that Fly Brotha or any of the countless other Brothas I might someday meet who were more dedicated to the fashion cause than I.

This turned out to be a truly edifying revelation. Now that I was freed—or more accurately, now that I had freed myself—from a largely superficial competition within my community that affects many of us, I could focus on things of genuine substance and value. I was officially out of the material race to the bottom of my bank account. My values would continue their transformation toward asset building, in pursuit of lifelong sustainable income, and I would continue seeking ways to put my money to work to generate that income. I was on a new path.

Transition to a new set of money values is a process that evolves and requires time to take into full effect. It was sheer serendipity for me that Mr. Fly Brotha in the brown suit turned down that street I was parked on that day. He will never know how his mere presence unexpectedly helped me, through my value shift, to become not only a better investor but a better person as well.

Does a person need to be ready for value change? I'd say, absolutely. Like any sort of addiction, being stuck on a particular set of values can only be altered or fixed if you're ready on a deep level to do so. Luckily, you don't have to hit rock bottom to be willing to improve your financial values or reset your priorities. You only have to do some soul-searching and be honest with yourself. I can't make you desire something better, nor do I honestly want to, not because I don't care, but because I believe everyone has to make their own choices about when and if they're ready for change. But am I trying to influence you toward a higher goal? You'd better believe I am.

While I speak a lot about my African American community, I don't care about your or anyone else's race when it comes to building wealth. I don't care about age. I don't care about income level. If you want to build wealth, you can do it, even from the bottom up. Countless others have proven this.

I'm only here to give you the knowledge and the encouragement you need to outline your path and follow it. Then, it becomes a question of where you stand on the nine elements of success: desire, faith, sacrifice, confidence, courage, emotional control, patience, consistency, and grit.

I know that bookstores are chock-full of titles in the vein of "Twenty-One Days to a Lifetime of Wealth" or "Three Weeks to Financial Security," but I don't believe we humans are that good at turning on a dime. Comfort is a tough act to follow, and for most of us, a voyage outside our comfort zone more closely resembles the slow and deliberate movements of an ocean liner rather than the quick pivots of a jet ski. I wish we could all simply drop all our bad habits overnight and get straight onto the correct path tomorrow, though even if we could, what's the guarantee that we wouldn't eventually falter and regress? That's why I offer you a strategy that will not only allow for a reasonable amount of time to change but also gives you the means to recover when you falter and regress. Because you will falter and regress, my friends. Not because you're inadequate, but because you're human, and because that faltering is a key part of the learning process that will eventually take you to the top.

The value transformation process, like all those outlined in this book, will take years to reach its full fruition, which adds to the amount of time it takes to achieve Destination Millionaire. The quicker your values transform, the more money you'll save and invest. The more money you save and invest, the quicker you'll achieve Destination Millionaire. This is a transformational process, and your behaviors will not change until you achieve that breakthrough in money values. Fortunately, like a finely tuned motorcycle, you can kick yourself into gear immediately by committing to habits that reflect the values you are learning to adopt. Here's how to begin:

1. LEVEL UP YOUR CIRCLE OF FRIENDS

Start by retooling and regrowing your circle of friends to favor people who possess the money values and behaviors you aspire to. I'm talking about the kind of friends who pass up trips to the mall or unplanned vacations to stay at home and read a book about financial freedom and investing. Have you ever heard that old saying that goes, "Show me your friends, and I'll show you your future?" I see a mountain of wisdom in that simple idea. You can't continue to hang with shoppers if you desire to be a saver. Your friends' influence is a powerful if not paramount factor in your behavioral choices. We are social creatures, and we learn to take our cues from those with whom we spend time. Changing your social circle won't be easy, though. Some of your family members and close friends whose influence triggers you to spend out-of-control may wonder why you've grown distant. You may feel lonely until you find the right new crew, and those folks may not exactly welcome you at first. But as you become more aligned with their type of financial interests, the doors will open. It's hard to overstate how vital this step is to changing your money values. Truth be told, you don't have to do much more than hang around them to begin to change your perspective. I'll give you an example: my own brother John Jr. He purchased his first house in his late forties; something that he might never have done had it not been for the influence of his good friend Andre. Andre worked at the post office but he was an assiduous saver and always paid his bills on time, resulting in a high credit score. In 2002, Andre started purchasing undervalued homes in DC. It was a time when you could buy houses with little-to-no money down if you had good credit and if the houses appraised for more than the purchase price. Andre grew up struggling in DC with a single mother and he never wanted to struggle again when he came of age.

He knew his mother couldn't afford to pay for his college, so he leveraged financial aid and scholarships in order to complete his education.

Andre's childhood experiences and lack of available financial resources gave rise to his Millionaire Mindset and money values. He became a millionaire by buying up every house he could get his hands on in DC. Over time the value of houses in DC skyrocketed and Andre's wealth reached the stratosphere along with it. He's since retired from the post office and spends his retirement time flipping houses in the DC area, not because he needs the money, but because he likes the game. My brother John Jr. had a breakthrough after hanging with Andre, and within six months of deciding to buy a house, he did exactly that. Next thing you know he had his Jeep Cherokee paid off as well. When I asked him what he was going to buy next, he gave me the kind of answer you'd expect to hear from a millionaire.

"Nothing," he replied. "I'm going to invest money in my 401(k)."

What's especially interesting about John's story is how the influence of his brother—me—turned out to be subordinate to the influence of his friend. It's often easier to listen to people we don't share a history with.

In addition to changing the close friends you spend the most time with, it's important that you create a wealth ecosystem. I like to call this your Money Team, a group of people and advisers who can help you along your journey to Destination Millionaire and beyond. Your Money Team includes millionaire mentors knowledgeable about investing, an independent financial adviser, an accountant, an estate attorney, and an insurance agent who can assist you when you need professional advice. We'll discuss ways to create this team later in the book.

Changing your crew works because when you change your social circle, the nature of the conversations you're having changes. Those conversations change your desires, thinking, and mindset because your new crew is discussing money outcomes that challenge your previous mindset. Many of the accomplishments that seemed so large to you in the past—too large, in fact—now appear more achievable because you're talking with folks who are doing it or have done it already. Changing your conversation will change your destination!

New surroundings require new ways of doing things. Here are a couple of key steps to implement as part of that adjustment.

2. LEARN THE WEALTH-BUILDING LANGUAGE

To participate constructively in your new surroundings, you will need to start learning about wealth-building techniques and the specific language that comes along with it in order to contribute to the conversation. You can do this by reading, studying, and listening to content on TV and to credible social media personalities (e.g., @millionairemoneymoves, The Bloomberg Network, CNBC, Tip'd Finance News, etc.) designed to increase your knowledge about wealth. Try to spend an hour or two each day reading a book, a financial publication, or listening to programming related to saving and investing.

At first it will be difficult. After all, you're learning a new language. It's no different learning how to speak "finance." At first you'll have a tough time understanding a lot of what you're listening to or reading, but in time it will become much clearer. It will likely sound foreign at first, like a whole new language. I liken it to my experience learning Spanish. I took exactly one class and then, brimming with misguided confidence, I visited several Spanish-speaking countries, assuming I could now communicate with the locals. The moment they started talking, rapidly and using a string of words that all sounded like one long word, my *cabeza* (translation:

head) started spinning like a top! I couldn't understand a thing. I stuck with it though, and continued to read, speak, listen, and learn Spanish. Now when I listen to someone speaking it, I'm able to catch three to four words in a sentence string and, with a little bit of gesticulating thrown in, understand precisely what they're saying. The pace of their speech feels slower now, not because they've changed, but because the neurons in my brain have learned to adjust.

Trust me, the first time you listen to someone talking about derivatives, equity positions, NFTs, or bond yields, your head may spin too. I have an advanced degree in business and a solid understanding of accounting and finance, yet there are still some subjects I don't fully understand. It's all a work in progress. But the same way I now have much more fun in Spanish-speaking places, you too will find enjoyment and confidence as you become increasingly financially literate. One thing I always like to remind folks is that we weren't born with the gift of speech. We learned to talk as children because we didn't worry about making mistakes or not understanding things along the way. My point is, we're all capable of learning a new language when we give ourselves a chance.

3. PRACTICE NEW BEHAVIORS

a. Start by taking at least 5 percent of every paycheck you receive and putting it in a savings/investment fund. If and when you get a raise, take 50 percent of your raise or bonus and add it to your savings/investment fund.

b. The next time your friends invite you to take an unplanned trip or to a weekly happy hour, opt out and invite a friend over to your house to sip on your favorite bottle of Brown

Estate and chat about your current year's financial goals.

c. Commit yourself to reading one hour a day about wealth building and finance. Commit another hour to listening to shows like Mad Money or Bloomberg News.

d. Identify five friends you want in your circle whose financial behaviors align with ones you desire or can learn from. Meet weekly with your new Fab Five to discuss their projects and ask if you can help them, perhaps by doing research.

The idea is to create a snowball effect by choosing actions that are small, achievable, and become larger and more effective as your new set of millionaire values solidifies. This is how you begin to live below your means and give rise to the most prevalent of all values shared by millionaires: frugality.

You will see that practicing your new values will impact your money outcomes immediately. You can track them too because you've committed in Chapter 3 to updating your net worth statement quarterly. Watch and enjoy the value of your assets growing by increasing your savings and reducing your liabilities. You'll notice the balance of your stock portfolio rising as you consistently invest in quality companies that pay dividends. You will begin to see the income and price appreciation you're deriving from the rental properties that you've invested in and own. These material acknowledgments that your wealth is growing, that you are getting closer to Destination Millionaire, will serve to fuel your efforts and change your mindset forever.

Continue these steps until they become natural, automatic, and effortless. In less time than you might think, you won't have to work at it any longer because these behaviors will have become part of your core values, the values of a millionaire.

Until then, I've identified five stages to the Value and Behavior Transformation process to help you assess the state of your current money values. They are:

STAGE 1: NUMB

- You continuously make bad money decisions and your spending doesn't create an emotional reaction beyond excitement about what you just purchased.
- You have no money in your 401(k), less than six months cash in reserve, and all of your credit cards are maxed out.
- Your spending is undeterred by high credit card interest, as long as you can keep spending.
- Your money decisions are based on your ability to come up with the money...period.
- Folks in the financially numb stage never build wealth nor achieve any of the outlined financial levels/goals.

STAGE 2: WOKE

- You're still making bad money decisions; however, you begin to feel something when you do.
- You're beginning to feel discomfort that your spending behaviors are not aligned with your financial goals (Comfortable, Financially Independent, Millionaire, etc.).
- An inciting event occurs, like learning that your best friend has built a nice-sized savings account or 401(k), or finding out your little sister (who makes less money than you) is buying a

house, while you're still living paycheck to paycheck. Perhaps it's a notice from the credit card company that they're closing your account for nonpayment. When you're "woke," these events make you take notice.

STAGE 3: QUEASY

- You start feeling sick to your stomach when you make bad financial decisions that do not align with your financial wealth level/goals.
- Bad spending behavior no longer gives you the pleasure it used to due to your heightened state of awareness.

I don't mean to imply that everyone is going to feel a signal in their gut; what's important to understand is that there is often an emotional component to change that manifests itself physically. It's a signal your brain sends you through your body. Value transformation truly begins when the intensity level of this state peaks though at this stage your actual breakthrough can happen at any moment. Coaching Guru Tony Robbins writes in his book *Money-Mastering The Game* that while a breakthrough can happen at any moment, "it can take years for the moment to happen." Mine happened on that bridge when I realized the folly of my Mercedes purchase.

STAGE 4: BREAKTHROUGH

- You decide once and for all to make the necessary changes in your money values and behaviors. This is a life-defining moment that alters your thinking about money forever.

- You begin to put good money values and behavior to practice.
- You work harder than you ever have to bring in as much money as possible.
- You are willing to live frugally in order to consistently save.
- You invest consistently.
- You begin to build wealth.

It takes several years to become a millionaire if you're starting from the bottom as I did. It takes time to develop the Millionaire Mindset, Millionaire Values, and change your money behaviors consistently. It also takes time for the value of your investments to grow. But now that you've reached this stage, it means the path ahead has been cleared, and it's only a matter of time and you will arrive at Destination Millionaire.

STAGE 5: EMANCIPATED

- Your behaviors and money decisions are consistently aligned with your financial goals (Financially Comfortable, Financially Independent, Millionaire, Rich, Ultra Rich, Billionaire).
- Your money values and behaviors are on autopilot.
- You weigh the impact on your net worth, savings, and debt balances before deciding to spend or not spend.

At what stage are you? Are you ready for change? If so, how badly do you want it? Is your desire for change at a level higher than 7 out of 10? Have you already experienced your breakthrough and find yourself fired up and ready to go? If you're not ready yet, that's okay too. I hope you'll consider the steps I've outlined above until you are ready to take the journey to Destination Millionaire.

MAKE MILLIONAIRE MONEY MOVES ("THE PLAYBOOK")

Now that we understand how developing a Millionaire Mindset and adopting millionaire values work, it's time to concretely start building wealth by integrating those elements and beginning to make Millionaire Money Moves. The combined power of those three catalysts: mindset, value and behavior change, and Millionaire Money Moves, is what will set in motion—and maintain in motion—your money working for you, your net worth increasing, and you becoming rich over time.

In my view, there are seven ways of getting rich or becoming a millionaire, seven specific paths—none of which is quick, easy, or free. Several of them are questionable, at best.

1. **Inheritance**—According to the US Census less than 1.9 percent, or 323,000 of the seventeen million Black households in the US,

have a net worth of $1 million or more. That's not what I'd call a reliable source of riches. Even if you were one of those less than 2 percent who received an inheritance, with how many relatives would you have to share the family fortune? What would you do to preserve your inheritance afterward? What are the chances it could sustain you for life?

2. **Lottery**—How many tickets would you have to buy? How much money would you have to spend? How many years would you have to continue buying tickets to hit the big jackpot? According to the National Endowment for Financial Education, about 70 percent of people who win a lottery or receive a large windfall go bankrupt within a few years. 'Nuff said.[23]

3. **Show Business/Entertainment/Athletics**—You may be the next Oprah, LeBron, Jay-Z, or Serena Williams, but in show business, entertainment, and athletics, the issue is not only being gifted and talented enough to "make it" (as incredibly difficult as that is) but also keeping your success going long enough and consistently enough to build and ensure long-term wealth. At any one time more than 90 percent of the membership of the Screen Actors Guild is unemployed. The average career of an NFL player is three and a half years. *Sports Illustrated* once estimated that 60 percent of NBA players are broke within five years of leaving the sport, while 78 percent of NFL players are either bankrupt or under financial stress within two years

---

[23] George Loewenstein, "Five Myths about the Lottery," *The Washington Post,* December 27, 2019, https://www.washingtonpost.com/outlook/five-myths/five-myths-about-the-lottery/2019/12/27/742b9662-2664-11ea-ad73-2fd294520e97_story.html.

of retirement.[24] So even if you make it under the bright lights, there's nothing in place to ensure you can hold on to your wealth. We want to be lifelong millionaires, not flashes in the pan.

4. **Entrepreneurship**—According to *The Economist* magazine, 47 percent of millionaires are business owners.[25] That's almost one out of every two millionaires. The reasons are many. Through entrepreneurship, you can earn significantly more income than any other way, and that income can be invested to generate even more wealth and income. What's more, selling a successful business can provide a huge windfall that sets you up for life. Yet along with its plentiful advantages, owning any business comes with its own set of challenges. Acquiring startup and expansion capital is difficult. The workload of a successful entrepreneur is typically heavy; twelve-plus-hour workdays and six-to-seven-day workweeks are not at all uncommon. Competition is plentiful; there are usually other businesses that do what you do, and you have to compete with them to win and retain your customer/client base. Business failure is a constant threat. By some estimates, as many as half of all businesses fail within their first five years.

5. **Real Estate Investment**—Real estate is a highly reliable method for achieving Destination Millionaire and beyond. It provides you with passive income, it doesn't necessarily require an enormous commitment of time, it features major tax benefits

---

[24] Pablo S. Torre, "How (and Why) Athletes Go Broke," *Sports Illustrated*, March 23, 2009, https://vault.si.com/vault/2009/03/23/how-and-why-athletes-go-broke.

[25] "More Millionaires than Australians," *The Economist*, January 20, 2011, https://www.economist.com/special-report/2011/01/22/more-millionaires-than-australians, p. 4–7.

on the income you receive, and the bar for entry is low (a down payment can be as low as 10–25 percent of an asset's price). Ever heard the old saying, "Well, they can't create more land?" It's true. Real Estate is all about supply and demand. Where supply is limited, demand increases for the property and thus the price and profits. I call real estate the gift that keeps on giving.

6. **Securities Investment (Stocks, Bonds, Options)**—Investing in securities can be the fastest path to great wealth. But it's risky, due to the vagaries of the marketplace, and it requires a lot of upfront capital to become a millionaire or strike it rich. That's why I like securities as part of a wealth-building strategy, not as a singular path to wealth. Fortunes can be lost overnight due to unforeseen circumstances, especially if they aren't correctly diversified.

7. **Alternative Investments Investing**—Alternative investments are a class of high risk, high-reward investments not listed on a public exchange." Alternative Investments are for folks who by most accounts have already passed the millionaire threshold and have become what are called "accredited investors."

I'll go into depth on each type of alternative investment in the Supplemental Chapter "Investing in Alternative Investments." For now, know that they include being an "angel" investor, which is someone who invests in early stage companies, investing as a venture capitalist (or VC), where money is pooled together to invest in later-stage companies looking to expand, go public or be acquired, investing in Hedge Funds, which encompasses a wide range of risky but potentially highly rewarding investments, and investing in Private Equity, which focuses on investing in privately held companies looking for expansion capital or acquisition capital in order to later be merged or acquired and sold at a sizable premium. Owing to the massive risks it engenders, investing in Alternative Investment is strictly limited to accredited investors, meaning folks who have enough cash to survive an enormous setback.

Of these seven paths to Destination Millionaire and beyond, three are highly improbable (inheritance, lottery, and show business/entertainment/athletics) while the other four are plausible, accessible roads to riches (entrepreneurship, real estate, securities investing, and alternative investments). Most importantly, they don't require any specialized gifts, talents, or luck, which is why my Millionaire Money Moves system focuses exclusively on them and will work for anyone.

Millionaire Money Moves are rooted in the universal law of wealth, which dictates that if you acquire appreciating, income-producing assets while minimizing your debt, your net worth will increase over time. That has been the path to wealth for centuries and it's the reason that the rich (who own most of the appreciating, income-producing assets) always get richer. That's why my system is specifically designed to change how you manage your resources from spending "your money" to spending "what your money makes." In its simplest form, the concept looks like this:

1. Increase the amount of income you earn as well as increase the quantity of income sources at your disposal.
2. Pay only mandatory, nondiscretionary expenses.
3. Reduce and/or eliminate nonmandatory discretionary spending as much as possible to generate money to invest.
4. Invest as much excess money as you can into assets that appreciate in value and generate further income on their own.

Imagine that your money's current job is to buy and pay for things. Not a hard thing to imagine I'm sure. What's different about the Millionaire Money Moves system is that it gives your money a new and better job. A promotion, if you will. Your money's new job is to make more money. Not by sitting in some bank collecting a piddling interest while that bank paying you the piddling interest makes oodles of dollars for itself by investing your hard-earned money. No. Those days are over. You're gonna make your money work much harder than that. It will still have to do its old job taking care of your expenses; only now, its main focus is going to be increasing your net worth and, thus, your wealth, through investment. You're going to put your money to work, so you don't have to.

The assets you'll begin to purchase with your income and newfound savings will become the money machines that generate greater income and make you rich. If you've ever wondered why the racial wealth gap keeps growing beyond the impact of racism, discrimination, and oppression, it's because we're not accumulating appreciating, income-producing assets. Full stop. It's high time for us to get busy buying assets that exponentially increase in value over time and offload the twin weights of bad debt and excess spending that are blocking our path to building wealth for ourselves and lasting legacies for the future. Simply put, we must begin to play the "get wealthy game" and move on from playing the "look wealthy game."

WHY MAKING MILLIONAIRE MONEY MOVES WORK

Millionaire Money Moves encompasses the new mindset and value changes you're putting into place in order to transition you from repeatedly making Million-Never Money Moves into making decisions that are completely aligned with your new values, money behaviors, and financial aspirations. Million-Nevers stay at or regress from where they are financially because their mindset, values, and behaviors never transform. They neglect or dismiss the need to earn more, save, and invest to build wealth.

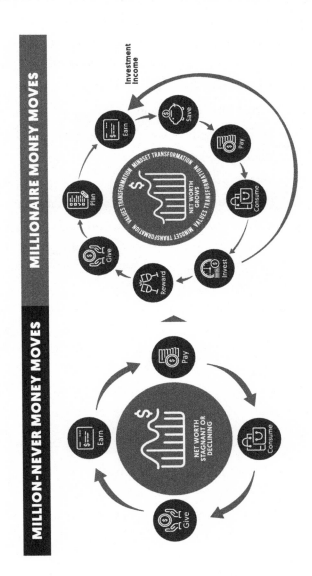

As this is a process of continuous improvement, it is cyclical in nature. The same way you didn't get into debt overnight, you're not going to get rich overnight either. But you will get rich. As you complete each cycle—whether it's over the course of six months, a year, or several years—you'll become more determined, knowledgeable, and efficient because you'll be able to clearly see your progress holistically. As you continue placing your money in assets that grow your wealth, your Millionaire Mindset, values, and behaviors further develop, and you become savvier and more responsive to opportunities to grow your income and wealth. Along with it, your confidence and courage grow, enabling you to intelligently take on higher risk/higher return investments. Simultaneously, as your money values and behaviors improve, you'll begin to save more, waste less, and thereby increase the amount of money you can profitably invest.

Let's dive in and see how each step of the process works.

PLAN

Millionaires plan to succeed. Million-Nevers fail to plan.

The Millionaire Money Moves system is built in steps, each of which is based on an if/then methodology. For example, when you reach "X" economic threshold—and only then—you can buy or invest in "Y." This way, not only do you avoid getting too far ahead of yourself, which can lead to financial difficulty, you set out a path that always points toward your end goals. Your final destination remains forever in sight, and each step along the way is informed by it. In a moment, I'll show you my M$M investment ladder which will clearly guide you through each of your future investment thresholds.

Equally important to the process is how a step-by-step approach normalizes your plan. As with any activity that requires a certain discipline—exercise, writing music, studying, and so forth—wealth building takes time to get accustomed to and accepted as a ritualized behavior. By setting it up in a structured way, you will quickly lock the process itself into your subconscious so that following your plan becomes second nature—an afterthought along the lines of, *I know I'll complete this step before moving on because that fits with my plan's design.*

One of the greatest weaknesses in most plans, including investment strategies, is a lack of realism and timing. That's why I will show you how to break your plan into realistic achievable steps, each of which triggers the next one, so you can measure feasibility rather than simply hoping you'll reach your goal as if guided by some unseen hand.

As you begin setting these goals, how can you know if they are even realistic? Experts believe the biggest difference between a goal and a dream is that a goal has a plan with a timetable attached to it. The approach to a goal is proactive, serious, and extremely deliberate. One way to look at this distinction in terms of your own journey is to decide whether—given the choice—you'd prefer to be a raft or a boat. Here's what I mean: some people are rafts, content to go wherever the ocean of life takes them. I've known many "rafts" who are happy living this way and they appear to be as happy as the people who choose to be boats. It's true. You can live your life either way and find happiness. The life of a raft is a life of acceptance, meaning you adjust to your circumstances rather than trying to shape them. The life of a boat, on the other hand, is based on strategy.

My choice was, and still is, to be a boat. I've been so specific about my goals that at times folks have criticized me for being *too* specific. Their critique is based on the notion that if you're too specific you'll never be happy unless you get exactly what you want, and if you don't ever get exactly what you want, you'll feel like your life has been meaningless. There's some truth to that. As with most things in life, a completely black or white, either/or approach can lead to paralyzing rigidity. So, I think the correct answer to the boat/raft question lies somewhere in the middle.

You want to be laser-focused on your goals, but adaptable. Sometimes it makes sense to use the power of the ocean rather than an outboard motor.

Now before I drown anyone in this maritime analogy, let me circle back and give you a clearer definition of what constitutes a goal. It's absolutely vital to understand what a goal is before embarking on its pursuit and choosing to be goal oriented.

Back in 1981, *Management Review* magazine published a ground-breaking article which laid out an idea called SMART goals. SMART is an acronym for:

- **S**pecific
- **M**easurable
- **A**chievable
- **R**ealistic
- **T**ime-Based

Here's a quick example of how a SMART goal works. The song "I'd Like to Teach the World to Sing" was the soundtrack to a famous Coca-Cola ad in the 1970s. That sounds like a goal, doesn't it—to teach the world to sing? But don't be fooled; that's a wish, not a goal. Compare that idea to this one, "Within the next six months, I'd like to teach a thousand people to sing, 'Lift Every Voice and Sing.'" Do you see how specific that is? Teaching one song (measurable) to one thousand people (may not be easy, but it's achievable) within the next six months (time-based and realistic). I can't stress enough how important it is to use this litmus test for each and every one of your financial goals. It's perfectly fine to wish for things, but wishing is no way to organize and plan your life or to build wealth.

KNOWING YOUR STARTING POINT

Now let's get to work. Everyone's starting point is different. Some folks may start off with a negative net worth; others will have a positive one. Where you're starting from doesn't matter; what matters is that you know where you're starting from so you can measure and be inspired by your progress. If you haven't yet done so, calculate your net worth as of today as well as your current income and sources of income so you know your precise starting point. Document your net worth and update it quarterly in a notebook, an Excel planning spreadsheet tab and/or in another suitable app. Once again, your net worth is the sum of your assets minus your liabilities. (You can refer to Chapter 3 for instructions on how to calculate your net worth.)

Here's an example of what that might look like:

EXAMPLE:

Current Net Worth: $25,000 (assuming assets equaling $225,000 in your Freedom Fund plus home equity minus $200,000 in mortgage, student loan, credit card, and car loan debt).

Current Freedom Fund (401(k), IRA, savings, stocks, or bonds): $100,000.

Current Income Sources and "Income for Life:"

- $22,000 Total Annual "Sustainable Income for Life" as follows:
  - $4,000 in annual income using the 4 percent rule from your $100,000 Freedom Fund
  - $0 in annual income or 5 percent from your real estate investment portfolio
  - $6,000 in annual income from your pension

- $12,000 in annual income from Social Security

Current Debt Level: $200,000 (assuming $200,000 in mortgage, student loan, credit card, and car loan debt).
Current Date: June 15, 20XX.
Current Age: 40

CHOOSE YOUR ENDGAME

As we discussed in Chapter 4, your endgame is where you aspire to be financially when you no longer wish to work. For planning purposes, your endgame should be broken up in these terms and look something like the following two examples:

EXAMPLE 1:

Net Worth Goal: $750,000 ($250,000 in cash, $500,000 in real estate, and $0 debt).
Freedom Fund Goal (401(k), IRA, savings, stocks and bonds): $250,000.
Income Sources and "Income for Life" Goal:

- $118,456 Total Annual "Sustainable Income for Life" as follows:
  - $10,000 in annual income using the 4 percent rule from your Freedom Fund
  - $25,000 in annual income or 5 percent from your real estate investment portfolio
  - $50,000 in annual income from your pension
  - $33,456 in annual income from Social Security

Debt Level Goal: **100 Percent Debt free**

Timing of Endgame:

Date: June 30, 20XX

Age: 55

EXAMPLE 2:

Net Worth Goal: $5 million ($2 million in cash, $2 million in real estate, $1 million in business valuation, and $0 debt).

Freedom Fund Goal (401(k), IRA, savings, stocks and bonds): $2 million.

Income Sources and "Income for Life" Goal:

- $313,456 Total Annual "Sustainable Income for Life" as follows:
  - ▫ $80,000 in annual income using the 4 percent rule from your Freedom Fund
  - ▫ $200,000 in annual income or 10 percent from your real estate investment portfolio
  - ▫ $33,456 in annual income from Social Security.

Debt Level Goal: **100 Percent Debt free**

Timing of Endgame:

By date: December, 31, 20XX

By age: 55

Take some time now, and write down what you want your endgame to look like in a readily accessible place that you can come back to, be it a notebook, a tab titled "Endgame" in your Excel planning spreadsheet, or somewhere secure (such as the Cloud). The targets are entirely up to you, but like any great marksman, you need to know what to aim for.

SELECT YOUR PATH TO
DESTINATION MILLIONAIRE

Which path to Destination Millionaire or your Endgame best suits your personality, interest, passion, skillset, and vision? Are you interested in Real Estate, or is being a landlord not your thing? What about investing in the efforts and talents of other entrepreneurs through Alternative Investments? Does Entrepreneurship sound more like your area of interest? How about keeping your day job and adding a financial future steeped in Securities Investing? Maybe you're interested in entrepreneurship and investing your profits in real estate and securities like I did. Don't worry about choosing or making the perfect plan or path right now; you will undoubtedly make changes along the way. But you can't get to any destination without a path(s). You'll need to identify your chosen plan as you prepare to develop your M$M Master Plan to Destination Millionaire, which we'll discuss shortly.

BUDGET LIKE A MILLIONAIRE
(M$M POWER BUDGET)

The next step in planning is to create your budget in order to kick off the process of transforming your income and savings into investment capital, and growing that investment money over time. We'll go into each of these areas in greater detail later on.

One of the most important things to know in creating a budget are your monthly expenses. How much money does it cost you every month to pay for whatever lifestyle you're pursuing—everything from your housing, to your healthcare, to your car, to your late-night jaunts to the corner store for cookies (well, mine anyway)? Your expenses include the amount of money you pay each month to service your debt obligations, plus any maintenance you may have to perform on your investments. In other words, what does it cost you to be you and to "do" you?

Think of your budget as your own personal accountant and bookkeeper who travels with you wherever you go and helps you make solid financial decisions. By solid I mean decisions that are exactly tailored to you and your life, not some nebulous idea of how much you should be earning or spending that predates your properly budgeted life. Your budget provides visibility as to where your money is going so that you can make improvements which will allow you to spend less and save and invest more. Budgeting is a tried-and-true technique to ensure you spend your money wisely based on who you are, where you're at financially, and where you're headed. It also helps you understand how sufficient and reliable your streams of income actually are. Obviously, your expenses and your income are likely to vary from month to month, though as you work your way to millionaire status, you'll notice yourself actively tracking every expense you incur or are even thinking of incurring. This is how that process starts.

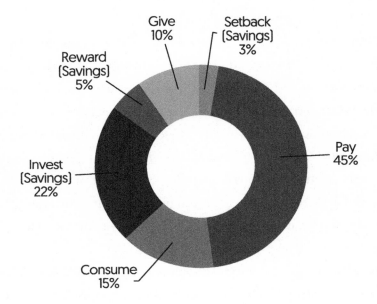

MILLIONAIRE MONEY MOVES
Power Budget
(For Givers)

Give
10%

Setback
(Savings)
3%

Reward
(Savings)
5%

Pay
45%

Invest
(Savings)
22%

Consume
15%

This is my M$M Power Budget, a budgeting framework I designed to allow you to manage the financial obligations needed to support you and your family, while at the same time positioning you to invest in your chosen path(s) to Destination Millionaire. Your investments are what are going to make you wealthy. Million-Nevers spend all of their income, don't invest strategically and consistently, and therefore never become millionaires. If you ever plan on reaching Destination Millionaire and beyond, you will have to earn more income and minimize your expenditures in order to invest as much as possible. This is the breakdown of my M$M Power Budget; we'll go into the rationale for each in further detail later on in this chapter.

Save (Setback Account) 3 percent of your take-home income—The M$M Power Budget calls for you to save 3 percent of your income in your Setback savings account. This account is reserved for times of financial hardship when you need to get your hands on cash quickly.

Pay 45 percent of your take-home income—This means paying for non-discretionary, required spending only and encompasses all the things you cannot function without, such as your rent, mortgage, transportation, utilities (gas, electric, water, etc.), internet, cellphone, and so on. You don't have much choice in what you Pay. These are the essentials to your life.

Consume 15 percent of your take-home income—The Consume category represents discretionary spending contingent upon your lifestyle. Discretionary items are items that you purchase to improve your lifestyle or satisfy your wants. By definition, discretionary items are a choice; you can either buy them or not.

Invest (Savings) 22 percent of your income in your Freedom Fund—This is where the rocket fuel is stored. Your Freedom Fund is what allows you to hit your number as I have and be free to do whatever you want with your time. You won't have to work for anyone but yourself, if at all. Wouldn't it be great at some point in your life to do whatever you want with your time? Well, if you plan correctly and execute your plan, that dream can become a reality, even when you're starting from the bottom as I did. Your Freedom Fund is where your 401(k), your IRA, and your after-tax investment accounts live. It's also a primary source of the capital used to invest in your chosen path to Destination Millionaire.

Reward (Savings) with 5 percent of your take-home Income—This 5 percent of your income is to treat yourself (travel, jewelry, shoes, car, boat, electronics, etc.) for achieving major milestones in your wealth-building plan. Call this your incentive fund, if you like; the point is that specifically putting 5 percent of your earnings into this fund prevents you from robbing yourself out of your savings and investment gains while still providing some material joy in your life. Let's face it, it's impossible and frankly no fun to save all the time. Sometimes you want to splurge and buy yourself something nice for your sacrifice. The Reward fund allows you to do so and stay on track with your dreams and life goals.

Give 10 percent of your take-home income—I believe that gratitude and giving are two essential keys to happiness. You may disagree. Whether or not you are a person of one faith or another, I still believe it is always a good practice to either give back or pay it forward to someone else. I'll go deeper into my reasons in a little while when we get to the section called "Give."

If you currently have the means and believe in giving 10 percent of your income to faith-based or charitable organizations that align with your values, use the budget structure provided above. For those folks who don't yet have the means or who prefer to give of their time and not a portion of their income, you should reallocate half of that 10 percent Give money (i.e., 5 percent of your income) to your Freedom Fund and use the remaining 5 percent to accelerate paying off your debts. Once you've significantly increased your earnings, have six to twelve months saved in your setback account, and have successfully got your debt category under control, you can choose to give any portion of your income you see fit up to that 10 percent, or simply continue to give your time instead (or both). That budget looks like this:

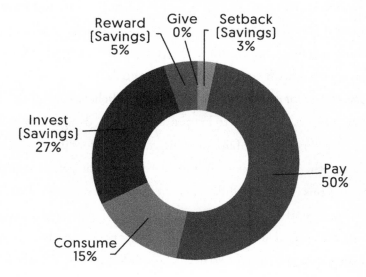

MILLIONAIRE MONEY MOVES
Power Budget

Reward (Savings) 5%
Give 0%
Setback (Savings) 3%
Invest (Savings) 27%
Pay 50%
Consume 15%

Along with these budget frameworks I've established a few rules you must abide by in order to stay on track.

M$M Power Budget Rule #1—Always pay yourself first. Every paycheck must go into your Setback, Reward, and Freedom savings accounts. You have to get in this habit if you're ever going to build investment capital, so get used to it now. I honestly don't care if all you can save is $5 per paycheck; if so, save it. In time when you get a raise or pay off some debt, you'll be able to save more. You must save money from each and every paycheck. No skipping allowed.

Think of it this way: when you fail to pay yourself, you're essentially saying that everyone else (the mortgage company, car dealership, utilities company, furniture store, clothing store, etc.) deserves your money except for you, the person working for it. I beg to differ. You're the one working for that paycheck; you deserve to keep some of the fruits of your own labor.

M$M Power Budget Rule #2—No more than two credit cards in your life. One VISA or MasterCard and one American Express. No department or specialty store credit cards are allowed. Credit card issuers are no dummies; there's a reason they try to lure you in with "save 10 percent" on your purchases if you get their specialty card. They know sooner or later you'll miss a payment, even accidentally, and they'll make it all back and more on the enormous interest you'll have to pay on your outstanding debt. If you own a business or have rental properties, you're allowed one additional credit card to make material or equipment purchases. However, you must pay off the balances upon use. If you already have more than this allotment of credit cards, then take out a scissors and cut the extra ones up right away. Go ahead, I'll wait. If you have outstanding balances on them, use the methods I outlined under Pay to pay off your debt as quickly and efficiently as you can. There is no better feeling than living fully in control of your debt. You don't need to hold onto the card to pay down the balance, so consign it to the scrap heap immediately. Experts will tell you that it's better for your credit score to pay off your debt by making regular payments over time instead of paying it off all at once. There may be some truth to that, but what I do know is that I'd rather be debt-free fast and allow my credit score to improve in time, than drag out principal and interest payments for the sake of a slightly higher credit score.

M$M Power Budget Rule #3—Do not accept credit (i.e., more debt) from anyone else. "No interest due for sixty days, ninety days, six months, or one year" are all invitations to unwanted debt. As a burgeoning millionaire, you're in the business of deferred gratification in pursuit of a larger goal, which means if you can't afford it now, assume you can't afford it later either, interest-deferral or not.

*M$M Power Budget Rule #4*—No withdrawals from your Setback or Freedom Fund accounts except in extreme circumstances like a job loss or major financial crisis. Those balances need to either go up or stay flat. If you have a financial crisis, you can delay putting money in those accounts, but you cannot take any money out unless your survival or the loss of a valuable asset depends on it. You have to do this to get in the habit of being a saver. You really have to be tough on yourself and follow my M$M Power Budget Rules if you're ever going to start building wealth.

The easiest and most efficient way to find savings opportunities is to optimize your budget. Find things you can do without, even temporarily, and put that money toward building wealth through investment. Before we move on, I want you to create a budget based on your current income and expenses and compare it to the M$M Power Budget. These are the steps:

Step 1: Know where your money is going—Working with your banking institution, compile six months of bank statements showing where your money is being spent.

Step 2: Group all of your expenditures into five categories (Save, Pay, Consume, Invest, Give). The money you save goes under **Save**. Non-discretionary expenditures (like rent, mortgage, transportation, groceries, insurance, utilities, home maintenance/repair, etc.) go under **Pay**. Discretionary/lifestyle expenditures such as entertainment, travel, shopping, eating out, and so on belong in **Consume**. Your 401(k), IRA contributions, and other investments go under **Invest**. If the expenditure is a donation to your favorite faith-based or charitable organization, or if it is money given to help out a friend or family member, it goes under **Give**.

Step 3: Calculate the percentage of your income being allocated to Save, Pay, Consume, Invest, and Give.

Step 4: Compare your past six months of allocations to the M$M Power Budget and identify which categories are out of alignment.

Step 5: Devise a plan to either lower your expenditures or increase your earnings (refer to (Sub) Chapter 7.2 "Earn") to align your budget to the M$M Power Budget and begin to invest your way to your Destination Millionaire.

Step 6: Automate your budget by using the leading budget apps and set up alerts and alarms to keep you vigilant.

Don't worry if your budget doesn't mirror the M$M Power Budget. What matters is that you know exactly how far off your budget is so that you can begin making changes in your earnings and spending to eventually align your budget with the M$M Power Budget.

Once you create your budget, document it in excel using the template shown below and provided on my website, www.cedricnash.com, or select a leading app to track your expenditures against your plan. The leading apps in the space of budgeting and personal finance are Personal Capital, Empower, YNAB (You Need A Budget), Acorns, Mint.com, PicketGuard, Dollarbird, Mvelopes, Wally, Good Budget, Spendee, and Albert. Take advantage of these tools where it makes sense.

This is the budget format that I created and used since 1990. The only things that have changed are the categories and the amounts.

Budget Planning Template

Pay Period 1	Planned	Actual	Pay Period 2	Planned	Actual
Income			*Income*		
Salary	$0.00		Salary	$0.00	
Pre-Tax Freedom Fund (401(k))	$0.00		Pre-Tax Freedom Fund (401(k))	$0.00	
Taxable Salary	$0.00		Taxable Salary	$0.00	
Taxes	$0.00		Taxes	$0.00	
Salary After Tax & Retirement	**$0.00**		**Salary After Tax & Retirement**	**$0.00**	
Expenses			*Expenses*		
Spending Allowance	$0.00		Spending Allowance	$0.00	
Sunny Day Savings	$0.00		Mortgage Payment	$0.00	
Pre-Tax Freedom Fund (IRA)	$0.00	Auto Pay	Escrow Account	$0.00	
Credit Card #1	$0.00		Pre-Tax Freedom Fund (IRA)	$0.00	Auto Pay
Insurance (Auto)	$0.00		After-Tax Freedom Fund Investment	$0.00	Auto Pay
Groceries	$0.00		Rainy Day Savings	$0.00	
Personal Property Insurance	$0.00	Auto Pay	Credit Card #2	$0.00	
Life Insurance	$0.00	Auto Pay	Long-Term Care Insurance	$0.00	
529 College Fund	$0.00	Auto Pay	Groceries	$0.00	
Total Expenses	**$0.00**		**Total Expenses**	**$0.00**	
Savings/Loss	$0.00		Savings/Loss	$0.00	
			Net Savings/Loss	**$0.00**	

Once you've optimized your budget as best as you can, I'll show you ways to further align your budget to my M$M Power Budget by increasing your income and adding additional income streams in the upcoming section called "Earn," as well as how to cut your expenses in the sections "Pay" and "Consume." By the end of this chapter, you'll be able to devise the right strategy to bring your current budget into Millionaire mode and begin saving and spending like a champion.

HOW TO STAY ON BUDGET BY IMPLEMENTING THE M$M POWER BUDGET

Let's face it, no matter how solid a plan we create, most of us struggle with staying on budget. There are seemingly endless reasons why. Friends convince us to go on an unplanned vacation, or savvy advertisers make us feel like we need that new pair of pricey shoes. The list goes on. Next thing we know our focus and motivation to reach Destination Millionaire gets derailed yet again. All that good planning went out the door. But here is a proven way you can stay on budget without having to agonize about your worst instincts winning the day. It looks like this:

1. Open up five accounts and utilize them in the following manner:

    a. Account #1 is your **Invest (Freedom Fund)** Account (22–27 percent of your income). This account should initially be your **401(k) account**. This will more than likely be with your employer unless you're self-employed, in which case you can open up a self-employed or solo 401(k). This account is where you will automatically direct 22–27 percent of your income. If you exceed the maximum deductible amount (currently $20,500 for workers younger than fifty, $27,000 for individuals older than fifty), you can put the excess money in your Freedom Fund by opening a tax-free IRA account. As your income grows, you can also open a separate after-tax investment account to invest funds that exceed your 401(k) and IRA limits. All of these accounts: your 401(k), IRA, and after-tax investment accounts make up your Freedom Fund. For self-employed individuals, the maximum amount you can put away in your solo 401(k) plan for 2022 is $61,000 if you're below age fifty. If you're older than fifty, you can add that extra $6,500 per year in catch-up contributions, bringing the total to $67,500.

b. Account #2 is your **Setback** Savings Account for emergencies (3 percent of your income). Unlike the type of little-to-no interest bank savings account you may be used to, this account should be an investment account at one of the discount brokerage companies, such as Schwab, Fidelity, TD Ameritrade, Robinhood, etc. Because you do not anticipate a setback arising in the near future, you can keep this money invested in the money market or invested in a diverse portfolio of quality stocks. It's important that this account remain liquid and available for any unforeseen emergency. Do not—and I repeat, do not—get an ATM linked to this account that can tempt you into dipping into your savings when your emotions swing out of control, as they will from time to time. Simply have 3 percent (setback funds) automatically withdrawn from your primary checking account (a.k.a. Pay Account #4, see below) on a monthly basis and you'll have it covered.

c. Account #3 is your **Reward** Account (5 percent of your income). This account prevents you from having to dip into your Freedom Fund or Setback funds to cover your reward spending. This account should be a separate investment account at one of the discount brokerage companies, such as Schwab, Fidelity, TD Ameritrade, Robinhood, etc. Brokerage accounts can all be linked under one login, giving you visibility to all your funds at any time. This is not a true savings account per se because once you achieve a major milestone in your plan, you will use these funds to fund your chosen reward. Therefore, the balance in this account will fluctuate from time to time. Simply have 5 percent (Reward funds) automatically withdrawn from your primary checking account (Pay Account #4, see below) on a monthly basis and you'll have it covered too.

d. Account #4 is your primary checking or **Pay** Account where your paychecks get deposited. Use this account to pay non-discretionary (required) expenditures like rent, mortgage, car payments, utilities, insurance, groceries, etc. A total of 45–50 percent of your take-home pay goes here, depending on which Power Budget structure you choose. Automatic deposits to all of your accounts can be set up from this one account. Meet with your banking representative to set up automatic deposits for all of your accounts.

e. Account #5 **Consume** Account is your secondary checking account for what you consume on a discretionary basis. In other words, this is where you can draw from to fund your lifestyle: entertainment, dining out, clothes shopping, and so on. Set up an automatic transfer to this account from your primary checking account so that 15 percent of every paycheck gets deposited. Whenever this account is empty, stay home and get more acquainted with Netflix or the sports bar and theater room you built in your basement until it replenishes to prevent yourself from dipping into your savings accounts.

For the **Give** portion of your budget, if you can't or don't want to set up an automatic withdrawal from your primary checking account, feel free to create a separate account solely for this purpose.

2. Once your accounts are in place, meet with your banking institution to set up automatic deductions to the appropriate accounts. I can't stress enough how important this is to keeping you on budget. Trust your plan and let the decision-making happen automatically.

3. If you're still struggling to stay on budget, because you're not earning enough to follow the M$M Power Budget, then consider putting more effort into earning more by following the advice I offer in Subchapter 7.2 "Earn" where I lay out how to earn more in your main hustle, side hustle, or with your investment income.

The truth is that you will never start building wealth and creating the lifestyle you desire until you can lower what you pay and consume, and thus be able to begin investing on a regular basis. Your investment assets are what's going to give you the income and freedom you need to do you.

CREATE YOUR FIVE-TO-TEN-YEAR M$M MASTER PLAN

I find it personally difficult to plan beyond five to ten years, as things can get kind of fuzzy beyond that first five-year block, though I believe it's useful to have at least a placeholder for some longer-term objectives in a proper high-level plan. You'll recognize from earlier that I wrote my first plan by hand in 1990.

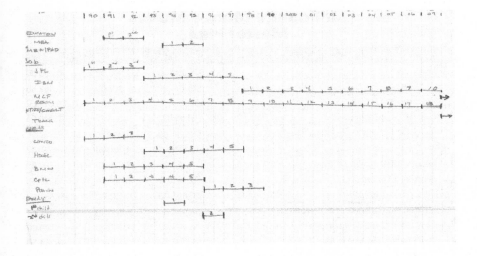

Since then I've developed a cleaner version of my planning template in Microsoft Excel that you can use and which allows you to document your goals by category.

Millionaire Money Moves
Master Plan

Income Assumptions	Annual	Semi-Annual	Monthly
Salary	$75,000.00	$37,500.00	$6,250.00
Taxes (25%)	$18,750.00	$9,375.00	$1,562.50
Take-Home Pay (75%)	$56,250.00	$28,125.00	$4,687.50
Annual Setback Savings (3%)	$1,687.50	$843.75	$140.63
Annual Freedom Fund Savings (22%)	$12,375.00	$6,187.50	$1,031.25
401(k) Contribution	$9,500.00	$4,750.00	$791.67
401(k) Employer Match 50%	$4,750.00	$2,375.00	$395.83
Investment Account	$2,875.00	$1,437.50	$239.58
Side Income - Tutoring	$16,640.00	$8,320.00	$1,386.67
Side Income - Computer Tech Work	$16,640.00	$8,320.00	$1,386.67
Income from Duplex Investment	$8,400.00	$4,200.00	$700.00
Annual Reward Savings (5%)	$2,812.50	$1,406.25	$234.38

Goals	Age:35 2020	Age:36 2021	Age:37 2022	Age:38 2023	Age:39 2023	Age: 2023
Net Worth Plan						
Net Worth						
Earn Plan						
Annual Increase						
Bonus Compensation						
Side Hustle Income						
Income from Duplex Investment						
Total						
Save Plan (30%)						
Setback Savings Account (3%)						
Setback Savings Account						
Freedom Fund (22%)						
401(k) Account						
IRA Account						
Investment Account						
Reward Fund (5%)						
Reward Savings Account						
College 529 Savings Plan						
State 529 Savings Account						
Pay Plan (Debt Payoff Schedule)						
Credit Card						
Auto Loan						
Student Loans						
Invest Plan (22%)						
Securities (Stocks and Bonds)						
Apple						
Berkshire Hathaway B						
INX - S&P 500 Index						
Real Estate						
Buy a Rental House						
Buy a 4-Plex						
Buy a 10-Unit Apartment Building						
Entrepreneurship						
Write the Business Plan						
Obtain Funding						
Secure the Location						
Start the Business						
Private Equity						
Business 1						
Apartment Syndicate 1						
Reward Plan (5%)						
Trip to Jamaica						
Rolex Watch						
New Mercedes Benz						
Purchase 40' Sunseeker Boat						
Give Plan (10%)						
Church (5%)						
United Negro College Fund (2.5%)						
Democratic National (2.5%)						
Personal Goals						
Complete Master's Degree						
Complete Financial Literacy Courses						
Get Promoted						
Learn Spanish						

Your categories will vary depending on the path you choose. Feel free to use any or all of the ones I use here; they're road-tested and can help you stay focused on achieving Destination Millionaire and beyond. As you can see, my planning spreadsheet is designed to align with the Millionaire Money Moves framework and M$M Power Budgets. It allows you to document and integrate your net-worth growth plan, Earn plan, Savings plan, debt pay-down plan, asset investment, and acquisition plan (real estate, private equity, stock, and entrepreneurial plan), Reward plan, Give plan, and for good measure, any personal goals you'd like to include as well. In this way, each area works in concert with the others. If it's important to you, then this is the right place for it to reside. That way, in one comprehensive document, you'll see how you're going to achieve your financial goals in relation to all the other areas in your life that you plan to improve.

I can't stress enough how critical this everything-in-one-place approach is. You need to logically prioritize your plans so they work together harmoniously, and by doing so, you'll significantly improve the probability of achieving your goals. Why? Because there are dependencies to wealth building and to life. In your case, it may be that you can't start your business until you have "X" dollars saved. Or you can't increase your savings until you complete your master's degree. My Master Plan template allows you to document when each goal begins and when it's completed. If a goal is dependent upon another goal being, say, 75 percent completed, then you can show that goal starting at the 75 percent mark.

At the top of the plan, you'll see a place for each year and for your age. I use these fields because I have particular goals I want to achieve by certain ages. I don't plan on working forever, and thus I want to stay focused on getting things done by a certain age. Trust me, it's an excellent motivator when you need one. The years you see that are blacked out represent years that have passed.

I want you to download this M$M Master Plan template at www .cedricnash.com and begin to fill it out. Get started right away. How do you want to live your life at each stage of your life? By when do you want to achieve your financial goal or Destination Millionaire? What type of assets will you need to acquire to achieve the income you want in order to level up and live the life you dream of? Planning costs you nothing while failing to plan will cost you everything, including the outcomes you desire. Will the future life you imagine for yourself and your family remain a dream, or will you make it a goal with a plan, a timeline, and a genuine shot at fulfillment? It's up to you to make the right choice.

Begin by plotting your net worth growth on the road to your Endgame, and then integrate it at the top of your five-to-ten-year M$M Master Plan. Insert your current net worth and a specific annual net worth goal at that rate for each year in the chart. You have to be intentional and honest with yourself to make sure that your growth rate is doable in light of where you're starting from and what your path to Destination Millionaire looks like. Otherwise, you won't arrive at the place in life you've imagined. Choose a percentage growth rate that you think is reasonable—5 percent, 10 percent, 15 percent, or whatever you know you can make happen. If you miss your goal in any one year, you can make it up in subsequent years. So, don't beat yourself up. Select a goal and begin to work toward it.

Millionaire Money Moves Master Plan

Goals	Age:35 2020		Age:36 2021	Age:37 2022
Net Worth Plan				
Net Worth	$25,000.00		$37,500.00	$75,000.

EARN

In business, there are two ways to generate profits: increase revenue and/or decrease expenses. More money in, less money out. The business of You is no different. To generate sufficient capital to invest and get to Destination Millionaire, you're going to need more income (achieved through earning and investment) and less money going out (achieved through budgeting, saving, and smarter spending).

There are two types of income streams: passive and active. Passive income streams require little-to-no direct effort on your part. As I once explained passive income to a golf buddy, "It means you make money while you sleep." Examples of passive income streams are securities dividends, investment interest, business profit distributions, rental income from residential or commercial properties, income from pensions, annuities, 401(k) withdrawals, and Social Security.

Conversely, active income streams require you to be actively involved in order to receive them. Active income comes from a job, essentially, even if that job is working in your own business. Side hustles, freelance income, salary bonuses...all of these are active income streams. To reach

Destination Millionaire, your "Earn" goal is to build up enough passive income streams to support the lifestyle that you want to live—forever. That means you must overload on your active income streams in order to invest in your passive income streams until they're large enough to support your lifestyle and your long-term financial goals.

I've found there are several reliable ways to find new income streams, starting with your main hustle. If you are already gainfully employed at a company and you're doing well, you can begin to look within your current place of employment for opportunities to increase your earnings. Here are some examples.

GET A PAY RAISE

In today's cost-cutting business environment, getting a pay increase can be challenging. Companies tend to offer pay increases slightly above the cost of living, at best, while many companies make raises contingent upon various performance thresholds. Rarely do significant raises arrive automatically, so the first step in getting a salary increase is to ask for one. If the answer is yes, then congratulations; you'll have just added to your Freedom Fund. Even if the answer is no, simply by asking for a raise you'll have opened up a discussion that can lead you to a raise in the future or, as the case may be, reveal that you may need to find work elsewhere to get to the salary level you seek. You lose nothing by asking so long as you do it in the right way.

Before you ask, prepare yourself to attain a successful outcome. Be ready to make the case for the value you bring to your team and/or your firm. In business, as in life, you rarely get what you deserve; instead, you get what you negotiate. Focus on ways in which what you do helps the company's bottom line because that's where the money for your raise is coming from. In your company or your department's annual budget, there's no "fund for people we like" though there's likely to be money available for "employees who increase revenue or productivity." I'm not saying it's unimportant to be nice or well-liked by your colleagues, but in your conversations about a pay increase, try to focus on how you either contribute to the company's growth or how you help it to cut costs.

You likely have more leverage than you think. Built into every new hire are significant orientation and training costs. And whenever an employee leaves a company, they take with them a piece of the company's institutional knowledge. Consequently, there is enormous intrinsic value in retaining someone who has already successfully solved specific problems the company has faced, in case—as often happens—similar problems arise again in the future. Experience pays, so why not let it help pay more for you? Most smart firms would rather make an effort to satisfy a good employee than spend the time and money to (hopefully) find and create another one.

OVERTIME HOURS OR SPECIAL ASSIGNMENT PROJECTS

Does your company offer overtime hours for your employment type? Are there special assignment projects where your company is willing to pay more for members of the project team? Ask around and you may find additional income streams you were unaware of. Overtime is typically paid at a higher rate than straight time, sometimes as much as double. Thus, it can be an excellent source of additional income to quickly cut down debt or enhance your Freedom Fund. Special assignment projects not only increase your earnings, they give you additional skills and experience that make you more marketable within or even outside of your company. If a project is a success and you've made a significant contribution to it, then you can more easily make the case for a nice raise based on your efforts. A rising tide lifts all boats.

COMPETE FOR A PROMOTION

Ever wonder why certain people get promotions while others are ignored or passed over? You'll likely find that the ones getting the promotions spend more time with the boss on the golf course, at happy hour, or at the company barbeque. My experience has been that not only are those folks golfing, drinking, and eating, they're keeping the boss informed about what they're accomplishing at work. Whether you realize it or not, every social engagement with your employer is a meeting in disguise. The folks who get promoted most quickly are those who stay in the boss's ear, feeding him or her ideas that make them look good to *their* boss. Take a cue from the word "promotion" itself: to get promoted you have to be a master at promoting yourself: your skills, your ideas, and your accomplishments. You have to be intentional about your career. It's too important to leave to chance. So, rather than wait for someone to tap you on the shoulder for the next higher-level position, tap your boss or HR person on the shoulder and let them know you're ready for that next level. If they disagree with your self-assessment, ask them what you need to do to get there. When you leave your career up to your boss, instead of you *and* your boss, you stand the chance of being passed over and not moving up at all. Build a relationship with your supervisors at work. Get advice from your company or an outside executive mentor or coach. Know the promotion requirements, qualifications, and timings. Develop a plan with your manager and HR department for your next promotion. Then make it happen. Remember that the additional 10, or 20, or 50 percent raise you will get is destined, through your investing, to become 100, 200, and 500 percent over time. Today's income stream at work is tomorrow's raging river of capital in your portfolio.

CHANGE JOBS WITHIN YOUR COMPANY

If getting a promotion isn't an option, then perhaps there are other opportunities within your company that your boss, HR department, or company mentor can connect you to. It's always easier when someone familiar and credible refers you to an opening rather than trying to approach it cold through an online application. As you may suspect, I recommend both approaches: the warm referral approach and the cold approach online. Do your homework to understand where your company is going strategically. Talk with your HR department to explore other areas within your company that could benefit from your company knowledge, your qualifications, and/ or your skills. Your company may be shifting directions and ramping up a team to set up a new division or product offering and may be in need of new talent. Applying for and securing one of those opportunities could result in a significant salary increase and/or bonus.

MAXIMIZE YOUR BONUS POOL

These days most companies offer a performance incentive for employees if the company meets their revenue targets and profit goals and the employee meets or exceeds their performance metrics. Often what you've received thus far is a percentage of your overall bonuses allocation. Is there a way for you to receive 100 percent or even more than 100 percent of your allocated bonus? In my business, for example, if our firm meets its performance metrics and an employee goes beyond what is asked of them, they can receive up to 125 percent of their allocated bonus. Find out if your company allows this and if so, sit down with your boss and develop a plan for you to earn 100 percent or more of your allocated bonus.

TAKE ADVANTAGE OF YOUR COMPANY'S 401(K)

One of the first tenets of becoming wealthy is to never leave money on the table. Some 21 percent of folks are not putting money away from their income for short or long-term goals like retirement.[26] Also, 48 percent of millennials with access to a 401(k) do not participate in their company's plan.[27] Maximizing your company's 401(k) matching plan allows you to increase your earnings exponentially because you're essentially earning free money. You can think of it as a tax-deferred wallet, a sort of "buy one, get one free," whereby you get paid as you invest in yourself. It's widely acknowledged that one of the biggest mistakes American workers make when preparing for retirement is failing to take full advantage of an employer match on company-sponsored plans. Rather than you having to fully finance your retirement, your company will match—in some cases

---

[26] Kathleen Elkins, "Here's the No. 1 Reason Why Americans Are Struggling to Save Money—and It's Not Debt," CNBC, March 15, 2019, https://www.cnbc.com/2019/03/15/the-no-1-reason-why-americans-struggle-to-save-money-isnt-debt.html.

[27] "Retirement Plan Access and Participation across Generations," The Pew Charitable Trusts, February 15, 2017, https://www.pewtrusts.org/en/research-and-analysis/issue-briefs/2017/02/retirement-plan-access-and-participation-across-generations.

dollar for dollar—whatever you tuck away in your 401(k). Not only will this burnish your retirement, it will free up more of your resources for investment and growth elsewhere. Add to the mix that your and your company's contributions are tax-free until you spend the money and it's a pretty sweet deal all around.

If you haven't already done so, reach out to your company's benefits department, find out if your company offers 401(k) matching, and assuming they do, make an appointment to fill out the 401(k) contribution paperwork right away. Not taking advantage of an offering like this is a huge financial mistake.

CHANGE COMPANIES

My last recommendation for actively increasing the income you earn at your current job is to consider changing companies every two to five years. Sometimes the only way to get your company to respect your talents is to find another company who will. One man's loss is another man's treasure. So, don't get down on yourself if your boss refuses to promote you, give you a raise, select you for a specialty project, or allow you to make more money working overtime. Take advantage of the myriad recruiting tools like LinkedIn, Dice.com, Monster, Indeed, or ZipRecruiter and find other companies that need people who possess your qualifications, skills, and experience. Some of the best places to connect with your company's competitors are industry events and conferences. You can and should use your attendance at events on behalf of your company to also build a network of folks who hire people like you at competitor companies. Try to help yourself as you do your current job; you'll find that other companies are always on the lookout for people whose learning curves are flatter thanks to their familiarity with the industry, business model, and technologies. Don't be afraid to do what you have to in order to do what you want!

SIDE HUSTLES

Whether you have a main hustle or not, the best way to actively increase your earnings is through a side hustle. Here's what I mean: In order to build assets and earn more, you have to be willing to do more. Since you need to pay down debts and increase how much you're saving and investing, it means you'll need to sacrifice personal and perhaps even family time to earn more money.

Thanks to technology there are now countless ways to earn extra money through a side hustle. Accessible part-time gigs are everywhere, including many you can do right from your home. For example, you can make, buy, or resell products to people all over the world on the internet. You can publish a book, make a movie, write a song, or create beats, and sell them online without the need of a publisher, record company, or film distributor. You can drive for Uber and/or Lyft and earn money in your spare time, in the evening, or on weekends. Have a license to do hair? You can work in a salon part time and make thousands of dollars working weekends and evenings alone. Own a piece of property or have an unused bedroom? You can rent them out on Airbnb or VRBO. What about working as a realtor? It's one of the oldest side hustles out there because you usually show houses in the evenings and on weekends when most home buyers and renters are available. Many licensed realtors sell houses on the side and make serious money. Are you good with social media? You can help small businesses manage their social media pages. Are you a certified fitness buff? You can get paid while you work out from your home, at a local gym, or even by working out with your clients in a public park. Have computer skills? Why not consult with businesses from the comfort of your home or in their office location on weekends. You can get a therapist's license and earn money counseling folks on Zoom from the comfort of your home or at a counseling center. No matter what your predilection or interest, there's a side hustle out there to help you up your net worth by increasing your investment capital. The opportunities to create additional streams of income are right in front of you. Think creatively, reapportion your time, and get your hustle on!

In addition to identifying your income streams and increasing the income you derive from each, there are a handful of other steps you must take in order to be sure your Earn Plan takes flight. They are:

- Determine which pathway to earning more works for you.
- Calculate the amount of income you'll receive from each source.
- Account for any dependencies associated with each new source (i.e., Do you need to get an updated car before you can drive for Uber or Lyft? Do you need to take five classes to pass a state exam before you can earn $2,000 a month as a mental health professional? And so on.).
- Develop a dependency mitigation strategy (i.e., How will you find time to take the additional classes? How will you obtain the money needed to pay for them?).
- Plot the amount and timing of the cash inflow from each income stream (i.e., when will each money source hit your account?).

As you finish each of these steps, you can comfortably integrate them into the Earn Plan section of your overall five-to-ten-year M$M Master Plan. The following is an example of how that might look.

Millionaire Money Moves
Master Plan

Goals	Age:35 2020		Age:36 2021		Age:37 2022	
Net Worth Plan						
Net Worth	$25,000.00			$37,500.00		$75,000.
Earn Plan						
Annual Increase			$843.75	$843.75	$869.06	$869
Bonus Compensation				$5,793.75		$5,798.8
Side Hustle Income			$8,320.00	$8,320.00	$8,320.00	$8,320.0
Income from Duplex Investment					$8,320.00	$8,320.
Total			$9,163.75	$14,957.50	$17,509.06	$23,307.88

Note how the amount and timing of each passive income source is integrated into the Earn Plan. As you begin to invest and earn additional income from passive sources in the form of rentals, dividends, interest, business profit distribution, pension, or social security income, be sure to include them in your Earn Plan.

Now let's tackle what to do with all that money you've redirected to yourself and your future.

SAVE

The best way to understand saving is to think of it as investment fuel that goes into your Setback Fund, your Reward Fund, your Freedom Fund (including retirement), and for parents or grandparents looking to give their kids a head start, your 529 College Savings Fund. Once your Freedom Fund reaches critical mass, it will provide you, through your investments, with the financial independence that goes along with what I refer to as "Income for Life." Saving is a commitment to consistently set aside part of your income so that you can use it to invest. Your net worth is the future you're constructing, and your savings are funding the bricks and mortar you're using to build it. Don't have enough for a brick every week? Then put aside enough for a quarter of a brick. What you'll find about saving is that once you start doing it, you'll begin to see other areas in your life from which you can draw further savings to add more bricks.

As you can see, the M$M Power Budget requires you to save a grand total of 30 percent of your take-home income: 3 percent for your Setback fund, 22 percent for Your Freedom Fund, and 5 percent for your Reward Fund. I know, that's a *lot* to save. But 10 percent ain't gonna do it if you want to get rich or retire, no matter what most experts may say. The math doesn't lie. At a savings rate of 10 percent of your annual salary per year, you'll accumulate:

- One hundred percent or one year of your annual salary (after ten years)
- Two hundred percent or two years of your annual salary (after twenty years)
- Three hundred percent or three years of your annual salary (after thirty years)
- Four hundred percent or four years of your annual salary (after forty years)

That means after forty years of working, you'll have only saved the equivalent of four years of your annual salary. Even if you're able to double that savings through compounding, you'll still wind up with only eight years of your annual income in your Freedom Fund. So, if you start at age twenty-five and retire at age sixty-five, you'll be broke by age seventy-three... only eight years after you retire. What will you do then?

Instead, if you were to save at a 30 percent annual savings rate and invest that savings into securities, real estate, entrepreneurship, and private equity, over the same thirty-to-forty-year period, you will have income that will support your dreams and outlive you. You may be wondering, as I first did, *How the #%@! am I going to save 30 percent of my income when I can't even save a nickel today?* I get it. I know it may feel impossible to save while dealing with all of the unplanned expenditures that come with supporting and raising a family and so forth. But I promise you, I haven't completely lost my marbles. The key is to take in more and pay out less. We just discussed ways to add new sources of income in order to augment your savings, and in a moment, we'll examine how to quickly knock down your debt through an accelerated debt payoff plan. So, bear with me...I only sound crazy.

As you know by now, my rule of thumb is the more you save, the more you can invest. The more you invest, the faster you'll get to Destination Millionaire and beyond. I understand that your budget may not currently look anything like my M$M Power Budget, but in time my Brothas and Sistas, and with consistent effort, you will get it there too. I know because I've done it myself. Create a plan, get started, stay focused, and get busy grinding; before you know it, you will be stacking cash like a Boss.

FREEDOM FUND SAVINGS
(SAVING FOR INVESTMENTS AND RETIREMENT)

Your Freedom Fund is the fund that is going to allow you to live life on your terms. This fund will be used to fund your investments (securities, real estate, entrepreneurship, alternative investments) and ultimately used to generate the income needed to fund your lifestyle in retirement when you choose to no longer work for your money and have built up enough money to allow your money to take over and do the work.

Let's start with your 401(k), which is the adult equivalent of a turbo-charged piggy bank and a central part of your Freedom Fund. Putting your pre-tax dollars into your 401(k) is one of the best, if not *the* best ways to make your money grow. It should be the first place for you to begin saving because you don't pay tax on that money until you withdraw it or retire. When you retire, you will almost certainly be in a lower tax bracket, and in the meantime, you can invest all that pre-tax money almost any way you wish, be it stocks, bonds, exchange-traded funds (ETFs), and so forth.

Whatever profit you make on those investments—including your principal—remains untaxed until you pull it out at retirement, presumably at a lower tax rate.

DETERMINING HOW MUCH MONEY YOU NEED IN YOUR FREEDOM FUND FOR RETIREMENT

Some experts believe you need twenty-five times your annual income by age sixty-five in order to have enough money to retire. I agree with them, especially if you use the 4 percent rule for making account withdrawals in retirement. That rule states that you can comfortably withdraw 4 percent of your savings in your first year of retirement and adjust that amount for inflation for every subsequent year without risking running out of money for at least twenty-five to thirty years. What's more, as a millionaire investor, your balances won't run out of money or be depleted at all, even if your investments earn a modest 6 percent return per year (4 percent living expenses plus 2 percent inflation is offset by the 6 percent profit your investments make).

There are three methods I recommend to determine how much your Freedom Fund will need: the Expense approach, the Annual Salary Replacement approach, and what I call the "Level-Up" approach.

THE EXPENSE APPROACH

To use the expense approach you need to create a separate budget to know how much money you need on a monthly and annual basis to live on. Start by choosing a retirement age for yourself and then see which items from your current budget you think you will eliminate by the time you retire. Can you pay your house off by then? Can you be debt-free by retirement age? Will college be paid off for all your children? Don't be too precise; err on the side of needing more than less. Since you will be retiring in the future rather than today, bear in mind that inflation will impact how much money you will need as well. (Given the current inflation rate of 2.24 percent per year, $1,000 in 2021 will be equivalent to $1,280 in 2031, a mere 28 percent more.)

Once you've created your budget, determine the annual salary you'll need by multiplying your annual budget by 1.25 percent if your retirement income will place you in a 25 percent tax bracket (1.30 percent if you'll be in a 30 percent tax bracket, 1.35 percent for a 35 percent tax bracket, and so on). If your annual expenses are, say, $60,000 after tax, and you're in a 25 percent tax bracket, you'd need $75,000 a year in retirement. Once you know the figure for your annual expenses, multiply it by twenty-five, and you'll arrive at the amount needed in your Freedom Fund: $1,875,000.

THE SALARY REPLACEMENT APPROACH

In this approach your assumption is that you want to earn your current working salary in retirement. Thus, you take your current annual salary before tax and multiply it by twenty-five to arrive at the amount of money you'll need in your Freedom Fund. If your current annual salary is $75,000, then you'll need $1,875.000 ($75,000 × 25). Keep in mind that your salary today will be going up. So, you may need to project your salary level at the time of your retirement and multiply that figure by twenty-five to arrive at the amount you will need then.

THE LEVEL-UP APPROACH

The Level-Up approach allows you to select how much money you *want* to earn in retirement. This gives you the option to set your retirement salary goal at a level higher than your current salary, so long as you're willing to strive for it. For example, say you're earning $75,000 a year currently; you might want to set your retirement salary goal to $100,000 a year. In that case, you would need twenty-five times $100,000, or $2.5 million, in your Freedom Fund to earn $100,000 a year in retirement before tax.

Whichever of these methods you choose, calculate the amount you'll need right away so you can plan and save accordingly. I recognize that at first glance the thought of having to save millions of dollars for retirement can be intimidating if not totally overwhelming. But look beneath the surface. You may have a pension, be paying into Social Security, have income from rental properties, or own a sizable stock portfolio that pays dividends. Each of these income sources can drastically lower the amount of cash needed in your Freedom Fund from savings alone. Document them carefully and you'll see that you have more and better resources than you think.

TRADITIONAL, ROTH, SEP INDIVIDUAL RETIREMENT ACCOUNTS

In addition to your employer's 401(k), there are three other account types you can use for retirement savings within your Freedom Fund: a traditional, individual retirement account (IRA), a Roth IRA, or a SEP IRA. While similar in many ways, there are some key differences in how each one works. Let's take a look.

At present, there's a contribution limit of $19,500 that may be put in your 401(k) plan each year. If you are fifty or older, you can make an additional $6,500 catch-up contribution as well. Once those limits are reached, that's when you should consider opening a traditional or Roth IRA in order to further contribute to your Freedom Fund and stash away additional money for retirement. In traditional IRAs, if after-tax dollars are contributed, they are tax deductible at the end of the year. IRA-deposited dollars can be invested in securities, and the gains they accumulate remain tax-free until you withdraw them from your account. The present "stash" limit in a traditional IRA is $6,000 per year if you're younger than age fifty and $7,000 per year if you're fifty or older, though that amount you can change annually.

A Roth IRA is where you may contribute after-tax dollars, and therefore, any withdrawals are tax-free (because you've already paid the taxes). Roth IRAs are best If you think your taxes will be higher in retirement than during your working years. Roth IRAs are not for everyone. As of this writing, if you make too much money (currently around $140,000 a year for singles and $208,000 a year for married couples), then you can't contribute to a Roth IRA at all. Almost all brokerage firms, whether physical or online, offer both traditional and Roth IRAs.

A Simplified Employee Pension (SEP) IRA is an individual retirement account opened by an employer, often someone who is self-employed. It allows an employee to make larger contributions than with a traditional or Roth IRA. It's also much less complex and allows employers to take a tax deduction for their contribution as with traditional IRAs.

As of 2021, the maximum contribution per year is the lower of 25 percent of your income or $58,000. Self-employed individuals especially may be able to contribute to both a traditional IRA and a SEP IRA. A good accountant (or a bit of research) can explain the rules governing each of these options in greater depth should you feel the need.

If your values align with you giving of your time and not of your money, then I suggest you allocate an additional 5 percent from the 10 percent of your give allocation and direct it to your Freedom Fund to accelerate your journey.

SETBACK ACCOUNT SAVINGS

Take a look again at the M$M Power Budget; it shows you how to apportion your savings so that you're prepared for any eventuality at the same time that you're building wealth. Your Setback account is designed to be a steady account, slowly building up until you have at least twelve months of your take-home income saved in anticipation of any serious, unexpected or uncontrolled setback like a job loss, health issue, or business failure. Most finance gurus will advise that you need six months' cash reserves. My experience has taught me that having a full year of cash reserves for setback situations is what's really needed to keep you from losing your financial gains. This account is indispensable because in your journey to Destination Millionaire, the unexpected will happen and you will need to have funds to get you through. Don't take this account for granted. I recommend saving 3 percent here because I'm assuming that everything is fine and dandy with your financial situation and with your current employer. A 3 percent rate doesn't anticipate a major financial downturn in the near future or that you won't have time to build up your reserve fund. Putting 3 percent of your income in your setback fund is like trickle charging the battery of your garage queen that you rarely drive. It slowly builds up your Setback fund for whenever you need it to give you a jolt of stability from unforeseen financial adversity. If an emergency rears its head before you have fully charged your Setback account, you can always rely on your Freedom Fund Savings account if you must.

REWARD FUND SAVINGS ACCOUNT

Your Reward account is where you'll put away 5 percent of your income to fund the discretionary purchases that serve as your rewards for achieving the financial goals in your M&M Master Plan. Think of this account as a bonus plan where your former impulse buys become trophy presentations instead. When you hit your milestones, you'll use this fund to purchase the material rewards—jewelry, Louis Vuitton bags, Harley Davidson motorcycles, or maybe those spinner wheels you've been wanting so badly—without losing your financial gains and deviating from your wealth-building Master Plan. Later on, we'll go over how to reap the benefits of deferred gratification and be happy, instead of being victimized by instant gratification and miserable.

THE 529 COLLEGE SAVINGS ACCOUNT

This process is how you set yourself up for retirement as well. Otherwise, where's the cash going to come from to help your kids with their college expenses or tuition? Few if any of us can save our way to retirement, however, we can invest our way there if we save enough to invest in the first place. For parents, the same goes for money for your kids to go to college. At minimum you need to open a 529 College Savings account now, and use this fund to build up savings for your children so they or you don't have to go into debt to pay for college. Meantime, your investments can do the work of supplementing whatever gaps you may face when the time comes to write those tuition checks (not to mention room and board). If creating a legacy is one of your reasons for wanting wealth, you'll need to keep the debt level of your kids as low as possible, especially when they're first starting out. I created college savings accounts for my kids when they were born and started contributing to them immediately. It allowed me to cover 100 percent of their college expenses without changing my lifestyle, which was my goal. The same year my twins graduated from college, I was able to purchase a 2019 Ferrari F488 without skipping a beat.

Saving takes some investigative work but by living smaller in order to save bigger, you free yourself up not only to invest more, but to do more in your life. Music legend Wynton Marsalis tells a story about how his father taught him to remember that if he could be "okay" in life with only a warm coat, food to eat, and his trumpet, then he could do whatever he wanted because nothing could ever stop him from being okay. It's a profound idea when you think about it. The less you need, the more you can do, and the easier it becomes to build bridges to your desired financial future.

BEST WAYS TO GET YOUR SAVINGS ON

Even now that I've successfully built my wealth, I'm always looking for new pockets of savings in my own life. I know that paying for what I don't really need is, to put it poetically, a form of oppression. I'd much prefer to invest in my own freedom or help someone else on the path to building wealth, wouldn't you?

You can make savings automatic by turning them into a ritual every time you get paid. Believe me, you won't miss the money you save if you do it regularly, though the swelling value of your Freedom Fund may cause you to experience a joy similar to when you were a kid, and that hollow sound in your piggy bank gradually became the dull "thud" that meant fullness and success.

Here are some best practices to get your savings on:

1. Pay yourself like you're the first bill on the pile. This way you can't run out of money paying everyone else in line.
2. Automate your savings by having them come directly out of your bank account with each of your paychecks. You'll quickly forget that money is being deducted automatically and over time, you probably won't even miss it.
3. Whenever you get a raise or a bonus, incorporate it immediately into your M$M Power Budget. Put 50 percent of your pay increase into your Freedom Fund by upping your automatic savings deduction. Assign 25 percent to your Pay (nondiscretionary spending) strategy to tackle bills and pay them off more aggressively. Keep the other 25 percent for whatever you desire, place it in your Reward Fund, or use it as extra pocket money. When your pay increases, your savings, investing, debt pay down, and discretionary spending should increase along with it.
4. We often get small, incremental raises and ignore them, which leads to increases in our discretionary spending and little else. Years later, our overall pay may have risen by 50 percent, but we have nothing of consequence to show for it because it didn't seem like much money at the time. So, whether they arrive in large chunks or in dribs and drabs, pay raises need to be managed with intention so their power and effectiveness can be harnessed and multiplied, over time.

5. Preach what you practice, and practice what you preach. Stop telling yourself that you "can't afford to save." If you can afford to spend, you can afford to save. Begin at the cashier's counter. Instead of buying that next discretionary item (shoes, handbag, jewelry, wheels, and so on), write yourself a check or use Venmo or PayPal to send the equivalent amount of that purchase to your Freedom Fund and invest it right away.

The following graph is an example of how to integrate your savings plan into your overall five-to-ten-year M$M Master Plan. Once you save enough to begin investing, your wealth will take a different form. You'll be transferring money from one asset type (cash) to another (real estate, a business, securities, or alternative investments), where that new type of asset has the ability to appreciate and generate significant income much faster than cash in the bank or a money market account can.

Millionaire Money Moves
Master Plan

Goals		Age:35 2020		Age:36 2021		Age:37 2022	
Earn Plan							
Annual Increase				$843.75	$843.75	$869.06	$869.0
Bonus Compensation					$5,793.75		$5,798
Side Hustle Income				$8,320.00	$8,320.00	$8,320.00	$8,320.0
Income from Duplex Investment						$8,320.00	$8,320.0
Total				$9,163.75	$14,957.50	$17,509.06	$23,307.
Save Plan (30%)							
Setback Savings Account (3%)							
Setback Savings Account		$843.75	$1,687.50	$2,806.16	$3,823.73	$4,744.02	$5,761.7
Freedom Fund (22%)							
401(k) Account		$4,750.00	$9,500.00	$15,093.75	$19,843.75	$24,619.06	$29,369.
IRA Account							
Investment Account		$926.00	$1,852.00	$11,098.00	$44,392.00	$21,270.00	$22,196
Reward Fund (5%)							
Reward Savings Account		$1,406.25	$2,812.50	$4,493.66	$6,073.73	$7,556.52	$9,136.7
College 529 Savings Plan							
State 529 Savings Account							

PAY

Most households' finances are tangled up, standing still, or going backward because they don't have "extra" money to save and invest. My goal is to help you reverse that trend and reduce your nondiscretionary spending to 45 percent of your income. You have to find a way to get moving in the right direction so you can invest in the type of assets that will generate the income needed to cover and exceed all of your household expenses. That's the only way you'll get to Destination Millionaire. You have limited control over nondiscretionary expenditures like housing, food, transportation, utilities, insurance, healthcare, furniture, and taxes because they are standard needs that everyone requires. But there's a lot you can do to minimize them or pay them off.

Step one—and it's a huge one—is to stop thinking about money to save being "extra." Your savings are not a surplus; they must be part and parcel of how you allocate the money you earn, not the money you hope to earn. Too many times, I've heard the lament, "How can I possibly save when I have to pay for X, Y, and Z expenses? You can't draw blood from a stone." The answer is that you can always save when you think of saving as a mandate instead of an afterthought. That's why paying yourself (a.k.a. your savings accounts) has to become the first stop for your paycheck or another form of monthly income stream. Once you've set aside your preplanned percentage of savings for the month, then you can address the rest of the nondiscretionary items you pay for. There are numerous areas of nondiscretionary spending for which you can find ways to pay less. Here are some of the "low-hanging fruit" to look at first.

HOUSING

Housing tends to be a household's largest expenditure at approximately 30–50 percent of total income or more. In my opinion, folks too often purchase or rent more house than they can afford because they misunderstand the meaning of the word "afford." When you can afford something, it means you can meet the expense of it, not that you can meet its expense and all the other expenses you have. It makes no sense to get a more expensive place to live simply because you can make the payments. If you're not saving money consistently, then I'm sorry to say you're not affording anything. You may qualify and meet the bank's requirements, but if the house's expenses are too great, then you can't afford to save and invest and consequently build wealth.

This disconnect is a huge problem and it keeps far too many households standing financially still. I understand the ego "jolt" of showing off to our friends that we've made it; in all honesty, it took me a while to learn not to be seduced by this and to be willing to buy a house priced at less than what I could qualify for so that I could invest in additional assets, use them to generate income, and eventually become a millionaire. It's a humbling feeling to watch your friends buy McMansions or rent fly cribs while you're living in a modest home. Over time though, your ego and self-esteem will recalibrate and you'll no longer be bothered by the attention your friends get for looking richer than you. Sometimes all it takes is seeing a friend go through financial hardship or a divorce, and being forced to sell their big houses or move out of their dope cribs. Living frugally is always the right choice until you no longer need to—not because you can "afford" to live large, but because your money is doing all the work for you.

While we're on the subject of housing, let's talk for a moment about mortgages. Our community got creamed by the mortgage crisis of 2008, understandably in many ways, in view of how historically unavailable mortgages have been for African Americans. In the same way loan sharks prey in neighborhoods on folks who can't get a credit card, mortgage brokers preyed on people who couldn't get a normal, fixed-term loan from a bank. But the truth is that subprime loans were a problem not because there were too many of them, but because they were too large and too variable for the people who took them on. Countless good people in our community took out loans for houses and condos far above their means, and completely outside of a thoughtfully planned road map to Destination Millionaire. Many ended up losing their homes, investments, and wealth along with it.

Whether you already have a mortgage or are looking for one now or in the near future, it is imperative that you shop around. Seemingly small variations in rate (0.25 percent or 0.5 percent) can have a huge impact over time. Even if you only save, say, $200 a month on your mortgage payment, over the life of a thirty-year mortgage that comes to $72,000 ($200 a month × 12 months a year × 30 years)! Not to mention the impact of compounding. That's not what I would call chump change.

As a rule of thumb, it makes sense to refinance your home (i.e., obtain a new mortgage at a better rate) whenever interest rates go down by 0.5

percent or more. Because there are fees associated with refinancing, not to mention a healthy amount of paperwork and time spent, it may not make sense for you until rates go down further. If and when you do refinance, take those monthly savings and put them into your Freedom Fund. Your entire wealth-building system should now be geared toward finding ways to increase the amount you save so you can increase the amount you can invest. Bigger savings, not bigger houses. I'm not saying you can't or shouldn't consider your house an investment, but too often in our community we *only* invest in our homes, missing out on greater financial returns elsewhere and risking our futures by having all our eggs in one basket.

If you're renting a house, condo, or apartment, you can always find places suitable for you and your loved ones for less than you are paying. Yes, you may have to move further away, however, those savings can set you on the path to investing in a house instead of investing in another millionaire's investment property.

HOME MAINTENANCE

Many people make the mistake of buying the home they think they can afford without considering the cost of its upkeep. Like it or not, that grass on your lawn is going to grow, those shingles on your roof will eventually need replacement, and those gutters along the side of your house are going to sag until they one day drop off. Why would a house behave any differently than a car, a boat, or a boyfriend (sorry, fellas, I'm afraid we need upkeep too)? Since your goal is to save more on nondiscretionary spending in order to invest, you absolutely must calculate home maintenance into your overall purchasing decision and see how much of it you can do yourself. Are you really going to repaint those doors (I hope so, but if not, factor in the cost of a handyman)? Are you going to mow the lawn every week or so (you can save a lot of money *and* get a free workout if you do)? A commitment to paying less to others and doing as much of your home maintenance yourself, when possible, increases your available investment funds while protecting the sizable investment in your home from inevitable wear and tear.

FURNITURE

Furniture costs can be enormous, and whether you rent an apartment or own a home, you will need a good deal of furniture to live in your home comfortably. I'm surprised at how often furniture is overlooked as a nondiscretionary expense; try living without it, and you're bound to be as surprised as I am. I recommend you buy your furniture slowly, with cash instead of credit, and that you be extremely careful not to overspend. There are several online sources where you can find quality furniture for far less than retail, such as Facebook Marketplace. I paid a pretty penny to Pottery Barn for my children's furniture set when I first set up their rooms. Now that they're in their twenties and all over six feet tall, those full and twin-sized beds don't fit them anymore. It was only when I sold their bedroom sets on Facebook Marketplace that I realized how much of a rip-off buying new furniture really is, and how much you can save by purchasing secondhand. The same goes for getting rid of your old furniture. It's often cheaper to sell it at a huge discount than to pay someone to move, donate, or dump it.

If you must buy furniture on credit, pay it off quickly and long before you need to upgrade it. You have wealth-building goals to achieve and you want to be sure you're sitting pretty financially instead of in that pricey lounge chair you can probably do without for now.

HEALTHCARE

Healthcare in the US is incredibly expensive and becoming more so every year. As you age and head toward retirement, your healthcare costs are only going to increase. Finding savings on healthcare is, as of this writing, a crapshoot at best. But there is something you can do to save money on your healthcare spending and, dare I say, it will also make a huge impact on your happiness. According to a recent study, people who begin to exercise before the end of middle age typically save between $824 and $1,874 on annual healthcare costs once they retire. And get this: the earlier in life they start their workouts, the more those savings can be.[28]

So, if the idea of working out, walking regularly, jogging, and so forth doesn't spur you into action, try thinking of it as money in your pocket instead. And not any ol' money either. What's fun about thinking like a millionaire is that you learn to see that money in your pocket as a seedling, not a tree. That nearly two grand a year or more that the average exerciser saves is different for a future millionaire like you; it goes into your Freedom Fund, so by the time *you* retire, it will have grown exponentially.

I think we're all familiar with all the other amazing, lasting benefits of exercise (longer, higher-quality life, increased self-esteem, better muscle tone, lower stress, etc.). Now you can add this one: cash in your pocket.

---

[28] Diarmuid Coughlan, et al., "Leisure Time Physical Activity throughout Adulthood Is Associated with Lower Medicare Costs: Evidence from the Linked NIH-AARP Diet and Health Study Cohort," *BMJ Open Sport & Exercise Medicine*, 2021, https://bmjopensem.bmj.com/content/7/1/e001038.

TRANSPORTATION

The cost of transportation, at 15.9 percent, is the second highest household expense in the American household. This includes the cost of buying or leasing a car, vehicle maintenance, and fuel.[29] While inflation varies and is tough to gauge, over time the cost of new cars has continued to rise. As I said when we talked about the mechanics of wealth, I strongly advise wealth builders to buy pre-owned vehicles. New cars drop in value by as much as 20–30 percent after the first year. What's more, you can save money on maintenance and repairs by finding certified mechanics trained to service your car's specific make and model. Why pay a premium price for service at a dealership, especially when oftentimes those same certified service specialists previously worked for a dealer's service team and know everything there is to know about your car? They can do the same work and use the same parts on your car but at a 30 percent lower cost than a dealer.

INSURANCE

Insurance is an area of spending that's easy to overlook, yet you do so at your own peril. Sh*t happens, and without proper insurance, your savings, your business, your home, and your very life are at risk. Children are often told, "it's all fun and games until somebody breaks a leg." Sadly, some people have that attitude toward insurance. They try to "wish" that everything will be okay, rather than plan for things to go wrong and be properly covered for

---

[29] "Average New-Vehicle Prices Up 2% Year-Over-Year in July 2020, According to Kelley Blue Book," PR Newswire, August 3, 2020, https://www.prnewswire.com/news-releases/average -new-vehicle-prices-up-2-year-over-year-in-july-2020-according-to-kelley-blue-book-3011 04310.html.

losses. Not you, Millionaire; you're working too hard to put your bright future foolishly at risk.

I'm not an insurance expert and thus I urge you to consult with one as you make your insurance choices. However, I can say that to be adequately covered, you'll need automobile, personal property, homeowners (or renters', depending on your housing situation) insurance, life insurance, health insurance, and possibly disability insurance. I know that sounds like a lot, and I won't lie and say it isn't or that it'll be cheap, so I think it's important we think about insurance in a fresh way. Insurance is not a question of if, it's a question of when. Something is going to happen to your car, your home, your business, or you, or your family members personally. It's inevitable. The issue is how well prepared you will be when it does. Success in life is about the ability to bounce back, but you can't bounce back from a bottomless pit. Insurance is necessary to provide you the foundation to make yourself whole again when trouble strikes, and ensure you can keep everything you've built rather than watch it be destroyed in the worst moments of your life.

Insurance comes in many forms and at many prices. There's a line of thinking that certain benefits are derived from sticking with your insurance company for the long haul, but the way I see it, insurers are like landlords who demand an increase every year. While their levels of service do vary, their products are about as different from each other as brands of gasoline. I think the best way to save money with insurers is to keep them competing for your business by having them requote your coverage every two years at the same time that you reach out to competitor companies as well. If you get a better quote from a competitor, you can share it with your current agent to see if they're willing to match or beat it. If they decline, simply change insurance providers.

Life insurance is a different case. It's not required by law, though I believe it should be considered a mandatory item for everyone, especially aspiring millionaires and those looking to create generational wealth. Life insurance is not for you as a beneficiary; it's for your family and dependents. Remember, the question is if, not when. Your eventual death, which is guaranteed to occur, can easily bankrupt your family or leave them with little to nothing, including the possibility of being thrown out of the house they live in. A payout from your life insurance (which can include the significant costs of your burial) will support and sustain them instead. Isn't that an investment worth making?

Life insurance comes in many forms, among them term insurance and whole life insurance. This is where a solid insurance agent can help guide you toward what suits your needs best. Be careful, though; the higher your premium, the more money an insurance company makes, so whatever your agent recommends, be sure to run it by your Money Team and get a second opinion.

A solid rule of thumb to determine how much coverage you need is to add up the expenses that you'll want covered in your absence: your income, your mortgage, your other insurance payments, your kids' college expenses, and any other essentials. Then subtract whatever you already have that your family could use (assets such as savings, stocks, etc.). Don't include your retirement savings because that's for your spouse later on.

Total that up and you'll have the amount of coverage you'll need. Chances are you'll be looking at a pretty high number, but if you shop around for quotes, which are free, you can find something that fits your budget *and* your contingency planning.

Term life insurance is cheaper than whole life insurance, but whole life insurance is permanent (as long as you continue to pay your premiums) and becomes an asset you can borrow against and eventually cash in. The decision is up to you; what I want to stress is that you need some life insurance *now*. If you can't afford full coverage, buy whatever you can afford and continue to augment it as your net worth grows. Don't get caught with nothing! And remember that over time your insurance needs are likely to change. You should therefore regularly review your coverage, at a minimum once a year.

The same is true of homeowners, renters, automobile, and health insurance. As daunting as they may seem when taken together, so long as the costs of insurance are broken out monthly into your M$M Power Budget, they will lose their power to overwhelm you. When something does go wrong, as I promise you it will, the comfort of your insurance payment will more than make up for the struggle to fit the cost of insurance premiums into your monthly budget. What's more, it will keep you from falling backward in your journey to Destination Millionaire.

Disability insurance is a true nice-to-have. It comes in different forms—short term and long term—and its function is to guarantee a continuation of some level of your income should you become incapacitated. You can buy both short- and long-term disability insurance, one to take you through any short-term medical problems and the other to replace part of your income should your disability extend. You may be entitled to some level of disability insurance from your employer, especially if you work for a large company. Ultimately, you'll have to decide whether you need this level of protection, but if you're a sole or primary breadwinner in your family, disability insurance can end up being a lifesaver.

When you become rich, and have a net worth of $11.7 million or more, including all assets and your insurance policy (assuming it's in your name and not the estate's), your heirs will be required to pay an estate tax commonly referred to as an inheritance tax (or "death tax," as detractors prefer to call it) from your estate in order to receive your wealth. For a married couple, that currently comes to a combined exemption of $24.12 million in net worth. Most of the estate's value is taxed at a 40 percent rate. This is where life insurance can be an extremely valuable asset. Rather than having to sell your assets at a potentially inopportune time (presently, the requirement is to pay the taxes due within six months of your death), your life insurance payout can be used to pay some or hopefully all of your estate taxes if you've planned correctly.

As with any insurance, make sure you choose a reputable insurance provider. Knowing the company's Comdex rating is a way to assess how well an insurance company pays out to beneficiaries. You should also reach out to your Money Team for a referral on a qualified insurance agent who can assist you in making critical decisions on insurance.

FOOD

Some folks consider food consumption a discretionary expense, as though eating were optional. Food is required for survival, which is why I take the opposite view, though let's face it, you have a lot of latitude as to how much money you need to spend on food. The average American spends 7.3 percent of their income on groceries and 5.6 percent of their income on restaurants and other meals on the road.[30] That's nearly 13 percent of your budget, on average. Because food prices are subject to so many variables

---

[30] Samuel Stebbins and Charles Stockdale, "These 20 Common Grocery Store Items Are Driving Up the Cost of Your Bill the Most." *USA Today,* April 29, 2019, https://www.usatoday.com /story/money/personalfinance/2019/02/28/average-grocery-store-bill-cost-is-driven-up-most -by-these-items/39094659/.

(drought, diseases, increased transportation, and refrigeration costs, etc.) it's nearly impossible to lower your grocery bills. The real opportunity to reduce your food cost is by lowering your cost of eating out. The average American household spends about $3,000 a year dining out, according to the Bureau of Labor Statistics.[31] (Remember that one person spending only on him/herself counts as a household too).[32] Restaurants mark their costs up as much as 300 percent in order to make a profit. In many cases, you could make a $15–meal in a restaurant for $5 at home. This may seem trivial, but that extra money could give a nice jolt (around $500 a year) to your savings for long-term or short-term goals, even if you only skipped one restaurant meal a week.

UTILITIES (GAS, ELECTRIC, WATER, ETC.)

Depending on where you live, you can save $1,000 or more a year simply by installing controls on your thermostat. Saving $1,000 a year over twenty years compounded with 6 percent interest would add $36,784 to your Freedom Fund. That may not sound like a lot, but if you're a single mother having a difficult time identifying savings, this is a solid place to look.

The quickest and most reliable way to save on your gas and electric bills is to install a programmable thermostat, preferably one you can control from your smartphone. Nest and Honeywell are two that I've used. I travel a lot and often forget to adjust my thermostat while I'm gone. These smart products allow me to adjust the temperature in my houses remotely and

---

[31] "Consumer Expenditures in 2015," US Bureau of Labor Statistics, April 2017, https://www .bls.gov/opub/reports/consumer-expenditures/2015/pdf/home.pdf.

[32] Amy Bergen, "The True Cost of Eating Out (And How To Save)," Money Under 30, July 22, 2021, https://www.moneyunder30.com/the-true-cost-of-eating-in-restaurants-and-how-to-save.

thereby save money from wherever I am. An hour or so before my return, I adjust the temperature again so that I'm comfortable when I arrive at home.

Another excellent way to realize savings on utilities is by installing a tankless water heater. The US Department of Energy estimates gas-fired tankless heaters save an average of $108 in energy costs per year over their traditional tank counterparts, while electric tankless heaters save $44 per year.[33] Installation costs are expensive compared to traditional water heaters but the savings in gas and water bills over time will easily pay for it and more.

CABLE, INTERNET, AND PHONE EXPENSES

In certain states, cable providers offer an app for Smart TVs that allows you to connect to TV via the internet and have access to basic cable at no additional charge. Cutting premium channels can also save you as much as $15–20 a month per channel. Promotional rates from cable, internet, and cell phone service providers only last for a certain term (usually six to twelve months), but they offer significant discounts. In most cases, at the end of the promotional term, you can call your provider and renegotiate whatever rate you default to or even switch providers and get *their* promotional rate. Or you can simply "cut the cord" and make do with the abundance of entertainment options available elsewhere.

Here are some additional tips to help you save your money for investment:

---

[33] Alan O'Neill, "Are Tankless Water Heaters Worth the Investment?" Abacus Plumbing, December 12, 2016, https://www.abacusplumbing.net/2016/12/tankless-water-heaters -worth-investment/.

1. Pare down the number of cable boxes you use.
2. Pay attention to hidden fees.
3. Nix the DVR.
4. Downsize and consider bundling your cable, internet, and phone plans.

Negotiate, negotiate, negotiate...remember, your providers are all offering you the same channels and broadband speeds and they are engaged in cutthroat competition with their competitors. Take advantage of their desperate hunger to keep you as a customer.

TAXES

In most states the amount of property taxes you pay is a factor of the assessed value of the property. Sometimes the government over-assesses the value of your property. This can cost you thousands of dollars over time, but you can challenge the government's assessed value of your property. To do this you will need to pay for an appraiser to appraise your property. If the appraisal value is less than the city's assessed value, then you can present your case to the tax assessor's office to have your property taxes lowered. You can also contact what's called a certiorari attorney, who can handle your tax protest on contingency (meaning they only get paid if you win your case). Either way, there are potentially large savings from lower tax payments awaiting your attention.

There are also several options available to lower what you pay in income taxes. You can deduct interest you pay on your mortgage interest, home equity loan, property taxes, mortgage insurance, or the points you paid to obtain your mortgage in the first place. It's not a dollar-for-dollar deduction (meaning you don't pay "X" dollars less in taxes for "X" deductible expenses), but the savings are still significant. You can also save by receiving energy credits for making your home more energy efficient.

Another reliable way to lower your income taxes is by starting your own business. When you own and operate your business you can write off (e.g., deduct from your taxes) all of the expenses associated with running your business, including a small portion of your mortgage or rent if your business is located in your home. Be it the leased car you use to get to work or to work appointments, the equipment you buy for your business, or any business-related travel or meals—all of that is tax deductible. The US tax code is strongly set up to favor businesses in a way it is not set up to assist salaried employees, so take advantage.

The tax code is weighted heavily in favor of investors like you. Money you earn from investments (including a sale of your home) is considered capital gains and is taxed at a lower rate than normal income. It might surprise you that Uncle Cedric isn't the only one out there encouraging you to invest and pay less on your taxes; the government is too—through the tax code. The key differentiator is whether an investment gain is classified as short or long-term. Short-term capital gains are investments such as real estate, securities, alternative investments, and entrepreneurship that are held for less than a year. They are taxed at an ordinary income tax level, which can be as high as 35 percent depending on your tax bracket. But investment gains held for more than one year and a day are considered long-term gains and are taxed at a lower rate, usually between 15–20 percent. Thus, patience in investing is not only a virtue; it can be a prime opportunity to save money by paying significantly less in taxes.

Finally, you can lower your taxes by changing the state in which you reside. Certain states like Nevada, Texas, Delaware, and Florida have no state income taxes. That's right; zero state income taxes. When I moved from California to Florida (via Maryland), I saved enough money on state income taxes (13 percent in the Golden State versus 0 percent in the Sunshine State) to pay off my waterfront house. Given how working remotely has taken hold, moving may be a worthwhile savings option for you to seriously consider.

DEBT

The "Pay" section of your M$M Plan must include a way to reduce and eliminate debt. But there is good debt and bad debt, and they're as different from each other as filet mignon and Spam. One of the principal goals in saving and investing is to eliminate all bad debt. Bad debt takes many forms: high-interest credit card debt, car payments, personal loans, and debts from unpaid tax bills.

On the other hand, good debt enables income and wealth development. For example, if I have debt associated with an income-producing apartment building, that's good debt because somebody else is paying for it, right? As of this writing, I'm about to construct a salon studio building for which I'm going to take out a loan of over $2.5 million. Don't let that big number fool you—that's $2.5 million of good debt because it's covered—meaning the payments or servicing of the debt are covered—by income from a sustainable rental business. You don't need to be a building owner to create and benefit from good debt though. Suppose the mortgage on your own home or condo is paid for in full or meaningfully reduced by an income-generating tenant unit or Airbnb? That's the kind of debt that allows you to have more of what you want without forcing you into a world of bad debt, bad credit, and bad living through crippling interest payments.

Nonetheless, while good debt can cover your own personal obligations, I want you to think of it in an even more robust way. Good debt, structured wisely, can be the engine that fuels your growth as an investor. Any assets you buy through debt which you would not otherwise be able to purchase in cash can still earn big rewards if or when they appreciate. And those profits are yours to keep. But you must be extremely meticulous about how you take on debt and how much of it you can handle. Income sources such as tenant incomes are subject to the same market realities as every other asset. Rents go up and down in cycles. Tenants may stop paying rent and assert whatever rights they believe they have to stay in your unit(s). In other words, sh*t happens in the real world. Therefore, when taking on the debt necessary to finance the purchase of a rental unit, for example, you need to be sure you've thought through ways to mitigate periods of crisis. There's nothing wrong with having a lot of good debt; in fact, it's true of every successful investor you've ever known or read about. But it needs to be well-thought-out and always backed by quickly available cash reserves.

THE BEST AND QUICKEST WAYS TO ELIMINATE BAD DEBT AND REPAIR CREDIT

Bad debt—and the paralyzing interest that goes along with it—are the sworn enemies of savings. When it comes to debt reduction, there are essentially two ways to go (because I don't believe in juggling debt through balance transfers or loan consolidations; if it's bad debt, it's got to go, go, go!). There's what's commonly known as the "Avalanche" method whereby you put more money toward paying your *highest interest rate* debts first, regardless of balance. The second method is called the "Snowball" method, in which you make all your minimum payments and then try to pay off your *lowest balances* first.

Here's how they look in practice. Each month, no matter which method you choose to employ, you must first make the minimum payment on each of your debts (to avoid late fees or finance fees). If you choose to use the Avalanche method, you would then put extra money from your main or side hustle toward paying off the debt with the highest interest rate until it's eliminated. You then do the same for the next-highest interest rate debt until it too is eliminated. You continue this process until all of your bad debt is paid off. The upside of this method is that you end up paying off your debt faster and spending less on interest. The downside is that it can take a long time to pay off your highest-interest debt, especially if the balance is also high. Debt fatigue may set in, not only destroying your morale, but in the worst instances leading to even greater debt.

Here's an example of how the Avalanche method works:

Student Loan: $5,000 at 6.00 percent (APR) interest
Auto Loan: $18,000 at 3.80 percent (APR) interest
Visa Credit Card debt: $11,000 at 24.70 percent (APR) interest

Using the Avalanche method, you'd pay as much as you could toward the Visa Credit Card first, as it has the highest interest rate. Then once that debt was eliminated (also known as "retired"), the Student Loan at 6.00 percent interest would be next in line. Use the money you were using to pay the Visa Credit Card debt off plus the minimal payment due on the Student Loan. After that debt was retired, you'd attempt to fully pay off the Auto Loan using the money that you used to make payments on all three loans.

I prefer to use the Snowball method because of how it can generate quick "wins" which supply the energy, drive, and inspiration to keep charging forward. Plus, if you want to renegotiate the terms of any of your debts, fewer debts will mean less renegotiation. The downside of this method is that in the long run, you'll end up paying more in interest and taking slightly longer to pay down your entire debt. So, you must pick your poison wisely.

Going back to the previous example:

Student Loan: $5,000 at 6.00 percent (APR) interest
Auto Loan: $18,000 at 3.80 percent (APR) interest
Visa Credit Card debt: $11,000 at 24.70 percent (APR) interest

If you elected to use the Snowball approach, you would pay off the Student Loan *first*, since it has the *lowest balance*. Once the Student Loan is paid off, you'd use that same money plus the minimum payment due on the Visa Card, until the Visa Card was paid off, and finally, you'd pay off the Auto Loan using the money you used to pay off the Student Loan and the Visa card plus the minimum monthly payment due on the Auto Loan. Another advantage of this method is that by reducing the number of accounts on your credit report with outstanding balances, it may help improve your credit score.

No matter which method you choose (and you may decide to try them both over time), paying down bad debt as aggressively as possible is the surest way to jump-start savings, get your finances headed back in the right direction, and increase your personal net worth.

STRATEGIES TO IMPROVE YOUR CREDIT SCORE

At some point in your wealth-building journey, you're going to need to use other people's money. Whether it's a loan from a friend or family member, a mortgage from a bank, or simply a temporary float from a credit card, your way to the top will require you to obtain some sort of credit. That means your credit worthiness is of paramount importance. Having a good credit rating paves the way to lower interest rates and fees, which in turn allow you to save and invest more.

Conversely, bad credit acts as a roadblock. Even if you're able to obtain financing with bad credit, you're assured of paying far more than you would have, if you only had a solid credit rating. Thankfully, there are a number of tried-and-true ways to improve your credit beginning with my favorite one of all: live within your means and pay all your bills on time. Period. Now, I know that's easy for me to say, so I want you to know that I say it with a large dose of humility. There was a time earlier in my life, right after college to be specific, when my bad money behaviors destroyed my credit. I didn't pay my credit card bills on time; I didn't pay my taxes on time; all because I wanted to use all my money to invest and build wealth. But as noble as that may sound, especially in a book like this, it was wrong-headed and it ultimately backfired. Cutting corners just ended up getting me cut.

Fortunately, I resolved my credit issue some time ago. My credit is now first-rate. I pay all my bills and taxes on time, not because I'm a paragon of virtue, but because I've come to understand how important good credit is to wealth building. I recognize that some folks struggle to pay their bills on time, and while I'm sympathetic, I'm not willing to leave things at that. No matter your circumstances, you have to fight with all you've got to keep your credit in shape. Otherwise, you end up trapped in a vicious cycle of increasingly damaged credit and increasingly higher fees and interest rates. And if you're Black or a person of color, that cycle becomes even more vicious thanks to the existing racial biases among credit agencies, which are known to negatively impact Blacks and women, such as the disproportionate number of high-interest predatory loans given to Black folk during the 2006–2008 housing bubble.

There have been countless other examples of people of color, with the same credit rating as their White counterparts, being steered toward higher interest and loan fees. To me, that doesn't make outstanding credit pointless; it makes it absolutely imperative. If you find yourself in a situation like that, you want to be sure you haven't brought a knife to a gunfight. Your armament, as it were, is an excellent credit score. You have to empower yourself, and the only way to do so is to pay all your debts on time and keep your credit score high.

Here are some tips to help you maintain or repair your credit score:

1. **Review your credit report regularly**—It's imperative to review your credit report regularly and quickly resolve any credit discrepancies in order to keep your credit score high. I do it religiously and you should too. My system works like this: once a year in January, I request a copy of my credit report and review it to make sure that I haven't had any identity theft issues. If I do (and sadly, it's become increasingly common), I resolve them as fast as possible. The same goes for any reported late payments or judgments that may have crept their way into my credit score. Mistakes happen and bills accidentally go unpaid. If you're not deliberate and systematic about erasing these stains from your credit report, they can end up hurting you for years. There is something else about this technique that I love. It's the way it says—to yourself and to others—that you take your obligations seriously and are trustworthy and reliable. You can pull your credit report for free once a year from the three main national

credit bureaus: Equifax, Experian, and Trans Union. Items that positively impact your credit score include a history of on-time bill payments, well-established lines of credit or credit card accounts, consistently low balances, and not too many requests for additional credit. On the flip side, outstanding bills, high balances, judgments, and collections will send your credit score plummeting.

2. **Download the Credit Karma app on your phone**—It gives you a free, up-to-the-minute estimate of your credit score. It also gives you insight into things that you can do to increase your credit score. The scores and credit report information on Credit Karma come from TransUnion and Equifax, two of the three major credit bureaus. Although it may not represent the average of all three credit agencies, it gives me an idea of where I stand. If my score is lower than I expect it to be, then I request a full credit report to make sure that I correct any discrepancies as quickly as I can.

3. **Get your bill-paying system under control**—If ever there were a place where the past is prologue, it's in your credit history; at least, that's the way lenders see it. To them, a good bill payer in the past is a solid credit risk today. Payment history is the leading factor in determining your FICO score. There are other factors as well, such as credit balances, usage, the age of your credit accounts, the mix of your credit sources, and the number of new credit inquiries made. But get a handle on paying your bills and you'll be well on your way to a credit score of 700 and above. Here's how: Avoid late payments like the plague. Set due date alerts in your calendar or better yet, make your payments

automatic from your bank account. One way or another, have a system in place to ensure your bills are paid on time every month. If you have a lot of bills to keep track of, consider consolidating the debt into a single credit card so you only have to make one payment. Not only can this help simplify your monthly payments, but it will also earn you additional reward points on your credit cards. Just be sure not to miss that one payment.

4. **Keep your balances low**—A good rule of thumb is to use no more than 30 percent of your credit line each month. Lenders refer to that as "credit utilization" and the lower yours is, the higher your FICO score will be. Ideally, you'll pay your entire bill off each month and use none of your credit line, but if you can't pull that off, try to stay below 30 percent and work your way down each month toward zero percent. Additionally, if you ask for and receive a credit limit increase, your utilization will automatically decrease as a percentage of your overall credit line. A simple phone call to your credit card provider will often do the trick. Just be sure you don't start spending more as a result.

5. **Limit requests for new credit**—Oftentimes folks like your employer or landlord will request permission to check your credit score. These are called soft inquiries and they don't impact your credit score at all. However, if you make multiple requests for credit, be it a new loan, or mortgage, or credit card, banks tend to see that as a sign that you need money and are therefore less credit worthy. Don't shoot me, I'm only the messenger, though as we said at the beginning of this journey together, we need to focus on the things we can control, and

this is one of them. If you want to raise your credit score, keep your new requests to a bare minimum (ideally zero), at least for a while as you work that FICO score upward.

6. **Boost your credit history**—There are several programs that can improve your credit history by reporting more positive financial things about you, such as your banking history, your utility payments, or in the case of renters, your on-time rent payments. Experian Boost, Ultra Fico, Rent Track and Rental Karma are but a few of the emerging services available to folks looking to boost their credit profile.

7. **Take action now**—If you have outstanding balances, do whatever it takes to pay them off. You can't afford to let your credit languish or deteriorate. Call your lenders and work out a payment plan you can meet or ask for an interest rate reduction. Avoidance will only prolong your misery. You can always temporarily reduce your spending in order to free up the cash you need to pay off any delinquencies.

8. **Hire a credit repair firm**—It's not always easy to negotiate on our own behalf, which is why it might make sense for you to hire a professional credit repair firm to talk to Visa or Mastercard or Uncle Sam for you. They are professional negotiators who understand how flexible creditors or the government are likely to be. Even if they can get your debt reduced by 20–30 percent (or more), it could be well worth the investment in their services. Ask your personal Money Team for a referral, or look for a credit repair firm online. Ask what their average reduction is and get them to provide you with referrals from other customers they've helped out.

Whatever it takes, repairing your credit and keeping it in good standing is one of the most important tasks for you as a wealth builder. It may take weeks or even months to do but the positive impact it will have on your future borrowing will be unmistakable. You're going to be buying assets to generate income and wealth; a solid credit rating cannot ensure you will get the capital you need and get it at the right price as well.

HOW TO INTEGRATE YOUR PAY PLAN INTO YOUR M$M MASTER PLAN

List any and all bad debts in your M$M Master Plan. Determine the amount you plan on paying toward each debt until it's completely paid off. Then choose the Avalanche or the Snowball approach to determine the order in which you pay.

Using a tool like Microsoft Excel, you'll now be able to easily see in what month and year you'll become 100 percent debt free, which is a great inspiration to tackle your debts head on.

Millionaire Money Moves
Master Plan

Goals	Age:35 2020		Age:36 2021		Age:37 2022	
Save Plan (30%)						
Setback Savings Account (3%)						
Setback Savings Account	$843.75	$1,687.50	$2,806.16	$3,823.73	$4,744.02	$5,76
Freedom Fund (22%)						
401(k) Account	$4,750.00	$9,500.00	$15,093.75	$19,843.75	$24,619.06	$29,369.
IRA Account						
Investment Account	$926.00	$1,852.00	$11,098.00	$44,392.00	$21,270.00	$22,196.0
Reward Fund (5%)						
Reward Savings Account	$1,406.25	$2,812.50	$4,493.66	$6,073.73	$7,556.52	$9,136.
College 529 Savings Plan						
State 529 Savings Account						
Pay Plan (Debt Payoff Schedule)						
Credit Card	$1,800.00	$700.00				
Auto Loan	$3,000.00	$3,000.00	$3,000.00	$5,100.00	$5,400.00	$5,400.0
Student Loans	$1,800.00	$1,800.00	$1,800.00	$1,800.00		

CONSUME

Shopping is fun. Travel can be wonderful. Dressing up and eating out in restaurants are two of the great pleasures in life. I think we can all agree on that. I bring them up because, for the purposes of your wealth journey, I want you to begin thinking about this type of consumption as what's called discretionary spending. Unlike their nondiscretionary brethren, these and several other expenses are entirely your choice to make, which means you have greater agency in determining what and how much of them are right for your wealth-building plan.

Bringing what you consume under control is challenging. In some cases, you will undoubtedly have to change your lifestyle. There is another alternative, which is to work your side hustles so that you can consume more, but that alone won't get you to Destination Millionaire, nor anywhere beyond. The bottom line is you're going to have to make some tough consumption choices, and what makes this especially challenging is how our society has made discretionary spending as easy as clicking a button on your phone, tablet, or computer.

Reduced spending converts your income into investment capital. You can find reductions in what you're paying for items like travel, dining out, storage fees, and many other areas where you probably spend more and more often than you need to. If you're currently consuming more than 15 percent of your take-home pay on consumable items, this means you need to devise a plan to either make more income or spend less on discretionary items. I can't tell you how your lifestyle should look, though I do want you to keep one overriding principle in mind. It's called alignment. You need your lifestyle to align with your wealth level, not your income level. You'll never build wealth by exchanging your income for lifestyle. For this reason, I strongly recommend you limit your overall discretionary spending to no more than 15 percent of your total income and use your remaining discretionary spend to accumulate assets. Here are several specific areas where savings to use toward your investments can be readily found.

EATING OUT

The average American eats an average of 4.2 commercially prepared meals per week.[34] At an average cost of approximately $12.75 per meal when eating out of the home versus, say, $4 for a home-cooked meal, you could save yourself $8.75 per person per meal by cooking more often at home. If you live in expensive areas, such as California, New York, Washington, DC, or Miami, you can expect these prices to be double or more. Multiply that potential savings by the number of people in your

---

[34] Trent Hamm, "Don't Eat Out as Often," The Simple Dollar, April 13, 2020, https://www .thesimpledollar.com/save-money/dont-eat-out-as-often/?tp=1#:~:text=The%20average% 20American%20eats%20an,month%20eaten%20outside%20the%20home.

household and by three meals a day and you'll see that what looked like a simple bite to eat is in reality a sizable bite out of your road to Destination Millionaire.

Eating out less often is a huge opportunity to lower spending on what you consume overall. Although easier said than done, I recommend you look at your credit card statements or compile your weekly receipts to see how many times you're eating out and how much you're spending when you do.

Now determine how much money you could save if you cut the frequency and amount you spend when dining out by, say, 25 percent or 50 percent. And don't stop there. Use a free app like investor.gov and calculate how much money that would be ten years from now, compounded at a 6 percent rate. See what I mean? That's the way to be serious about finding savings in what you consume so that you can save and invest to achieve Destination Millionaire.

HAPPY HOUR
(UNTIL THE CREDIT CARD BILL ARRIVES)

A recent survey by Alcohol.org[35] asked American workers what they spend on afterwork drinks. On average, they reported spending $3,035 per year. I'm neither a teetotaler nor someone who doesn't understand the "investment" that afterwork drinks can sometimes be, but when so many American workers are struggling to put away even 10 percent of their income in their company's retirement plan, I can't help but see most

---

[35] "American Workers Spend More than $3,000 a Year on Afterwork Drinks," American Addiction Centers, accessed June 14, 2022, https://www.alcohol.org/guides/afterwork-drinks/.

of those drinks and hors d'oeuvres as misplaced spending. And that's to say nothing of the big ballers paying $3,000 and up for a bottle service section where they're served $60 bottles of Vodka, Hennessy, and Tequila for $1,000 a bottle just to look cool in the club. Okay, I couldn't resist saying something, but you get my drift. Being *actually* rich is much flyer than playing the part. But don't only take my word for it; ask Bernard Arnault, the multi-billionaire who owns a controlling interest in LVMH, the parent company of Hennessy, Moet-Chandon, Louis Vitton, Dior, and a whole host of other brands we frequently consume. The cool and smarter play is to get rich along with Arnault, not to make him richer than he is. So, do your homework and consider investing in LVMH stock instead of overpaying for another bottle of bubbly.

To reduce what you spend on happy hours, I recommend you start with minimizing the number of days you frequent them. Maybe you can limit it to once a week and only on Fridays. Or maybe you do two happy hours a month at your favorite expensive spot and you find a cheaper spot for the other two. Maybe you have two happy hours a month in your basement bar with your best friends or at your friend's basement bar. Invite them to bring a bottle of their favorite spirits to save you even more money. There are so many ways to save in this area. The choice comes down to how bad do you want to be a millionaire and what sacrifices you are willing to make to achieve Destination Millionaire and beyond.

ENTERTAINMENT

It's difficult to track how much you spend on entertainment if you don't plan for it in advance. Be it a comedy show, a round of golf, a concert, a day on the slopes, or a night at a jazz club, the price of entertainment can easily balloon your budget far beyond what you can afford as a burgeoning millionaire. Controlling these costs is particularly tough because most tickets and entrance fees are paid with a credit card.

On the other hand, there are more entertainment choices available now than ever before, so as with all the discretionary spending you do, it pays to shop around, be extra-selective, and above all, be creative. Maybe you can purchase less expensive seats for that show or sporting event. See if you can replace expensive entertainment activities with something more modest, like a movie night at home. Find ways to be entertained that cost less; the options are there for the asking.

To lower how much you spend on entertainment concretely, I suggest you review your credit card and bank statements over the past six to twelve months and highlight any and all entertainment-related expenditures. Enter them into an Excel spreadsheet or a ledger, whatever works best for you. Use this to calculate a monthly average for what you spend on entertainment, and then try to identify specific ways to minimize your entertainment expenditure by 25–50 percent.

If you need further motivation, do the math I outlined in the sections above and figure out how much your savings today will be worth ten years from now. You may find, as I do, that counting your money is a lot more entertaining than it looks.

PERSONAL CARE

A recent study conducted for Groupon shows that women who regularly invest in their appearance spend an average of more than $225,000 in a lifetime. Men of a similar ilk spend about $175,000. Mind you, I'm a person who believes that personal care is important, but when I see a number that adds up to the same cost as four years of college tuition, it gives me great pause.[36]

So what to do? Do we merely write this category off because—hey—it feels good to look good? Or do we take a millionaire's approach and seek out the savings beneath the hairdos, the fingernails, and the moisturizers? You know my vote; now let me explain my platform.

I know firsthand through my ownership of hair salons and salon studios that Americans spend a fortune on personal care, and it's the kind of spending that doesn't go away because customers consider it an important way of treating and de-stressing themselves. Personal care decisions are fundamentally personal, as their name suggests, though I want to urge you as a budding millionaire to consider some alternate possibilities. For instance, can you cut your number of trips to the salon in half, or experiment with alternative hairstyles that don't require hair care services as frequently? Can you consider learning how to treat and style your and your family's hair on your own, which will save you big money even with the cost of shampoos, conditioners, and other related products? Or what about this: why not link expensive treatments like massages and reflexology to the Reward plan in your M$M Master Plan?

I realize how sensitive this issue can be as personal care has a lot to do with self-esteem, but don't let that prevent you from trying out less expensive alternatives that can keep you AND your net worth looking sexy and beautiful at the same time.

---

[36] Chelsea Haynes, "True Cost of Beauty: Survey Reveals Where Americans Spend Most." Groupon Merchant, August 3, 2017, https://www.groupon.com/merchant/trends-insights/market-research/true-cost-beauty-americans-spend-most-survey.

TRAVEL

In 2001, the United States Travel Association (USTA) identified the African American market as the fastest growing segment in the travel industry. That's good news for Black folks, and bad news for the Green Book (the last of which was published in 1996). According to a report by MMGY Global,[37] African Americans spent $103 billion on leisure travel in 2019 alone. In other words, the new "Bling Thing" is a question that starts like this: "Have you been to…"

The trouble is, unplanned travel can be a huge budget-buster for anyone looking to save and invest to become a millionaire, which is why you need to be especially wary of friends who always find a reason for an unplanned "girls" or "boys" trip. You know the ones I'm talking about. Before you know it, they'll have you spending too much money traveling and too little saving and investing. I'm not saying you can't have a good time with your favorite peeps, but any traveling you do must be planned and budgeted for annually, and included in both your M$M Master Plan and yearly plans.

As you plan that travel, take full advantage of credit card, airline, and hotel points to save money. I once went on an all-expenses paid vacation for two to Dubai by using my American Express points. We flew first-class on Emirates Airline and had a limo pickup to and from the airport each way. The cost of the first-class airfares alone would have been $23,000 per person had I not used my points. That's no misprint; it would have cost me $23,000 per round-trip ticket. I paid for our hotels with my Marriott Reward Points. That's what I like to call "balling hard on a budget" because

---

[37] "The Black Traveler: Insights, Opportunities & Priorities," MMGY Global, September 2020, https://www.mmgyglobal.com/the-black-traveler-insights-opportunities-priorities/.

that's how millionaires roll. Simply because it looks lavish doesn't mean you have to or should spend your hard-earned money to get it.

Book your trips as far in advance as possible to take advantage of discounted rates. The closer you get to your departure, the higher the airfares and rental car fees are bound to be. Look on sites like Airbnb and VRBO for lodging at far less than hotel rates. If you must book last minute, seek out apps like Hotel Tonight, which lists that night's unfilled hotel rooms at a significant discount. If you travel abroad, get the best foreign currency exchange rate by using an ATM to get cash in the local currency rather than at a bank or foreign exchange office.

Finally, and perhaps most importantly these days, remember that travel does not have to be a performance. The more you feel you need to see x, y, or z place so you can post something on social media about it, the more you'll be spending your time—and travel budget—for the benefit of others. So, have fun, see the world, and focus on the joy and enrichment of the person who worked so hard for the money to pay for this wonderful time. You.

RIDESHARE

I have a friend who used to say, "When I get rich, the first thing I want is my own driver." Little did he suspect back then that someone would invent a service like Uber or Lyft. Yet lo and behold, each of us can now feel like we've got a driver at our own beck and call whenever we need to get somewhere (including my friend, though he never did get rich).

Millennials especially seem to be enamored of the Uber/Lyft lifestyle. According to Betterment though, for the average twenty-something, the replacement value of all their Uber and Lyft ride spending over a twenty-five-year period would amount to over $235,000, even if it were conservatively invested.[38]

Every wealthy person I've ever met with a personal driver knows exactly what they pay their driver each month. But do you know how much you're paying for your Uber and Lyft rides every month? How much cheaper might it be to drive or take public transportation (or, dare I say, ride a bike) so that you too can become rich someday? I realize folks have places to go and people to see, but the more we do so within the means which allow us to accumulate wealth, rather than spend the wealth we don't have, the faster we'll get to the people we need to see at Destination Millionaire. Starting with ourselves.

EDUCATION

Public versus private-school education is a touchy subject in many households. Couples often struggle, understandably, to agree on the right choice for their beloved child(ren). What often gets lost in those discussions, however, is context. Your children's education doesn't happen *outside* of your wealth-building journey, and it too often takes on a starring role, to the detriment of your own retirement planning and wealth-building strategy as a whole. We all want our kids to get the best education possible and conquer the world, but we can consider a range of strategies to enable the next generation without disabling our own futures in the process.

Millionaires start by doing the math. Thirteen years of school (K–12) plus four years of college or university adds up to seventeen years of

---

[38] Megan Leonhardt, "Giving Up Uber Could Save You $323,000," *Money*, February 7, 2018, https://money.com/uber-lyft-cost-323000-long-term/.

potential educational costs per child. Given a rate of $15–25K per year for the first thirteen years of private school, plus anywhere from $15–20K per year and up for in-state colleges (to say nothing of private or out-of-state colleges whose costs can easily reach far above $50,000 a year), it makes sense to explore not only what alternatives to private school are out there, but *which solutions have the highest likelihood of leading to the overall positive outcome you so fervently desire.*

Private education is no guarantee of success, and in our community especially, people too often make the mistake of thinking, *I'll pay for private school through high school so my child will get a free-ride scholarship through college.* There is no such *quid pro quo* in the American education system, and at the astronomical prices of higher education today, that type of thinking amounts to a risky bet at best. Public school can be a viable option that will also save you thousands of dollars which can be put toward your financial future and retirement. It's a serious, costly mistake to believe that the "best" schools are only accepting kids from private schools. Getting into an excellent university has far more to do with how a kid performs academically overall, the courses they've challenged themselves to take, their leadership skills, community service work, and a host of other factors that have nothing to do with dollar signs or preppy wardrobes. One shining example is CNN political commentator Abigail "Abby" Phillips, who attended Bowie High School just around the corner from where I live in Maryland. Upon graduation, she got into Harvard and is now a highly respected figure in the world of broadcast journalism. Bowie High is in a public school district that has consistently struggled to compete with other school districts in the state. Naturally the exception doesn't necessarily prove the rule, but there's no doubt that numerous kids' public school education—and opportunities down the line for college—have been dramatically enhanced with strategies, such as enrolling them in as many AP courses as they can comfortably take on and hiring tutors. This is what I did for my kids and they've all graduated from accredited universities and are moving on in their careers, leaving me debt free and positioned to live a lavish life during retirement. Even if public education, enhanced by tutoring, doesn't ultimately lead to a scholarship for your child, it does preserve the money you would have spent on private school for college, and allows you to grow that money for thirteen years before you have to use it. Furthermore, going to private school may actually impede your child's chances of getting a full-ride college scholarship because it's hard to demonstrate a need when you can afford to pay—or seem to have been able to afford to pay—for private school education. So, there's a lot to think about.

I know some folks change zip codes in order to place their kids in neighborhoods that offer access to better public schools. This is a good strategy only if you can afford to pay up to double for your house because the cost of housing is typically highest in areas where the public-school systems are the best. Sure, you can sell your house in thirteen years and downsize, though that all depends on where the prices of houses will be in thirteen years. The assumption is that your home's value will appreciate more in a neighborhood with great schools as compared to a neighborhood with okay schools. But you can never predict what the housing market will do (or when). You may end up having to pay a significant premium for your house or having to sacrifice for thirteen years in terms of the size of your home. My point is, there's a trade-off for whatever choice you ultimately make, so do so thoughtfully, and with a calculator close at hand. I also recommend you speak to a college recruiter now. If anyone knows what it takes to get into college, it's the people who hold the keys to the kingdom.

STORAGE FEES

When we think of storage fees, most of us have in mind one of the myriad self-storage places dotting the American landscape. Sure, we all need *some* storage space, but given the amount of money spent on off-site storage (by some estimates, upward of $35 billion per year), it's clear that our stuff is making other people millionaires instead of us. The storage facility owners make money in their sleep, with minimal employees and near-zero maintenance costs (which also explains why building and owning storage space is currently a hot real estate investment play).

I think it's safe to say that most people end up living in their home or apartment for a lot longer than they first expected when they moved in. Unfortunately, the same is true with renting storage space. Even though it's called "temporary" storage, the average duration of a rented storage unit is around fourteen months, with nearly half of tenants renting for over a year, and some for much longer.[39]

To my mind, holding on to personal items in storage is a psychological and financial trap. That's why I have a rule of thumb that I use to determine whether to "keep it" or "dump it." If I haven't gone down to my storage area in my house in a year or more (and I say "storage area" because I refuse to waste money on a storage unit), then I throw it all away and never look back. I'm not unsentimental at all; I simply don't see the point in paying rent (or occupying otherwise useful space at home) for anything that isn't an active part of my life. What I'm here to tell you is that you may easily

---

[39] Shira Boss, "What Your Stuff Is Costing You," AARP, January 3, 2018, https://www.aarp.org/money/budgeting-saving/info-2018/clutter-cost-fd.html#:~:text=Monthly%20storage%20fees&text=According%20to%20other%20market%20research,four%20rooms'%20worth%20of%20furniture.

find as much as $1,000 per year extra in your Freedom Fund to build your future with by foregoing costly storage space. So, do yourself a favor and dump the junk!

DRY CLEANING

I can't tell you exactly how much your dry cleaning costs, but I can tell you it ain't cheap. It may also not be as necessary as it may seem. You can decrease the amount of money you spend on dry cleaning, simply by purchasing clothes that don't require special treatment in the first place. Have you considered if you're willing to essentially pay a fee each time you wear an item of clothing that requires dry cleaning? Take a moment before buying and check the label; perhaps you can pass on buying an item, knowing how much it'll cost you in dry cleaning down the line.

If you already have a closet full of dry-clean-only clothing, or absolutely must have a new item tagged with those deceptively expensive two words, then there are some workarounds available to you, such as buying an appliance to do your dry cleaning at home. If even that's too much, you can try gently hand washing items. When I caught on to how much money I was spending dry cleaning my nice T-shirts, I decided to wash them at home and hang them to dry in the hot sun of the sunshine state. Guess what? My T-shirts look great and I don't even have to iron them because they dry quickly and wrinkle-free in the sun. Just sayin'...

If or when you decide you must go to a professional, then shop around for dry cleaners and look for lower prices (though be careful you don't end up sacrificing quality and customer service). You can also look for cleaning deals on sites like Groupon and Living Social. The savings from these sites can be as much as 50 percent on dry cleaning.

Last, try to negotiate your price with the owner of your dry cleaner. If you've been a longtime loyal customer, you never know what savings the owner may offer you for remaining a loyal customer.

Now that you've evaluated how you can lower the amount that you consume, it's time to develop a strategy to consume just 15 percent of your income so you can consistently make Millionaire Money Moves. The following steps will help you get there.

1. Determine your overall spending by making a careful review of your bank and credit card statements. Isolate the discretionary items and highlight them (your credit card company may even do it for you). How much are you actually consuming compared to how much you thought you were consuming?

   You may be surprised. To get an accurate amount, go back six (or, even better, twelve) months and find out how much money you spent on discretionary items. Then...

2. Calculate the percentage of your income that you are spending on each discretionary expense; then, add up the total to determine the overall percentage of your income that you consume by choice alone.

3. Rank your discretionary expenses in order from most important to least. Be honest with yourself. As you're ranking them, think about which expenses you could live without and still "do you." Try to choose at least two expenses to control or eliminate for the next six months, on a trial basis. Once you get these two expenses under control, choose two more until all of your discretionary expenses are under control.

4. Go back and examine each and every expense one more time. If you aren't able to eliminate any more of these, how much can you reduce their frequency or the total amount you spend on them? Remember, you're trying to get the entire package down to 15 percent of your income. I know it's not easy but the best place to find savings and thereby investment capital is the place where you get to make the choice.

5. Create your own Strategic Consumption Plan. Start with the details of your income. If you're married, you and your spouse can create separate plans and sit down to see where you can find easy agreement on items to cut or reduce, then hammer out a compromise on whatever's left. Remember, a family who plans, saves, and invests together stays together. If you're unable to get your discretionary spend to 15 percent of your income, write down a plan to make up for it by increasing your earnings to the point where you'll still achieve the 15 percent of your income goal.

Consume
Reduction Strategic Plan

Income Assumptions	Annual	Semi-Annual	Monthly
Salary	$75,000.00	$37,500.00	$6,250.00
Taxes (25%)	$18,750.00	$9,375.00	$1,562.50
Take Home Pay (75%)	$56,250.00	$28,125.00	$4,687.50

Rank	Consume Description	Spend	Income	Rank	Strategy for Lowering or Eliminating	Spend	Income
1	Eating Out 4x per Month	$400.00	8.53%	1	Cut Eating Out by 25%	$200.00	5.33%
2	Happy Hours 4x per Month	$260.00	5.55%	2	Eliminate Happy Hours Completely	$0.00	0.00%
3	Shopping	$200.00	4.27%	3	Cut Shopping in Half	$100.00	2.13%
4	Entertainment Activity 4x per Month	$225.00	4.80%	4	Cut Entertainment in Half	$112.50	2.40%
5	Personal Care (Hair, Nail, Cosmetics, etc.)	$200.00	4.27%	5	Cut Personal Care in Half	$5.000	1.07%
6	Travel	$500.00	10.67%	6	Cut Travel in Half	$250.00	5.33%
7	Ridesharing Uber/Lyft	$100.00	2.13%	7	Eliminate Ridesharing	$0.00	0.00%
8	Storage Fees 10' x 10' Space	$90.00	1.92%	8	Eliminate Storage by Throwing Away Storage	$0.00	0.00%
9	Dry Cleaning	$75.00	1.60%	9	Wash Clothes at Home	$0.00	0.00%
	Total	$2,050.00	43.73%		Total	$712.50	16.26%

6. Implement your strategy and check your progress in a month and then in six- or twelve-month's time. As you've heard me say several times, change doesn't happen overnight; it's the result of consistent, sustained effort. If you find you've over-consumed, focus on the specific items that put you over the top and do your best to tame or eliminate them altogether. Remember, this is the list of expenses you don't absolutely need.

7. Continue making adjustments to your discretionary expenses until you achieve your goal.

INVEST

An article published in *Financial Therapy*, entitled "Investment Behavior: Factors that Limit African Americans' Investment Behavior," cites three major impediments to African American investment: a lack of investment capital, insufficient financial literacy, and an overall fear of investing.[40] While I don't disagree with these findings, I'd like us to take a look at each of these so-called impediments the way a millionaire would, and see what can be done to overcome each of them.

LACK OF INVESTMENT CAPITAL

In previous chapters we've seen how we can address a lack of investment capital by creating it ourselves: earning and saving more at our jobs and

---

[40] Crystal Hudson, John Young, and Sophia Anong, "Investment Behavior: Factors that Limit African Americans' Investment Behavior," Financial Therapy Association, (2018) 9:1, https://newprairiepress.org/cgi/viewcontent.cgi?article=1127&context=jft#:~:text=These %20factors%20included%2C%20but%20are,financial%20knowledge%20and%20risk% 20tolerance.

side hustles, paying and consuming less, and taking that money and investing it (which in turn generates additional income). We all know that the game isn't fair. We generally earn less and are promoted less frequently than our White counterparts who have the same qualifications and education as us. And it's also true that less than 1 percent of all venture capital goes to Black-owned businesses.[41] That means the majority of us will have to raise our own capital to invest, it's going to take us longer to reach our goals, and we're going to have to work harder, which is nothing new to the Black experience as a whole. The way I see it, we can either look at those undesirable conditions as reasons to back down from a life-changing challenge, or we can see them for what they truly are: impediments, not dream killers. There are countless Black entrepreneurs in the world, including Yours Truly, figuring out how to obtain the capital needed to reach their financial aspirations in spite of all the inequalities and obstacles daring them to give up. We are past and living proof that it can be done. The only question for you as an investor is how hard are you willing to work for your capital? How badly do you want it? How much of your time and money are you willing to sacrifice in order to make more so you can invest more? The means are at your disposal and the money is within your reach. The choice is up to you.

BECOMING FINANCIAL (AND WEALTH) LITERATE

While financial literacy is an important part of building lasting wealth, most millionaires would agree that on its own, financial literacy is not

---

[41] James Norman, "A VC's Guide to Investing in Black Founders," *Harvard Business Review,* June 19, 2020, https://hbr.org/2020/06/a-vcs-guide-to-investing-in-black-founders.

enough. There are numerous resources out there teaching financial literacy: books, classes, and online content abound. Many of these resources are free. All that's needed to become financially literate is the desire and effort to do so, which includes a commitment to keep learning for the rest of your life. Before you know it, you'll be as fluent speaking the language of finance as you are ordering a meal at a restaurant.

To my mind, financial literacy should be seen as a spectrum, not a single point. My grandmother had an eighth-grade education, yet she became financially literate enough to save for and eventually buy a house that's now worth millions. Though Grandma was a wise woman, it wasn't her education, genius, or luck that made that kind of success happen for her. It was her desire and effort. She learned what she needed from the materials available to her and guess what? It was enough. I think too often we stare at a seemingly unreachable summit (often "unreachable" because someone *told* us so) and miss seeing the staircase sitting right in front of us, inviting us to take the first step. The information we need to become sufficiently literate in finance is readily available to us, much of it free of charge and all of it begging to be consumed.

Yet what's also needed in our community, and is too often overlooked, is what I call "wealth literacy." You can think of it as financial literacy with a purpose—to turn our financial literacy into something lasting and enduring across generations. What must we do once we become wealthy so that our wealth grows and expands over time rather than dissipating?

My investment process is designed to teach you not only what it takes to get rich, but how to turn your wealth into a vehicle for lasting prosperity. I believe we are capable of whatever we put our minds to, personally and as a community. When we needed our civil rights enacted, we organized the largest march the world had ever seen. When we needed to get rid of a tyrant President, we banded together, stepped into the breach, and triumphed. There's never been a challenge we haven't been able to face and overcome. So, before we get started, I want to address—Millionaire-style—the third, so-called impediment facing our community: fear of investing.

CONQUERING FEAR OF INVESTMENT

As African American investors, we have every reason to be cautious. Our fear of the banking and financial systems is justified. Unfortunately, that fear is paralyzing us—devastatingly so—and that inaction is a major reason why it seems impossible for us to grow sufficient wealth in this country. We need to find a way to eradicate our mistrust of investing, and the banking and financial institutions that surround it, so we can put all of our available capital to work on our behalf. We can make the system build wealth and work for us as it has done for so many others.

I read a quote a while back that talked about "conquering fear with action." I used to believe in that idea wholeheartedly, but over time, as I thought more about it, I recognized the flaws in that line of thinking. Action alone, although it sounds good, doesn't eliminate the fear, especially if it leads to disastrous outcomes. What really eradicates fear is action combined with knowledge, the type of knowledge available from fact-based research and experience. Yet, our fear of investing can be overcome only if we get to the root of where that fear comes from in the first place.

Is it a fear of losing all your money? Is it a fear of failing and looking stupid? Is it a fear of the unknown? Is it a fear based on what your family, friends, and mentors have instilled in you based on their investing experience, or what they were led to believe but never confirmed themselves?

It's sad because often what we fear stems from what we've been told to fear without us ever finding out for ourselves if what we are afraid of is even real or worth being afraid of.

Investing takes courage. There's no way to make your personal or company portfolio grow if you allow a fear of investing to rule the roost. Back in Chapter 5 we learned how to get our courage up and reduce fear through research and action. That's what professional investors do. They don't act on whims; they carefully read company prospectuses and talk with corporate management, colleagues, and industry experts prior to investing. They glean publications like *The Wall Street Journal* and *The Economist* to look for trends that may signal how a particular industry is likely to fare in the long and short term. Years of practice have taught them that information is capital, capital is power, and power can overcome fear. Once professional investors do their research, they jump all in and keep at it—learning and adjusting along the way. We need to do the same. Sitting on the sidelines or investing small amounts of our capital won't get us there. It's time we act the part by jumping all in, keeping at it, and adjusting until we get where we desire to go. If it can work for other communities and individuals, it can certainly work for us.

While there are innumerable investment vehicles out there, chances are your wealth journey will involve one or more of these four:

1. Securities (stocks, bonds, commodities, Exchange Traded and Mutual Funds)
2. Real Estate (residential and commercial)
3. Entrepreneurship (creating and operating your own business)
4. Alternative Investments (angel investors, venture capital, hedge funds, and private equity).

It's now time to show you how to use the excess capital that you've created—by earning more and paying and consuming less—to become a millionaire by investing in and acquiring securities, real estate, entrepreneurship, and alternative investments.

I'm often asked questions like, "How much money do I need to get started investing? What should I invest in? How much money do I need to start flipping properties? How can I get into buying multi-family and commercial properties? If I want to start a business, how much capital do I need and where can I get enough to initially fund my business? How do I find real estate syndication groups to invest with? These questions, and many others of that ilk, led me to create the M$M Investment ladder. The chart you see below not only explains how to become a millionaire starting from the bottom, but it also provides you with a framework to use as you begin making Millionaire Money Moves and increase your net worth. The ladder's levels should be seen as guidelines, not absolutes, as your own will vary according to things like the geographic locations where you are investing. Let's take a closer look at these investment and savings thresholds which I've designed to guide you confidently into the investment marketplace as you head toward your financial goals.

MILLIONAIRE MONEY MOVES
Investment Ladder by Available Capital

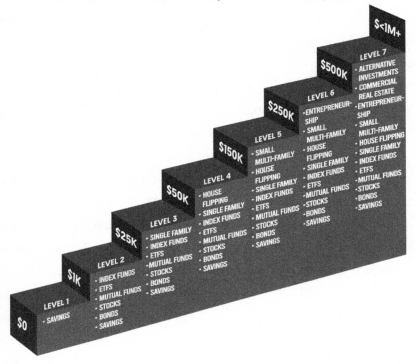

As you can see, the first step in turning yourself into a Level 7 millionaire investor is to reach $1,000 of savings, which is the threshold between Level 1 and Level 2. That's no misprint; *once you've saved $1,000 in your Freedom Fund, your investment journey is ready to begin.* At that point, you can begin to invest in securities: index funds, Exchange Traded Funds, mutual funds, stocks, and bonds. Later, when your savings reach Level 3, between $25,000 and $50,000, you'll open yourself up to being able to invest in real estate, either by purchasing a single-family home, vacation property or duplex as your primary residence, or as an investment property from which to earn rental income that can be reinvested. As you continue to save and move up the investment ladder to Level 4, you'll gain the ability to add rental properties and house flipping as ways to generate more income and investment capital. The goal of the M$M framework is to get you to level up to Level 7, whereby you'll be well diversified as an investor in securities, real estate, entrepreneurship (if you desire), and alternative investments (angel investing, venture capital, hedge funds, and private equity). The ladder is an investment pathway to becoming a millionaire starting from the bottom.

To further guide your journey to Destination Millionaire, I've provided four supplemental chapters in a Millionaire Money Moves Supplementation Investment Guide. Each contains concrete instructions about how to invest the excess capital you've generated in securities, real estate, entrepreneurship, and alternative investments, and become a millionaire for real. The process works like this: once you reach $1,000 in savings, you'll have arrived at Level 1 on the M$M ladder and you're ready to begin investing. Go immediately to Supplemental Chapter 1 in the next book for specific details on how to begin investing in securities (stocks, bonds, commodities, index funds and exchange traded funds).

When you reach Level 3 on the M$M ladder ($25,000–50,000), go to Supplemental Chapter 2: Investing in Real Estate, where you'll learn how to become a millionaire by investing in real estate.

When you get to Level 6 ($250,000–500,000), move on to Supplemental Chapter 3: Investing in Entrepreneurship (Starting a Business) to learn how to become a millionaire as an entrepreneur.

Once you get to Level 7 ($500,000 to $1 million-plus), it opens you up to the world of Alternative Investments. Proceed to Supplemental Chapter 4: Investing in Alternative Investments to learn how to invest as an angel investor, venture capitalist, hedge fund investor, or private equity investor. By this time, you will already be a millionaire (which, as you'll see, you'll need to be in order to qualify as an accredited investor) and well on your way toward Destination Ultra Rich or Billionaire.

You're welcome to read these supplemental chapters at your leisure or as a reference guide to go back to when you're ready. Now that your money is starting to work for you and generating additional income, let's explore how you can reward yourself for all of the hard work and sacrifice you've made while maintaining and even increasing your gains.

REWARD

On the road to greater wealth, rewarding through greater consumption must be avoided at all cost. Rewarding investment and specific financial targets is the only way to go. Most folks get their paycheck, pay their bills, and spend the rest of their money on consumer items: new clothes, a new iPad, new sneakers, and so on. They're not investing that money; they don't really know what to save it for; so, what the hell? They may as well buy something with it. Their incentive, if any, is built into the idea that *I'm gonna get my paycheck and buy that new (fill in the blank) which will make me feel better, more satisfied, or rich.* In other words, M$M Pay is followed directly by M$M Consume. Avoiding this trap becomes especially challenging when you've successfully increased your earnings, either through increased effort in your main hustle or by taking on a side hustle. As more money piles up, so too does the desire to consume more. This is why it's so important to master emotional control and balance when it comes to financial decision-making.

Your long-term goal should be to increase your investment portfolio and build up enough capital so that your money—not your labor—starts making the money you use to occasionally splurge. But you have to sacrifice, at first. That's a key part of the Millionaire Mindset. We're all human beings and we need motivation to do the right thing; otherwise, we're a lot more likely to do the "not right" thing. That's where the concept of reward comes into play.

Every self-made millionaire I've ever met buys stuff, and sometimes that stuff costs a boatload of money. What's different is that their purchases are usually tied to or at least commensurate with the attainment of one financial goal or another, rather than money whose sole purpose is conspicuous consumption. They're not trying to show off and honestly, neither should you, except as a way of validating your own achievements to yourself. You want to link your next big purchase to achieving a certain goal, a certain level of savings, or a certain level of investment income. For example, "I'm going to buy this car only once I've successfully purchased 'x' shares of IBM stock or once I've increased my net worth to 'x' level." The idea is to build up to your reward, as opposed to impulsively rewarding yourself every month or every time you get a windfall of money. The key is to break out of the pattern of buying things habitually or reflexively and instead make your large purchases well thought out and all about being proud of yourself. Continue to be nice to yourself, but take temptation and put it on the back burner until you can execute it as validation. My reward approach is designed to balance the need to save and invest with the emotional desire to spend money on the things that give you pleasure, satisfaction, and—in some cases—the baller attention some folks desire.

It's easy to overspend. Let's face it, in the world of Bling, it can be a struggle to keep yourself grounded. The lure of shiny, fancy objects is as ubiquitous as the air we breathe. In places like Miami, New York, and Los

Angeles, to name just a few centers of Blingosity, Rolls-Royces, yachts, and other forms of supreme richness abound. Honestly, I don't begrudge anyone their $500,000–car, though I strongly dislike the way it makes me and folks like me want to keep up. I realize that much of this seeming wealth is often a mirage because many people with a decent income can lease houses, cars, and boats by making the monthly payments. But based on their net worth, they can't actually afford this kind of lifestyle. So, if driving a Rolls-Royce is what you've always dreamed of, then at least do yourself the favor of having the income from your hard-won assets pay for it and make those hefty monthly payments a reward for tangible achievement in investing, not flashiness. As I so painfully learned in my story about that Mercedes, you may decide that pride in yourself—and not your purchases—is all the reward you want or need.

INSTANT GRATIFICATION VERSUS DEFERRED GRATIFICATION

Instant gratification is what Million-nevers do. As soon as they earn enough money to purchase the things that they believe will gratify them, they pull the trigger and buy them. They end up with lots of shiny, expensive things that maintain no value as a result. Acquiring assets, the central task in wealth building, requires capital, and it's impossible to amass the amounts of capital required to invest in securities, real estate, entrepreneurship, and private equity if you spend your money instead of amassing and investing it. I understand how difficult this is; as I've said, I've been a repeat offender myself. Therefore, to stop me from spending my available capital on "things" instead of assets, I practice deferred gratification. If you look closely, you'll see that it's what all millionaires do. It's simply the practice of delaying the accumulation of material items until certain earning or investment goals are reached, goals specific to my M$M Master Plan. This prevents me from losing focus and ending up with a bunch of worthless stuff and little-to-no assets.

I find that deferring gratification actually enhances a person's emotional satisfaction and appreciation because it ensures that you've been wanting this reward for some time now. This is why I recommend establishing sizable and meaningful rewards. Waiting until you achieve a goal before you make a purchase gives you a stronger sense of gratitude for whatever you've bought because you'll have sacrificed and worked long and hard for it. That feeling of satisfaction is far more lasting, and includes the added benefit of knowing that you are rewarding yourself responsibly and building wealth along the way.

As you can see, I have my M$M Reward Plan directly integrated into my five-to-ten-year M$M Master Plan. If you look at my example, you'll see a "trip to Jamaica" contingent upon completing my master's degree. Purchasing a Rolex Watch is slated for after I've successfully launched my business. I'm purchasing a Mercedes-Benz after purchasing a four-plex investment property. I'm buying a forty-foot Sea Ray Boat once I've purchased an apartment building. All my rewards are attached to achievements that increase my income or my assets, and thus, my net worth. This prevents me from consuming irresponsibly.

Millionaire Money Moves
Master Plan

Goals	Age:35 2020		Age:36 2021		Age:37 2022	
Invest Plan (22%)						
Securities (Stocks and Bonds)						
Apple						
Berkshire Hathaway B						
INX - S&P 500 Index						
Real Estate						
Buy a Rental House						
Buy a 4-Plex						
Buy a 10-Unit Apartment Building						
Entrepreneurship						
Write the Business Plan				Done!		
Obtain Funding						
Secure the Location						
Start the Business						
Private Equity						
Business 1						
Apartment Syndicate 1						
Reward Plan (5%)						
Trip to Jamaica				Buy	Done!	
Rolex Watch						
New Mercedes Benz						
Purchase 40' Sunseeker Boat						

The goals in the Reward section of your M$M Master Plan can be as small as a pair of red-bottomed shoes or as large as a private Gulfstream G650 plane. That's totally up to you. If your assets are continuing to appreciate, and the income you generate from them can cover your rewards, then you can afford them (assuming there's no outstanding bad debt you're carrying). Simply being able to make the payments doesn't mean you can afford something; these other conditions must be true as well. If your assets and the income derived from them are stagnating or depreciating, and your debt is growing, then you can't afford to be rewarded, nor do you honestly deserve to be. At least not yet. It's as simple as that.

HOW TO REWARD YOURSELF
INTELLIGENTLY

When you do reward yourself, you need to make use of your ever-growing Millionaire Mindset and always buy "smart." The following are my rules for how I reward myself when it's time:

1. Buy smart. Strive to make your money go as far as possible by hunting for the best price for your reward. Don't make the purchase without first shopping around.

2. Pay for your reward with cash, frequent flyer and hotel points received from your two to three credit cards. Avoid financing your reward and thereby paying interest.

3. If you must finance your reward, finance it for two years or less to keep your debt and the amount of interest you pay to a minimum.

4. Evaluate the impact to your net worth before you purchase your reward. Make sure you're not losing your wealth gains by purchasing your reward.

5. If I can buy one of my rewards tax-free (sometimes with an out-of-state purchase) or on sale by waiting for it a little longer, I'll wait for it. I'll also shop around for a better price. The internet is an amazing tool for finding items cheaper by comparing the prices of the same item. Whenever possible I'll play one offer against another to get sellers to match or beat their competitor's price. Am I always 100 percent honest about what the other guy has offered me? No, Your Honor, I am not. Guilty as charged. But it never hurts to let a vendor know he ain't the only game in town (or the world, thanks to the internet).

Shopping smart is being frugal, and I do it because I value my money. As a millionaire, I want to make it last as long and go as far as it can.

GIVE

Giving is a way of showing gratitude, paying forward the blessings and opportunities that you've received from God and others. The M$M Power Budget recommends that 10 percent of your income be allocated to giving. This is if giving of your money aligns with your values. If you lack the means to give money or prefer to give of your time, that is equally noble and completely up to you. Giving is a fundamental pillar of making Millionaire Money Moves. Here's why: in order to reverse the racial wealth gap, we've got to think not only about ourselves but beyond ourselves as well, and that thinking has to be concurrent and not merely consecutive. "Let me get mine, then you can get yours" is a broken philosophy that's holding us back as a community, but also, as individuals. On the one hand, there are countless moral reasons to give to others.

As much as the world of finance may appear to be a dog-eat-dog free-for-all, it is fundamentally a highly interdependent system built on relationships. Giving—in the form of money, time, or resources—is the glue that binds those relationships together. Like all the other Millionaire Money Moves, it needs to be done with intelligence and care. According to a report by the Kellogg Foundation, Black households give 25 percent more of their annual income than White households.[42] That means that the potential for impactful giving is already an entrenched part of our culture. I think the feat for us is finding the proper balance between how much we give, how we give, and how much we hold onto in order to create the potential for future giving. While it's true that, as the old saying goes, "You'll never see a U-Haul behind a hearse," giving without a well-thought-out plan can diminish rather than increase the likelihood of financial success for you and for our communities. There is a money crisis in our community and we need to pool together all of the financial resources available to us in order to respond to this crisis.

According to some researchers, Black folks spend in the neighborhood of $10 billion a year on gifts. That level of generosity is a deserved source of pride to be sure. Yet if we're serious about changing our future, we have to reexamine all the available giving options, including how much and what we gift to our friends and families. For instance, what if instead of buying friends and family gifts we bought them shares of stock, a savings bond, or we donated money to their retirement fund, or their kid's college fund? Gifting in that manner would have a lasting impact, and when our loved ones retired they'd never forget the gift we gave them—Financial Peace. Will they remember the Gucci socks we bought them at Christmas instead? I have my doubts. There's nothing wrong with buying material things as gifts, but doing so exclusively only favors obsolescence over growth, and that's a big mistake. It's reactive, not proactive.

Giving or paying it forward is a critical step in the wealth-building

---

[42] "Culture of Giving: Energizing and Expanding Philanthropy By and For Communities of Color," W. K. Kellogg Foundation, accessed June 14, 2022, https://www.d5coalition.org /wp-content/uploads/2013/07/CultureofGiving.pdf.

process, whether you are a person of faith or not. There are several ways you can give back and pay it forward; the most common is through church tithes, offerings, youth programs, or building funds or by assisting family and friends. There are many organizations in your community that could use help.

If giving money aligns with your values, here is how I suggest you do it. However, if giving your time, effort, and expertise is more your thing, I've articulated several ways to do that as well. You can do one type of giving or both; it's purely a personal choice and one that may evolve over time as well.

CHURCH (TITHING) AND CHARITABLE ORGANIZATIONS

My own Christian upbringing has led me to believe that when you give from the heart, God grants you favor. You too may have your own moral convictions about why giving is good. Whatever the case for you personally, there are also many powerful financial reasons to make sure that giving is as much a part of what you do—now—as getting is. In other words, you can and must do good and do well at the same time.

Favor comes in many forms. Sometimes favor opens doors to opportunity. Sometimes it grants a long healthy life. Sometimes it provides peace in your soul. Sometimes it gives you a leg up when you most need it. The largest recipient of African American giving is the Black Church. The church has been one place where the Black community has historically been able to pool financial resources together for the construction of church buildings, schools, senior housing complexes, and more. Through our church organizations we've proven that we have the ability to leverage financial resources to do big things in our community. Think about this, though: what if we could continue the good work of the Church in its traditional manner of volunteerism while also creating separate for-profit limited liability corporations where members could pool together their financial resources to build and grow their personal wealth through investment syndications? The Black Church successfully performs that same function, but solely for the benefit of expanding and growing the church. They do this with parishioners who volunteer their expertise, time, and money to accomplish the church's mission. Imagine if the church could benefit both the church and its parishioners by creating opportunities for wealth building? We often have a difficult time coming together outside of the Church to pool our money together to invest in entrepreneurship, real estate, private equity, and securities. I believe a good part of that difficulty is due to the lack of sufficient trust and credibility among ourselves to create widespread partnership deals for apartments, senior housing, and schools *outside of the church.* So, why can't the Church, as a trusted agent, bridge that gap by being the conduit for community and personal economic development in both for-profit and nonprofit areas? I strongly believe that, if the Church leadership could trust the process, it could grow its parishioner base, improve our communities, and be the needed catalyst to creating significant and lasting economic wealth and prosperity for us and for our communities.

What about giving to the other organizations that have paved the way for us in the past and will continue to do so in the future? Black Lives Matter, the NAACP, The Black Wealth Summit, and My Brother's Keeper, to name but a few of the dynamic national and local nonprofits helping out Black folks. My company mostly supports local charities. I personally like to see the value of our impact wherever we donate, to see our investments put to work to improve the community in which we work and live. We support our local food bank by providing labor for a day where we sort food donations provided by the local grocery stores. We also support our local county by donating backpacks to young people who are in need of a nice new backpack and school supplies. We provide food for needy people in our county during the Thanksgiving and Christmas holidays. Supporting nonprofit organizations is a personal choice, but it's also tax-deductible, which means Uncle Sam will reward you for your generosity. I recommend you dig deep, seek out, and donate to organizations that align with the changes you want to see in the world. It's one of many ways to give without having to exceed the 10 percent of your income allocated to Give.

POLITICAL DONATIONS

The same is true in the political realm. Aspiring office holders need contributions to their campaigns to get elected. That's a plain fact. There's a reason politicians are called lawmakers; it's because their votes have a dramatic impact on our personal and professional lives. I think all giving is a personal choice though I believe that if we want the laws to change in order to rectify the injustices we face and level the playing field, we're going to have to make political donations of time or money, whichever is most readily available. Money doesn't only talk in politics, it echoes. Rare is the political leader who doesn't seek reelection at some point, and when that point is reached, the first question they ask is, "Where's the money to support this campaign going to come from?" When we support local politicians with our time and money, we're in a better position to hold them accountable and ensure that they are advocating for the interests of our community. Our giving has to be substantial enough that politicians can't simply ignore or deny our needs. This is the only way we are going to realize the changes we desire in our communities. Our impact on elections has to be so great that ignoring us results in a loss of support and therefore election losses. We can't allow ourselves to be peddled for votes and then brushed aside once the election is over. We have to play the political game as the big-money organizations do if we're ever going to have an impact.

GIVING (OR LOANING) MONEY TO FAMILY AND FRIENDS

Don't loan more than 25 percent of your monthly income to friends or family. That's a fixed total, not 25 percent per month. So, if your monthly income is, say, $2,400, you should never have more than $600 loaned out to friends or family. Once you hit your $600 maximum, you need to collect from the people who borrowed from you before you lend to anyone else. You can simply say, "I don't have any more money to lend, but if you can get Ray Ray to pay back the $300 I loaned him, I can lend you $150 of it." This is incredibly useful any time your family or friends ask you to lend them money because, without feeling guilty or lying, you can honestly say you don't have any more money to lend. I know how difficult this may be for folks who value their family above all else. And while you may be helping a family member out of a pinch, you're not helping them or the rest of your family build generational wealth by loaning them money every time they ask for it, whether they pay it back or not. The best way to help them is to teach them to manage their money so they don't have to constantly borrow money from friends and family. If they can't or refuse to be taught, there is nothing you will do for them by giving or loaning them your hard-earned cash.

I want you to respect your money, not worship it. We often work at extremes; either we disrespect our money by giving it away too easily, we spend it frivolously, or we worship it as though it were the be-all and end-all of our existence. I believe there is a healthy middle ground and we have to fight to find and stay within it. That's the place where we can build wealth, while still being good people and good financial stewards.

Here are a few other things to keep in mind when loaning money:

- Don't loan money to people with chronic money problems. It never helps them meaningfully and it adds you to their endless wheel of money problems. The choice to loan or not is yours but don't expect to get paid back anytime soon if you do. Consider this as well: the challenge of collecting money you loaned in order to help them out financially frequently becomes a major burden to you. And despite your best efforts, you may never get the money back.
- Be clear about whether what you're giving is a gift or a loan by asking the recipients of any loans to sign a promissory note. This is simply a contract stating the terms of your loan, including a payback date. I know this sounds formal, but you need documentation of how much you loan and your terms for repayment.
- If someone fails to pay you back, use this as a teaching moment and express to them that you can never loan them money again because they've failed to respect you and your attempt to help them out.
- Stick to your guns. When you tell someone that you've loaned out too much money and folks are not paying you back, don't be dissuaded by pleas like, "But I've never borrowed money from

you" or "I've always paid you back." Your response has to be a firm, "NO, I'm sorry." You've imposed your lending limits the same way all financial institutions do. You either have to stick to those limits or wind up doing the miserable work of collections agencies, with your friends or family no less.

- Keep your lending to friends and family to a minimum. You may feel you "owe" it to them to loan money, though the truth is that it's generally not a two-way street. Chronic borrowers never have money to lend you in your time of need. They're always behind the eight ball and owing folks.

GIVING BY PAYING IT FORWARD
THROUGH MENTORING

"There is no such thing as a self-made man.
We are made up of thousands of others.
Everyone who has ever done a kind deed for us, or
spoke one word of encouragement to us, has entered
into the make-up of our character and of our
thoughts as well as our success."

—GEORGE BURTON ADAMS

I realize you may not be able in your situation to give money to anyone right now, or perhaps you've already allocated the 10 percent from your M$M Power Budget, but as you see, there is more than one way to give and foster growth in the lives of others. You can volunteer your time or become a mentor. Even though the tangible results of these types of giving may be less apparent on the surface, they can easily become the greatest gifts of all. There's no doubt that in my life, and in the lives of every millionaire I've ever met, the contributions mentors have made had everything to do with the success of those to whom that time and wisdom was directed.

Through the giving of one of my longest-standing mentors, Mr. Alfred Glover, I learned about giving's exponential power, or as you'll see, how $300 can turn into $500,000. Mr. Glover is a retired Black Army colonel who grew up in South Carolina. He fought in Vietnam and then retired to Fort Ord, California—a military base near where I grew up. Mr. Glover became a wealthy man buying properties in Monterey along with his partner, Mr. Rockwell, a White fellow from nearby Carmel. They developed houses all through Seaside and Monterey, including my little town of Seaside Hills, which was where the wealthier Blacks lived and enjoyed views of Monterey as well as Carmel Valley (where the ultra rich White folks lived).

Mr. Glover has always been a community man. In addition to being a successful entrepreneur, he's fought his whole life for equality and economic opportunity for African Americans living in Seaside. He built his own opportunities by starting a bank from scratch and then selling it. Eventually he bought an office building, which later encouraged me to buy an office building for my business and portfolio of investments as well. They say imitation is the most sincere form of flattery. When it came to Mr. Glover, I knew that brand of "flattery" had a good chance of turning to gold over time.

Right before I was about to begin college, Mr. Glover's daughter, Patrice, pulled my sister Karla aside and said, "My dad wants to talk to your brother Cedric. He heard he's about to go away to college."

It was well known that Mr. Glover was a man of few words, so if he wanted to talk to you, it meant he truly had something to say. I went up to his house and found him outside watering his lawn by hand, as most folks in Seaside didn't have underground sprinkler systems.

As I approached him, he said, "Young man. I heard you were about to go to college."

"Yes, sir," I said. "I'm about to go to Cal Poly, San Luis Obispo."

"Well, I just want to let you know that if you need anything, you give me a call. We're here for you."

"Okay. Thank you, Mr. Glover," I said.

And that was it. Mr. Glover later saw to it that I received a $500–scholarship from the Alpha Phi Alpha fraternity before I left for college. I pledged Alpha, though I knew deep down that Mr. Glover had a deeper message for me that day which was this, "Your community thinks highly of you, you are out there representing us, and we will do our part to make sure you succeed." This is such a key element to mentorship so it's worth taking a closer look. Not only does a mentor expect you to treat them with respect but also to treat *yourself* with respect. The knowledge, wisdom, and care that they are passing on to you has value that extends beyond you. The way that value appreciates is by you giving it its proper dignity, doing your utmost to be worthy of its gift, and ultimately passing it on to someone else deserving. Giveback is payback.

I didn't call Mr. Glover to ask for anything until one summer when I had a girlfriend in the Bay Area. This was back when long distance calls actually cost something and either she or I must have had a lot on our mind because I managed to run my phone bill up to over $300 in one month. Jeez! My roommate began hounding me for the money to pay our bill but I felt too ashamed to ask my dad for the money. I decided to turn to Mr. Glover instead.

I went to his office around noon the next day and I said, "Mr. Glover, I need $300."

I didn't tell him what it was for. I was far too embarrassed about it.

He said, "Okay. Come back in a couple of hours, and pick up a check."

"Thank you," I said, "but I've got to do something for you in exchange. I've got to work for it. I don't believe in handouts."

"That's fine. You can pick up the weeds around my office."

I went outside and cleaned up for a while, clearing up the weeds in the cracks of his driveway. I came back that afternoon to pick up the check for $300.

When he gave it to me, I said, "Mr. Glover, I really appreciate this. I've got to find a way to pay it back to you."

He said, "No. Pay it forward. Make sure you help somebody else out when you're in a position to do so."

I paid my phone bill off right away but I never forgot Mr. Glover's admonition. Many years later, when I went into business for myself and finally began to prosper, I started giving money to other kids from my church and community to assist them with college expenses. All told, I've probably "paid forward" close to $500,000 by now. Through Mr. Glover, I learned that, as the Bible teaches, "to whom much is given, much is expected." [43]

There's another side to mentoring which is being a mentor to others. Being a mentor is enormously fulfilling though it is full of its own particular nuances. The better you understand them the more effective you'll be as a mentor, and the more satisfaction you'll derive from your own mentoring work. To begin with, mentoring others is not about pushing your dreams

---

[43] Luke 12:48.

and ideas on someone else. It's really about leveraging your ideas, personal contacts, and resources to facilitate the dreams of your protégés. Here are some other tips for effective mentoring:

1. Find young people who move you in some way. A mentoring relationship should be natural, not forced. As a mentor, you must possess a strong desire to help them achieve their goals; otherwise, you'll have a hard time being consistent.

2. Listen to the people you mentor. Understand what's going on in their life. Explore their dreams and aspirations. Don't judge or try to alter their dreams. Encourage them to choose a big dream and help them develop an action plan and timeline to achieve it.

3. Don't be a dream killer. You may not believe their dreams are achievable, but keep that to yourself. Your job is to help facilitate their dreams; their job is to do the work. I think we're often guilty of imposing limitations on what young people can achieve based on our inability to achieve big things. Support their vision; let the world tell them yes or no. You never know who you're mentoring. They could have what it takes to be the next Robert Smith, P. Diddy (a.k.a. Sean Combs), Oprah, or President Barack Obama.

4. Don't try to make them be your version of success. They will be more inspired by their own vision of success, not yours. You can expose them to a host of things including your profession to see what moves them, but allow them to decide what they want to do and who they want to be in life.

5. Be consistent and committed. Don't drop the ball. If you say you're going to meet with them, show up. Be prepared and on

time. Demonstrate through action that you're there for them and will be there for them going forward.

6. Be willing to leverage your access, contacts, and resources to help them. If your boy has a business and can afford to hire your protégé, make the introduction. Do what you can to help them gain employment and alleviate financial pressure they may be experiencing. Before you make that introduction, prepare your protégé for success. Review and help them update their résumé. Practice interviewing techniques. Explain the importance of the right appearance for a job interview. Do what you can to enable them to experience what success feels like.

7. Be available. When they call, call them back. When they need you to come to their rescue, come to their rescue. I have an older cousin who lives in Danville, Virginia. When he was eighteen years old, he was sentenced to ten years in prison because he was in a car with a couple of friends who foolishly decided to rob a gas station. Anthony had no intention of robbing anyone; he just happened to be in the car. If he could've called a mentor to take him out of that situation, his life would be completely different. Some of these young folks just need someone to call when they're in need.

Mentoring and inspiring your protégés to pay it forward has a profound, compounding effect. The impact of mentoring one person can grow exponentially into impacting thousands if not millions of others. Therefore, don't allow an inability to give more than 10 percent of your personal income to hold you back from the fulfillment of giving through mentorship and the chance to truly change the world.

GIVING AWAY YOUR WEALTH

Although we can't take it with us when we go, we can still be smart about how we pass our wealth along to minimize taxes and avoid expensive legal issues, so we have more money to create generational wealth and/or to donate to our favorite charities. As you might expect, giving your wealth away has enormous tax and legal implications.

If you fail to create a legal will before you die, you will be considered to have died "intestate" at the moment of your demise. I can hardly think of a greater mistake any wealth builder or family leader can make than to die intestate. If there is no will, whatever you own will go into what's called probate court where a judge will be required to decide what goes to whom. Aside from the considerable legal costs and aggravation that goes along with it, probate court means your dying wishes will be up to someone else's interpretation, and that process alone can take months or years to resolve. What's worse, and this is all too common, family members can end up fighting over what they believe they're entitled to rather than receiving what you've decided to give them. A family at each other's throats is not the kind of legacy you want to leave.

Remember what I said earlier: it's not a question of if, it's a question of when. Therefore it is absolutely imperative that you prepare a proper will—now—either in collaboration with or reviewed by an estate attorney. Not only can they help you plan for the best way to distribute your wealth, they can assist you in creating instruments like trusts or living trusts, which will control and protect your legacy from profligate spending.

Warren Buffett famously said about his own children, "You want to give them just enough money so they feel they can do anything, but not enough so they feel they can do nothing." Obviously you may feel differently about your legacy, and your estate attorney cannot only help you create the distribution you desire, but also do so in the most tax-efficient way.

Here's one small example of how a professional can save you money and steer you in the right direction: the IRS currently allows a person to gift up to $15,000 a year, per person, to family members without any additional tax having to be paid. This is one of the strategies wealthy folks have used for decades while they are alive to save on taxes and pass along their wealth to their families and friends. That $15,000–figure fluctuates regularly, but it doesn't go away. Imagine how much of your legacy and wealth you can pass on over ten or twenty years through this one tactic alone.

Fighting family versus grateful, wealth-building family—I know what I'd choose.

FINDING AN ESTATE PLANNER

Estate planning is a specialty and not all attorneys are experienced in estate planning. You'll need someone specialized to plan and prepare your estate. Start by asking one of your millionaire mentors for a referral, or ask an attorney you trust who they would use to manage their estate. Generational wealth isn't simply about passing on the money. It's more about educating and instilling the right principles, values, and practices in your heirs so they can preserve and grow your family wealth for generations to come. Your responsibility is to educate your children about money and how it works. Watch and monitor how they spend their own money and take advantage of teaching moments to gently prod them in the right direction. And in the spirit of "trust but verify" that we've carried through this book, consult with your estate planner to set up trust accounts that preserve and protect your wealth in the long run and minimize your heirs' ability to squander the nest egg you are leaving them. Rules are the things that prevent chaos.

INTEGRATING YOUR GIVE PLAN TO YOUR M$M MASTER PLAN

Once you've explored how you want to give, and how much of your income you are able to devote to it, create a Give Plan so that it becomes a priority. If you're unable to give 10 percent or more at the onset, or you need to aggressively pay down your debts and increase your income to be able to give later on, you can still make a pledge now to give more when you're better able. Write your Give Plan directly into your M$M Master Plan. List the organizations or persons that you intend to give to regularly and try to spend some time with these organizations to ensure they're using your gift wisely. Insert how much money you pledge to give on a monthly, semiannual, or annual basis for each of the organizations or persons to whom you desire to give. Not only won't you miss that money, but it will also come back tenfold as rich as it has for me and countless others.

Millionaire Money Moves Master Plan

Goals	Age:35 2020		Age:36 2021		Age:37 2022	
Reward Plan (5%)						
Trip to Jamaica				Buy	Done!	
Rolex Watch						
New Mercedes Benz						
Purchase 40' Sunseeker Boat						
Give Plan (10%)						
Church (5%)	$1,406.25	$1,406.25	$1,864.44	$2,154.13	$2,281.70	$2,571.6
United Negro College Fund (2.5%)	$703.13	$703.13	$932.22	$1,077.06	$1,140.85	$1,285
Democratic National (2.5%)	$703.13	$703.13	$932.22	$1,077.06	$1,140.85	$1,285.8

EXECUTE

Creating a plan is one thing, executing your plan is everything. It's so important that it deserves its own subchapter. Now that you've created your Millionaire Money Moves Master Plan, it's time to execute it. At some point in your journey to Destination Millionaire and beyond, life will throw you a curveball or two. The key to handling them is to not allow the unpredictable nature of life to derail you from your journey. There will be setbacks aplenty, like the ones I have experienced and discussed in Chapter 10, but you must always find a way to keep going in spite of them. Here's a methodology for executing your plan that I recommend:

STEP ONE—BREAK DOWN YOUR PLAN

In addition to my Master Plan I create a one-year plan for each year in my Master Plan. This allows me to focus on accomplishing the things I need to make each year a success. At the end of ten successful years, guess where I wind up? At my ten-year goal. You can even go a step further and break your Master Plan into quarterly and monthly goals. This is especially helpful at first, not only for tracking your progress but for building up your morale for the long term as well. Achieving small goals that lead to your larger goals is a lot less overwhelming than looking at what you must accomplish over a seven-year timeline. Mountain climbers epitomize how well this methodology works. Faced with an enormous challenge at the outset, they break each climb into small, achievable steps, which then build confidence as they tick each step off their list until they reach the summit. Any changes in surface or weather conditions along the route are carefully worked into the plan at regular intervals as well. In this way they execute their plans and tweak them for maximum efficiency and risk tolerance.

Millionaire Money Moves
1-Year Plan

2022 Goals						
Category Age	Annual Goal	Beg. Yr. Balance	End of Yr. Planned Balance	End of Yr. Actual Balance	Status	Approach
Reward						
Trip to Jamaica	$0	$0	$0	$0	Completed	
Personal Savings/Investments						
Liquid Cash & Private Equity	$0	$0	$0	$0	Exceeded	
Schwab IRA	$0	$0	$0	$0	Exceeded	
401(K) Savings	$0	$0	$0	$0	Exceeded	
Total	$0	$0	$0	$0	Exceeded	
Debt Pay Down						
Visa	$0	$0	$0	$0	Completed	
MasterCard	$0	$0	$0	$0	Completed	
Auto Loan	$0	$0	$0	$0	Completed	
Student Loans	$0	$0	$0	$0	Completed	
Total	$0	$0	$0	$0	Completed	
Asset Purchases						
House	$0	$0	$0	$0	Failed	
Purchase a 4-Plex	$0	$0	$0	$0	Descoped	
	Annual Goal	Beg. Yr. Balance	End of Yr. Planned Balance	End of Yr. Actual Balance		
Set Back 1 Yr.'s Income Goal	$0	$0	$0	$0	Exceeded	Goal of 12 Mos. Cash Reserves
% of Goals Completed					90%	

In that spirit, I document my results from the previous year every January. As you can see, I note which goals I exceeded, completed, failed to complete, or descoped, meaning removed temporarily from that year's plan. I copy my balances from the previous year over to the beginning balances in the current year. Then I document how much I plan to save in each savings category. That goes under my "annual goal." I then take the sum of my beginning balances plus my annual goal and place that number in the End of Year Planned Balance. In January of the following year, when I update my annual results, I add up the balances from my accounts and place them in the End of Year Actual Balance column. If that sum is greater than my End of Year Planned Balance, meaning I've exceeded my goal, then the status of this goal is highlighted in blue. If the number is equal to my End of Year Planned Balance, meaning I've met my goal, the status is highlighted in green. If the number is less than my End of Year Planned Balance, meaning I've failed to hit my goal, then the status is highlighted in red. If the Goal was Descoped, the status is highlighted in yellow. I use the Approach column to document how I plan on accomplishing my goal in the coming year. Is it through saving $300 per month, saving my tax refund, or taking on a side hustle?

Once I'm done documenting which goals I've exceeded, completed, descoped, or failed to complete, I calculate my completion percentage. My target is 100 percent, although I'm content with completing 85 percent or higher. Remember that whenever a goal is descoped, it gets removed from the total you use to calculate your completion percentage. Any uncompleted tasks get moved into next year's annual plan. That forces me to always keep my goals in plain sight.

STEP TWO—WORK ON ACHIEVING PLAN TASKS AND GOALS EVERY DAY

Achieving goals is tough business. If it were easy, everyone would be millionaires. You have to chip away at your goal every single day because it is impossible to know how much effort and how long it will take to complete the tasks that lead to achieving your goals. There will be rough patches that will stall your progress. There will be unexpected problems that you'll have to create solutions for like finding more capital, getting a seller to agree on your purchase offer, or winning the next deal needed to keep your business afloat. You will lose faith, patience, and confidence along the way. This is why you have to find a way to continue to work on the tasks in your plan daily. Whatever you do, keep moving forward. Take baby steps if you have to, so long as it's a daily routine.

STEP THREE—TRACK YOUR PROGRESS

A guy who worked for my company for five years named Randy Randazzo would always say, "What is measured is treasured. What is inspected is respected." I don't know where he got this saying from, but it has a real ring to it. I recommend measuring and inspecting your progress at short intervals—monthly, quarterly, or biannually—to keep yourself on track and allow yourself ample time to make any necessary adjustments. There are several ways to track your progress as you make Millionaire Money Moves. In addition to making updates to your M$M Master Plan you also need to track your spending against your budget and your net worth growth. There are several tools in the marketplace that you can use to track your progress. Some are free and others charge a small monthly fee.

I personally used excel spreadsheets, however in today's app-centric world, you will find it more efficient to track your net worth using an app on your phone that links to all of your accounts and can provide you with a real-time estimate of your net worth. The leading apps are the same ones I mentioned earlier: Personal Capital, Empower, and so forth.

STEP FOUR—ADJUST YOUR PLAN

As you execute your plan, descope a task or goal whenever it makes better sense to complete it at another time. You can even delete the task or goal altogether if you realize it's no longer required to achieve your endgame goals. For instance, you may have planned to make a large purchase, like a fourplex as you see in the above graph, but based on the performance of your investments the past six months, it seems more prudent to wait and pay off some additional debt first. That fourplex purchase would be marked "descoped" for that particular year. The point is to be flexible if it serves your purpose. Make continual "in-game" adjustments to clear your path to success along your journey.

STEP FIVE—STAY FIRED UP AND COMMITTED

There will be times when your motivation will falter and your focus will drift. That's the way ambition works sometimes. The secret is to adjust, not quit. Never give up on a goal no matter how many years it takes you to complete that goal. Place it on your list for the following year if need be. Don't be so rigid that you make your life miserable. Several of the goals in my plan have taken me many more years to accomplish than I ever thought they would. Heck, this book is a perfect example. It's simply impossible to predict 100 percent of the time how long a goal will take to accomplish. It's impossible because goals are dependent upon other things happening on time as well. If those things get delayed, then our plans get delayed along with them. It happens to everyone and should be seen as simply part of the process and nothing more. If you need encouragement or a quick energy spark, visualize how achieving your goals will make you feel inside and read books and articles about folks who've achieved their dreams. Make sure to surround yourself with people who are getting big things done.

Focus, execute, tweak, repeat.

CHAPTER 8

NAVIGATING OBSTACLES
AND SETBACKS

"Adversity introduces a man to himself."

—**ALONZO MOURNING**, former NBA great

The road to financial success is full of unexpected turns, blind alleyways, and dead ends. Whether they arise in business or in your personal life, the many obstacles and setbacks you will face can and will adversely impact your journey to Destination Millionaire and beyond. The most important thing to remember whenever or wherever these setbacks occur is this: resist the urge to panic and overreact. The solutions always outnumber the problems if you have the patience and initiative to seek them out and give them a chance to work.

Several of the most common difficulties I've witnessed on the road to Destination Millionaire are job loss, divorce, family or personal health problems, large unplanned expenditures, bankruptcy, stock market downturns, prolonged real estate vacancies, and business closure. As you know, I've experienced several of them myself. The easiest solution to most of these issues is to have twelve months of cash reserves in your Setback Fund to protect you until the problem subsides or gets resolved. But not everyone will have that twelve months of cash set aside when adversity strikes. And not every setback will last twelve months or less. So, what can you do if you don't have enough cash at hand to recover from an unexpected setback, or if cash reserves alone won't solve your issue? Luckily, there are many available ways to navigate and overcome obstacles so long as you don't panic and use your feet before you use your head.

Major challenges like a job loss, a serious illness, a foreclosure, or even a collapsed roof—to name but a few—can be financially and emotionally devastating. Unfortunately, people too often give up in the face of them because they either don't know where to look for solutions or they don't believe there are sufficient ones out there to be found. That's one reason—and a big one at that—why there are so few millionaires and so many Million-Nevers.

Before you consider running away from your problems or giving up on them, I want to urge you to take a moment to stand down and search out solutions that you may not see at first. You have a lot more resources available than you think. Remember, nothing is ever as good or bad as it first seems. In difficult moments your mindset (desire, faith, commitment, focus, emotional control, patience, consistency, courage, and grit), and millionaire mentors are pillars that can support you and keep you on the road to your financial goals.

Let's take a deeper look at some of these potential crises as well as possible solutions to keep you on track and headed forward toward greater wealth.

JOB LOSS

Most people can lose their job at anytime, and few of us have contracts guaranteeing a severance to survive on until we find new work. What's more, folks often get laid off even if they haven't done anything wrong, owing to things like position elimination, new management strategies, and so forth. When you're trying to build wealth starting from the bottom, and the bulk of the money you're saving and investing to get to Destination Millionaire is coming from your main hustle, losing your job can seriously derail your plan and devastate your ego to boot. That's why I want to offer a few solid strategies to use in the unfortunate event of a pink slip.

1. GET WORD-OF-MOUTH WORKING IN YOUR FAVOR

Job loss is never easy and no matter the circumstances of your termination, it's hard not to take the whole thing personally. Whether you've been fired or laid off, you'll eventually have to face the disappointment and anger that often go along with losing your job. It's almost impossible not to feel wronged in some way, or worse, to feel as though there's something wrong with you. But rather than allowing yourself to slip into the murky quagmire of the blame game, you can take concrete steps to mitigate the damage of a job loss and open up pathways to new and (frequently) better employment.

In the immediate aftermath of losing your job, you may feel the urge to confront your former boss or manager. Unfortunately, that's essentially guaranteed to get you nowhere and it's also unlikely to do much to restore your damaged pride. Talking badly about your former employer won't help either; no one wants to hire someone they think may make similar complaints about them one day. It's usually best to say to prospective employers something like, "We had a parting of ways," or "We left on good terms" and leave it at that.

When it comes to job loss, you are truly not alone. If you were to interview all the people you've ever known you'd be hard-pressed to find someone with any sort of lasting career who hasn't lost their job at least once. Look no further than someone like Steve Jobs, the founder of Apple Computers, who got fired—get this—from the company *he created*, before returning triumphantly years later to build Apple into one of the most successful tech companies of all time. Think he wasn't furious when they let him go?

Or take the story of my frat brother, Paul, who worked for Southwestern Bell (now AT&T) for twenty-plus years and got hit with a surprise layoff only eighteen months from his pension fully vesting. Imagine how painful that was. Overnight he found himself in a world of hurt through no fault of his own. However, rather than do something rash or foolhardy that might have cost him down the road, he kept his eye on the bigger picture. I asked him about it sometime afterward and he told me, "I cleared a virtual space in my closet and set my pride there. I told myself that I will be back to get you, but I need to get to work reaching out to my network to find my next job."

I think Paul's decision is an example we can all learn from. If you lose your job, move your pride out of your way, at least temporarily, and put together a list of people in your professional network. The folks you've worked with or had business discussions with over the years. Start reaching out to them immediately. Whether you're aware of it or not, you've built a number of valuable relationships at your places of employment, many of which will endure long past this one painful moment. Take time to reach out to those people and see if they'd be open to writing a recommendation for you or keeping their eyes out for any future openings. Out of sight is out of mind, especially in the job world, so keep yourself in the sights of those who may be willing and able to assist you.

You need to minimize the time you think about the job you lost and maximize the time you think of your career as a whole. During this period of transition, keep a notepad or use the voice memo function on your phone to document all the ideas you come up with to improve your situation. When you're calm and at peace is often when the best ideas tend to enter your mind.

You also have a social network of people who you can and should leverage right away. People with whom you go to church, play sports, or serve in the community, as well as the folks you party with or you're connected to on social media. Reach out to them and tell them the news. Initially, you may feel a bit embarrassed but it's important to move past this because people can't help you if they don't know you're in need. Holding it in and trying to act like "this don't happen to me" won't help you solve the problem. You're far more likely to find an opportunity through your existing networks than you are posting your résumé into the black hole of an online employment-site algorithm.

2. ADD A PASSIVE JOB SEARCH OPTION TO YOUR ACTIVE ONE

I know I just referred to online employment sites as "black holes" but that's the way of the world today. So, go ahead and update and post your résumé on all the leading job board sites as a backup. Recruiting firms use sites like LinkedIn, Monster, Dice, ZipRecruiter, and CareerBuilder to comb through candidates they think they can place. Several large companies use these tools to search for talent as well. They can't find you if your résumé isn't posted. And here's a little secret: with a bit of research online or by hiring a career counselor, you can learn how to tailor your résumé and get it past the initial layers of Artificial Intelligence that job sites use to analyze resumés and determine job eligibility before passing them on to the real decision makers. (You didn't think there were *people* reading all those résumés at first, did you?)

Consider posting your résumé on these job sites as a passive way to seek employment but not a primary one. While you're waiting for the email response from a posting, you need to be out hustling for leads from your personal and social networks.

3. LEVERAGE YOUR INTERNAL HR DEPARTMENT

Here's another resource you may not have considered: the HR department of the company that let you go. They may have an internal opportunity elsewhere at the company. As crazy as that sounds, it happens more often than you'd think. Maybe the company is pivoting into different markets and needs to retool new departments with talent who possess specific skills. Perhaps there's an opening in a different office. You may still have to reapply so they can evaluate your skills against the new position, but you will automatically have three things working in your favor: you're familiar with the company's "institutional memory" and culture, you've shown you can be loyal even in the toughest of circumstances, and you're demonstrating professionalism that is greatly prized in the business world. Anyone can be bitter; it's much harder to see the bigger picture and place purpose before pride.

Put yourself forward and be ready to compete. You can use your job loss as a personal challenge to prove to your company that they'll be lucky to have you back.

4. GET YOUR HUSTLE ON AND PUT UP SOME NUMBERS

Let's face it, looking for a job can be overwhelming and depressing. You may not feel comfortable revealing your true feelings about it either, for fear of frightening your family or your kids. The only way you're going to feel better is to restore your hope, and the way to restore hope is by getting out there and talking to prospects. You have to be consistent about it until you get to the yes that puts you back on the payroll. Start by setting a goal each day for the number of resumés you're going to send out, as well as one for the number of HR departments you're going to speak to, and the number of people in your network you're going to call, email, or meet with. Count every single one and keep that list visible throughout the day. Don't worry about finding a job, per se; worry about hitting that goal you set and striving to exceed that goal by at least one per day. Your job right now is finding a job—one of the hardest jobs of all—so your metric needs to be how hard you're working at that, not only what you find as a result. At the same time if you feel you're knocking on the wrong doors and coming up empty, simply reset your targets and continue putting in the work.

5. START YOUR OWN BUSINESS

If all else fails, consider starting a business. You heard me right; that's what former New York City mayor Michael Bloomberg did. He was fired when the company he worked for merged with another one. He wasn't needed anymore. When no one called him back for a new job, he decided to start his own business. Fifty-plus billion dollars of net worth later, guess who's laughing now?

We're all much more resourceful than we think, especially when we connect with the networks we already have in place. My frat brother Paul's network eventually came through for him. He found another job internally and has been at it for several years since. His pension is now safe and secure. He told me that while his network provided him with the opportunity, he learned he also had to be in the right mindset to sell himself and properly showcase his capabilities and skills. He wouldn't have been able to do that holding onto the disappointment and defeat of losing his previous job. When it finally came time to return to his virtual closet and reclaim his pride, he found it not only undamaged, but resurrected by his ability to overcome.

DIVORCE

Some 40–50 percent of first marriages in the United States end in divorce. The divorce rate for subsequent marriages is even higher. If you get divorced after age fifty, studies show that you can expect your household income to drop by about 25 percent if you're a man and 40 percent if you're a woman.[44]

Divorce can be devastating to everyone involved: couples, kids, and in-laws. It's particularly damaging financially when you're trying to build wealth and increase—or at least maintain—your net worth. Arguments over money are widely acknowledged as the leading cause of divorce (even before infidelity), so it's little surprise that splitting up assets in a divorce is difficult and expensive. Depending on the markets you're invested in (stock, real estate, etc.) the timing of your divorce may force you to sell assets when prices are low. This could mean losing out on equity. If you

---

[44] Catherine Fredman, "12 Mistakes to Avoid When Divorcing Over 50," Investopedia, August 30, 2021, https://www.investopedia.com/personal-finance/mistakes-avoid-when-divorcing-over-50/.

were the only one saving for retirement, half of your account balance will likely be split, forcing you to work harder and for longer to prepare for your own retirement. If you're married to a big spender with large credit card debts, you could be on the hook to pay half of the other party's debts. And if you're either the primary breadwinner, a parent, or both, you'll wind up with less available income due to alimony or child support payments.

By now, you may be thinking it's cheaper to keep him or her. You are most certainly right, which is why I recommend you do everything possible to save the marriage if you feel it's right for you and are willing to put in the work to repair and sustain it. But saving the marriage for financial reasons alone won't work in the long run. Therefore, before you choose to divorce and separate your assets, I strongly recommend the following steps:

1. See if you can agree on which of you would be best to manage your finances. Is it you, your spouse, both of you together, or a third-party financial planner who can develop a financial plan that you both agree to and can commit to following? It's sometimes necessary and easier for a couple to follow the advice of a neutral expert you both accept.

2. Make a list of the things you already agree about. It will allow everyone to focus their energy on the things you still need to resolve, and it will help demonstrate that even though you may think you two can't agree about anything (as couples often feel at the time they divorce), in reality, you can.

3. If divorce is inevitable. Avoid costly legal fees by trying one of these two methods:

a. Mediation—In which a professional mediator helps you resolve any differences about how your assets are to be divided (as well as determining issues like child care, alimony, visitation, etc.). All final decisions are reached mutually between you and your spouse.

b. Arbitration—In which you each present your case to a professional arbitrator whose final decision you both agree to abide by.

Fighting it out in court—the third way to settle a divorce—will almost certainly enrich your lawyers while further impoverishing both of you. I speak from experience. I couldn't help thinking how the $100,000 we ended up spending on legal fees could have been better used to fund our kid's college education instead of funding our attorneys' kids' college education. It may be necessary in your circumstances, but given how costly (not to mention antagonistic) it can be, it may benefit you to try one of the other two options first. A licensed mediator or arbitrator is required, like an attorney, to know the laws of the state in which your divorce is being settled.

To stay on track, it's essential you get your divorce terms settled as quickly as you can, pay what the courts or arbitrator/mediator requires, and begin planning how you're going to make up the slack with less income and fewer assets in order to continue building your wealth. Once you officially know your post-divorce obligations, get busy working and paying whatever you are required to pay going forward (alimony, child support, etc.).

I also have a special message for my female readers. Sistas, if you're the spouse who has primary custody of your children in a divorce, then you need to hire a mediator, arbitrator, or lawyer and find out what is actually due to you. I know of too many women who do themselves and their kids an enormous disservice by trying to work out a "side deal" with their husbands or the father of their kids because they're afraid to anger him or engage in a messy, drawn-out court battle. You can't afford to be shortchanged. You must not leave money on the table that's essential to being able to raise your kids. As is, single Black women under thirty-five have a median net worth of approximately $100. You read that correctly: $100.[45] Raising your kids on your own, with one salary or with limited support from your children's father, will only make you and them poor. Divorce hurts women financially more than it does men for this reason, so it's imperative you get all that you're entitled to *by law*.

I often hear Brothas talk about purposely not working hard because they don't want to go to court and be required to pay more child support, or they claim that the mother of their kids is wasting the money they're providing and they don't want to fund her wasteful spending. That's a cop-out that only hurts you and your kids. Children need financial support. If you're not going to be there all the time, at least make sure they have the financial resources in place to live a good life. I know firsthand how unpleasant and difficult paying an ex-spouse can be. I got divorced when my twin boys were seven and my younger son was only five and a half. Their mom and I weren't getting along financially or in any other way, for that matter, and it was an agonizing decision to divorce because I didn't want to leave my boys nor be financially harmed. I was thirty-eight years old with a net worth of about $3 million, and I was scared

---

[45] Emily Moss, Kriston McIntosh, Wendy Edelberg, and Kristen Broady, "The Black-White Wealth Gap Left Black Households More Vulnerable," Brookings, December 8, 2020, https://www.brookings.edu/blog/up-front/2020/12/08/the-black-white-wealth-gap-left-black-households-more-vulnerable/.

I would now have to start all over. But in the end, it was the right choice for me to make.

I looked at my net worth statement, came up with a plan, and focused on growing my business and restoring and building up my net worth while simultaneously providing for my kids. I never missed an alimony or child support payment. Eventually my ex-wife's new boyfriend and his kids moved in with them but I didn't stop sending support checks. I'd be lying if I told you I didn't think about it—*how did I know he wasn't benefiting from the fruits of my labor?* But taking money away from her would ultimately hurt my sons' quality of life, so I forced myself to focus on their needs and disregard all the rest as much as possible. In addition to paying my required child support and alimony, I saved for their college—tuition, books, housing, food, cars, gas, and spending money.

All these years later, two of them have graduated from college with no school debt whatsoever. Our younger son has the money to fund the rest of his college expenses which have grown significantly since it began sitting in his 529 college savings account. I wasn't ordered by a court to pay for my sons' college (and now, graduate school). I elected to because I wanted to make sure they were equipped for success in life. My dad set a precedent by paying for my college so I felt obliged to do the same for my children. I've let them know that they will have to pay for my grandchildren's college when they have kids.

All through my post-divorce life, I've found ways to take nice vacations, treat myself to some "toys" (sport cars, boats, watches, etc.) and purchase an ever-growing number of appreciating assets. My net worth today is significantly higher than the $3 million it was when I needed to divorce. My message is that, if you stay focused and are willing to work hard, you can do both, do right by your children and still do right by yourself.

FAMILY OR PERSONAL HEALTH ISSUE

If you're not financially prepared with a long-term disability plan, funeral insurance, or a treasure chest of cash in the bank, a family or personal health issue can wreak havoc in your life and set your wealth journey back significantly. Not only will the bills pile up; often, your ability to generate income will suffer due to the emotional impact of a health crisis. It's hard to focus and dedicate time and effort into building wealth when a loved one's health takes a sudden turn for the worse or when someone dear to you is on their deathbed; the time and expense to care for them is enormous.

Here are three ways to weather your unexpected healthcare or funeral expenditures and still protect your existing financial gains.

1. Shop around. Doctors are paid based on the services they provide, so it's often useful to get second or third opinions from other capable doctors. Even if the diagnosis is similar, the costs from one facility to another can vary dramatically. You want to make sure that you are properly diagnosed and in the best facility, especially before you begin any invasive or expensive medical treatments.
2. If you don't have a health savings account (HSA) where you've stashed money away for medical emergencies, or if your account balance is not large enough to cover your medical shortage but you have a 401(k) or 403(b) employer retirement plan, reach out to your employer and consider applying for a 401(k) hardship withdrawal. This can save you the 10 percent penalty normally associated with early withdrawals from your 401(k). Believe it or not, it's up to the actual administrator of your plan whether to allow this kind of withdrawal.

3. If you have a whole life insurance policy (as opposed to a term policy), you can potentially borrow money against it at a far lower rate than a credit card loan.

For the loan and withdrawal options I've outlined, it's important you consult with an accountant as well as your life insurance and 401(k) representative to be sure you're aware of any tax, repayment terms, or credit rating repercussions that might be triggered by either of these financial moves.

LARGE UNPLANNED EXPENDITURE

Imagine a scenario like this: you've been saving and investing like mad and managed to squirrel away $10,000 in your Freedom Fund account when all of the sudden the roof on your house starts leaking and needs immediate replacement. Or the government sends you an audit notification and you learn you owe thousands to Uncle Sam in back taxes, penalties, and late fees. Or that trusty old car you've been relying on throws a rod and needs its engine replaced.

Why do these large expenditures always seem to sneak up on us at exactly the wrong time? Honestly no one can say, but sneak up they do, so let's look at how to pay for these types of unplanned expenditures without derailing your wealth-building train while doing so.

1. Can you use your credit card to pay for the expenditure? Paying for unplanned expenditures is one of the main reasons to have a credit card in the first place, so long as you haven't previously used too much of its credit line on expensive, unnecessary purchases. Keep in mind that as your debt amount

increases, your credit score and your net worth will lower until the debt is paid off. So, if you do go the credit card route, treat that balance like an enemy that must be eliminated as soon as feasibly possible.

2. Can you take the money out of your savings account? That may be the simplest solution if it's available to you, though bear in mind that a withdrawal will lower the total value of your assets which in turn lowers your net worth. You may also no longer have cash available if another major emergency occurs, so you'll need to replenish your savings account as soon as the unplanned expenditure is paid off. I try my best not to take money out of my savings account because it tends not to return as easily as it departs. Tapping into your savings account has to be a very last resort because this is the seed money you need to get you to Destination Millionaire.

3. Can you call a friend or family member and ask for an interest-free loan? The savings on interest alone compared to a bank or credit card loan may make this the best option for you. This solution has the added value of not increasing your debt-to-income ratio because banks and credit agencies won't be aware of personal loans from friends. That means your credit score won't be negatively impacted. Like all loans though, a personal one from a friend or family member increases your liabilities, which in turn lowers your net worth. Be sure to pay your friend off quickly so you can count on them (and they on you) in the future should you need to borrow again.

4. If a personal loan isn't an option, can you take out a short-term (one to three years) personal loan with your bank or credit

union? Credit unions are open to allowing members to take out personal loans. The interest rates are reasonable and they are fast and easy to obtain.

5. If you have the money in your 401(k) can you take out a loan from your plan? When you pay the loan back, the interest is paid to you which increases your 401(k) balance. Also, 401(k) loans don't get reported to credit agencies. A word of caution, though: be careful about becoming too reliant on borrowing money from your 401(k). Its purpose is to save enough money to support your retirement needs, not to function like a personal ATM. Be sure to consult your 401(k) administrator or tax accountant before you pursue this route as any withdrawals may be subject to tax implications or penalties.

Do you have (and I hope the answer by now is yes) an investment portfolio at a brokerage house? If so, you can borrow against the funds in your investment account without selling any of your stocks, thus allowing your investments to keep growing. You'll pay the brokerage firm a competitive interest rate and the loan will never appear on your credit report. Your debt-to-income ratio remains unchanged as far as lenders are concerned, and you can pay it back as you would any other type of loan.

If you're lucky enough in the near future to be expecting a salary bonus, tax refund check, insurance or escrow overpayment refund, or a payoff from a personal loan you yourself made to a friend, you can use any of the six options above and pay down your loans or credit card balances quickly when you receive that "bonus" money. But watch out; bonus money is a slippery currency if your money values have not transformed. Since it's technically a "reward," you may feel tempted when you get your hands on it to reward yourself with one or more expensive lifestyle items instead of paying off the balances you've accumulated to cover your unplanned expenditure. Don't fall into that reward trap; it can easily snowball into a series of bad financial decisions that send you back to your starting point. Focus instead on the impact your decisions will have on your overall net worth. (Pay your balances off, and your net worth will go up!)

BANKRUPTCY

There might come a time in your financial life when you decide that filing for bankruptcy may be the only solution to your financial problems. If so, you may be wrong. Bankruptcy has significant negative consequences. It will temporarily ruin your credit rating (though that can be rebuilt) and limit your ability to secure a mortgage down the road. You may have to sell off some of your hard-earned assets for less than they'd be worth in better times. Your bankruptcy may hinder your relationship with your creditors and it won't magically erase all your debts, especially child support or alimony.

I recommend you avoid filing for bankruptcy at all costs. My concern is that you'll never develop willpower or learn anything lasting by not confronting your financial situation head-on. Learn how to navigate these setbacks now and you'll be prepared to handle future setbacks yet to come. Avoidance teaches avoidance, nothing more. Sure, bankruptcy will temporarily wipe your financial slate clean, but you won't have acquired the necessary knowledge to avoid having to file for bankruptcy again (and as it so often occurs, again and again and again).

If instead you take concrete steps to work your way off the precipice of bankruptcy, you will come out stronger and better for it. Start by calling all of your creditors and explaining to them that you're experiencing financial hardship and want to deal with them directly rather than avoid them through bankruptcy. Let them know you appreciate what they did for you by trusting you and offering you credit, and remind them that you have every intention of paying them back. Ask if they can lower the interest rate on your debt or spread out your payments by giving you more time to pay back the loan and get your financial house back in order. You'll be amazed at how willing your creditors are to work with you. Banks and credit card companies understand from experience that people often fall upon hard times. If they never practiced forbearance, or renegotiated the loans they made, they'd run out of customers to loan their money to in no time. Even if you're unable to pay a loan back in full, or at the previously agreed upon rate of interest, your lenders will be glad not to have to write the loan off as a total loss and they will continue to think of you as a trustworthy customer in the future.

My own brother wanted to file for bankruptcy back when he was in over his head. I told him, "Why do that? You borrowed the money; pay it back. You'll learn nothing by avoiding it." To my great and lasting surprise, he listened and took his debt head-on until it was fully paid off. Shortly afterward he purchased his first home and ever since then he's been in full control of his wealth journey. I don't think he would be where he is if he hadn't worked through that difficult time rather than throw in the towel.

STOCK MARKET DOWNTURN

Investing in the stock market has long been one of the fastest ways to get rich. It's also a way you can rapidly lose your shirt, not to mention your life's savings, in the event of a severe market downturn. In the last hundred years alone there were a number of dramatic crashes in the stock market, including the 1927 crash that set off the Great Depression, the internet Bubble which burst at the end of the last century, the 2008 Real Estate Crash that set off the Great Recession, and the Pandemic Downturn of 2020. In all likelihood you too will experience at least one more serious market downturn, perhaps not as severe as the ones I cited above though, even so—to a savvy investor a serious market downturn is often an opportunity disguised as a disaster. What matters is what you do whenever a market "disaster" strikes, and equally important, what you don't do.

It generally takes most folks a number of investments over many years to get rich in the stock market. Many of us also have our 401(k) retirement plans firmly invested in the ups and downs of the stock market through mutual funds. If you're a person nearing retirement, a severe downturn in the market could be potentially devastating. Yet the stock market—like the mythical Phoenix—has risen from its own ashes time and time again. This means that, even when things may look disastrous, the right strategy cannot only help you ride out a cyclical downturn; it can lead to a period of enormous prosperity when the market eventually recovers. Here's what I advise you to do (and not do) whenever the market takes a severe downward turn:

1. Take a chill pill. Sit tight. Start to come up with a short-term mitigation and a long-term strategic investment plan. The worst thing you can do right now is panic and sell everything in your portfolio at a loss. Remember that you don't lose in the market until you sell your stocks for less than what you paid for them. So, if you run off and sell right away, all you'll be doing is

locking in your losses. I understand your desire to mitigate your losses but selling everything as soon as you realize the market is heading south is the wrong strategy. For now, your losses are only on paper, not in cash.

2. Conduct an immediate review of your portfolio. Which of your stocks are worth holding onto? Research the companies in your portfolio and find whatever you can about what's going on with those companies right now. Did something bad happen to your specific companies? Market downturns behave like rushing rivers in that they tend to sweep away "innocent" companies along with them. But just as some boats can handle rushing rivers and emerge unscathed, the same is true of certain stocks. So, you have to read, read, and read some more to determine whether your particular stocks can handle the turbulent financial waters. Listen to and evaluate what the Wall Street experts and economists are saying. Do you have a wealth adviser? If so, have them share their own research about the future prospects of your companies. Do you already have a millionaire mentor savvy in stock investing? If not, read the next chapter where I'll show you how to find a couple. He or she will not only have years of experience with market "booms" and "busts," they may be invested in some of the same stocks as you and may know more about how those companies are doing. Once you've made a thorough analysis, hang on to the stocks you think are temporarily undervalued, buy more of them if you're confident in their eventual comeback, and sell the ones whose futures—based on your research—no longer look promising.

3. Find inexpensive quality stocks and buy them! That may seem counterintuitive, like buying seeds in the midst of a drought, but it's a tried-and-true strategy known as "buying the dip." Naturally you need to hunt for these deals but the hunt will be well worth it in the long term. Even if you have to take some losses in this downturn, there is plenty more time on the clock to make up for your losses over time, by buying temporarily underpriced stocks at a bargain price. For example, when the 2008 crash happened, all the major bank stocks tanked. Within a few years, nearly all of them had not only returned to their previous prices but far exceeded them as well. So, take a deep breath, dust yourself and your portfolio off, and keep investing!

I remember back in 2010 I was invested in the stock of a bank called Washington Mutual. One day the stock doubled and I was flying high. The next evening, I heard on the news that the market was about to take a downturn. I had a flight scheduled to land at 9:30 the next morning, right after the time the market was scheduled to open. Not only couldn't I sell my stock until I landed, by the time I reached my destination, I'd lost nearly all of my investment in the stock. (Washington Mutual eventually collapsed and got sold to JP Morgan Chase.)

Around the same time, Berkshire Hathaway B had split fifty to one, making the new per-share price a more accessible $70 per share. I took the money I had left from my Washington Mutual sale and purchased Berkshire Hathaway B. Eleven years later, I still own that stock only now it's trading at $284 per share. Boy, do I wish I'd purchased a whole lot more of it, as I've learned that, over the long term, you can't lose if you keep fighting and continue investing strategically.

PROLONGED REAL ESTATE VACANCY

Investing in rental properties has a lot of advantages which may be why it is such a popular option for folks seeking financial independence. Rental income is steady, predictable income and long-term appreciation of a rental property is a solid bet as well. Yet despite these and numerous other benefits of buying and leasing properties, there are times when being a landlord is so difficult it can make you wonder why you got into real estate in the first place. The rental market is a fluid one. For instance, tenant vacancies rise when competition from brand new properties with better or more numerous amenities are built within walking distance of your property or properties. Increases in the affordable housing supply or shifts in mortgage rates can lead to higher home ownership (and, consequently, a smaller pool of renters). Severe unpredictable crises such as the COVID-19 pandemic or a plunge in the stock market generate job losses, and thus existing renters may no longer be able to pay their rent (while eviction moratoriums can temporarily disable your one clear recourse to collecting rent again).

Commercial rentals are often even tougher because commercial tenants have remarkably specific needs based on items like foot traffic, proximity to their customer base, overall square footage, and a host of other unique tenancy criteria. Commercial vacancies can easily run into the months or years before the right tenant can be secured.

So what can you do if a prolonged vacancy threatens your wealth-building journey? Here are a few strategies to employ whenever you find yourself either unable to collect rent from your existing tenants or unable to fill your available rental properties with new tenants:

1. Start by checking in with any non-paying tenants and find out what's preventing them from coming up with the rent. Did they

lose their job or suffer some other kind of financial setback? You'll be amazed at how an open dialogue initiated by you can persuade your tenants to be honest with you, which can lead to finding a mutually acceptable solution. Naturally, not everyone will be honest or even willing to meet you part way but the only way to know is to ask them directly, and the sooner you do, the better. You need to be clear about exactly where things stand in order to determine the best way to proceed. Sometimes you can even help a tenant help themselves (which in turn helps you). I once had a tenant who owned a hair salon that had been shuttered by government order due to the pandemic. I suggested she file for a COVID-19 business loan and in the meantime pay me what she could whenever she could. She had a valid issue. I tried to show some understanding and helpfulness, and once she received her loan and her state government allowed salons to reopen, she paid me the balance due in full. Remember, it's a negotiation and the best negotiations are the ones that lead to a win for each party involved.

2. Consider lowering the rent or renting by the hour or day to pop-up vendors. That may sound like anathema to a lot of folks but it's better to have 80 percent of something rather than 100 percent of nothing. Your objective is to do what's necessary to keep yourself afloat until things pick up. In all likelihood, that's what your tenant's goal is too. Even if you have to temporarily bring the rent to a level that covers only your mortgage and operating expenses, you won't miss out on any appreciation of your property and you'll still have the opportunity to raise the rent to market rate in the future.

3. Reach out to your banker and share your situation with them. Don't be shy about it; the bank will already know if you're not paying as regularly as you used to. I find it better to communicate and set expectations accurately. This will increase your credibility with the bank and help you obtain financing from the same bank when you spot your next deal because you'll have proven to be trustworthy even when the going gets tough. Let them know what your tenants—and by extension you— are experiencing. In all likelihood, your banker will temporarily accept 60 percent of your payment (or whatever you're presently capable of paying) rather than nothing. Their desire is to keep you as a customer. Give them a timetable as to when you expect things to return to normal. Ask your bank representative if they would be willing to lower your interest rates. I've had several situations in which the bank adjusted my interest rate for a small fee without me having to refinance my loan. Banks offer this as a courtesy to good customers when interest rates drop significantly, and doing so has no impact whatsoever on your credit score. The last thing they want is to lose you to a competitor bank that offers you a lower rate. If they won't adjust your interest rate, perhaps they'll allow you to refinance the property at a lower rate. They make a few quick bucks and you get the relief you need. It's imperative that you explore all the options available to you because there are far more than you probably realize.

When times turn tough, you have to keep up the fight. It pains me to no end to see the number of African Americans who began building real estate portfolios before the 2006 housing bubble, and then they had to surrender those hard-won assets when the bubble burst in 2008. If only they'd been able to hang on, their property values and net worth would have returned and in almost all cases dramatically increased over time. I was purchasing properties during this time too though I managed to hang on during the 2008 crisis. The payoff was enormous, to say the least. When trouble strikes, you have to fight with everything you have to hold on to your gains. You may not see how you'll get through it yet, but keep fighting and you will eventually find a way.

Sometimes all it takes is your own mistake to trigger a major crisis. If so, the remedy remains the same. I once found myself with a completely empty four-unit property and two-car garage with no one to pay rent. I was on the hook for my full mortgage and all the utilities because I'd realized too late that my heaters and water heaters had been unknowingly damaged in a building flood the previous winter. By the time I learned of the damage, it was winter again and I was unable to provide any heat. My tenants were forced to move out and I didn't have cash reserves for new heaters because I was barely keeping things afloat. What's worse, if I couldn't get the heaters repaired or replaced right away, the pipes would freeze over and burst, causing major flooding throughout the building. Had that occurred, my insurance wouldn't have covered it because I would have known about the situation and failed to act. So, doing nothing was never an option. I had to use my credit card and spend $20,000 to install four new hot water heaters and four new furnaces, plus money for a hotel, gas, and food (the building was three hours from where I lived at the time). To make matters worse, I was looking after my grandfather then and he needed money too. My back was against the wall and I felt horrible, though I hung in there. I tell you, had someone offered me a way out, even with no financial gain to me, I probably would've jumped at it. That's just how bad things can get when you're on the journey to Destination Millionaires. But you have to find a way to keep charging forward. Take one step, then another step. Keep taking steps forward until you're out of your situation. Or as Winston Churchill so eloquently put it, "If you're going through Hell, keep going."

When I emerged from my "Hell," I was eventually able to get things restored and rent out the apartments and the garages. Nowadays I'm making a positive cash flow on the property and I get calls weekly asking if I want to sell the building. I have only three more years before the property is paid off and it's now worth about $2 million. I'm so glad I fought through it. I urge you to find a way to fight through your setbacks. Property that provides income and capital appreciation is worth fighting for.

BUSINESS CLOSURE

Being forced out of business by a recession, a pandemic, a market downturn, or any number of other major crises can happen to anyone, regardless of race. But research has shown time and again that when American business owners get disrupted, Black business owners get disrupted disproportionately harder. Much harder. The COVID-19 pandemic is the most recent case in point. The National Bureau of Economic Research reported that within the first few months of pandemic-related lockdowns, Black business ownership declined by a colossal 41 percent.[46] Our lack of equal access to capital and to key stakeholders due to systemic racism further

---

[46] Michael Sasso, "Black Business Owners' Ranks Collapse by 41% in US Lockdowns," *Bloomberg*, June 8, 2020, https://www.bloomberg.com/news/articles/2020-06-08/black-business-owners -suffer-41-drop-in-covid-19-lockdowns#xj4y7vzkg.

magnifies our tenuous position as business owners. These are precisely the resources that would allow our businesses to stay the course during tough times.

Building a business requires Herculean effort, so before you ever decide to throw in the towel on a business you've worked so hard to build, here are some suggestions to mitigate your circumstances and help you at least construct the building blocks for your next business down the road.

1. Assess your situation carefully and determine the true impact to your business in both the long and the short term. During tough times we're often scared, overwhelmed, and unable to think straight. Try to relax and take time to think long and hard about your situation and your options. Is what you're experiencing a temporary issue or will it impact your business permanently? Would the long-term prospects of your business look strong if you could find a way to make it through this rough patch, or has your market shifted and you need to completely rethink your business plan, target market, or product, and service offerings? The only way to survive is to assess not only the nature of the threat, but its duration as well.

2. Assemble an emotional and/or spiritual support team. Speak with your family, counselor, mentors, and/or religious leader. Let them know what you are going through and what you plan on doing to stay open and keep things going. There is nothing more sustaining than having a support team on your side when your business is falling apart. Your passion and your dreams are at risk of being crushed. Now is not the time to isolate yourself or your worries. As I've said before, people need to know you're

in need in order to be able to help you. Perhaps members of your family can work more or take on a side hustle to help relieve the stress of meeting your family's financial needs while you are navigating a potential business failure. The more pressure you relieve, the more strength you'll have to get things back on track or close them down constructively.

3. Create a game plan designed to keep you afloat and plan conservatively. It's essential you don't underestimate the time or money needed to return your business to normal. Assume your circumstances will require more time and money than you think you need to get the business back to normal. This will provide you with a cushion in the event your estimates are off. When you negotiate with your suppliers, your landlord, your clients, and your staff, plan for an additional 20 percent, 30 percent, or even 50 percent more than you think you need. Come up with a realistic plan and formally document it in writing. Create an impressive presentation, rather than a few thoughts scribbled on a piece of paper. When the people you work with and do business with see an impressive presentation, it will instill confidence. These are the folks whose help you'll need to assist in your recovery. Discuss with them how and when your business will return to normal. Your employees don't want to lose their jobs, your lenders don't want to lose their clients, and your suppliers don't want to lose their customers, so you all have an interest in a temporary sacrifice in exchange for a return to collective prosperity.

4. Once you have the support and the money in place, begin executing your plan immediately. If you have to make some

adjustments along the way, that's fine; in the meantime, every minute counts. Be sure to keep your support team as well as your employees and suppliers informed of your progress. People left in the dark tend to assume the worst.

5. In the end if all else fails and you're forced to go out of business, inform your employees, landlord, clients, and suppliers right away. How you handle this situation will have ramifications long into the future so be gracious and thorough. Business is a relationship game and you should assume the relationships you've made will last for the rest of your time in business. Be responsible and to the extent possible make sure all employees, suppliers, and vendors are paid what they are due. If you can't meet your obligations right away, present them with a plan detailing how and when you will. Do all you can to make the transition smooth for them as well as you. People tend to remember their last encounter with you most vividly. Knowing that you left on good terms and tied your affairs up responsibly and graciously, you can confidently return to those same contacts and ask for their assistance or collaboration once again. One failed business venture doesn't mean you won't be back again. You'll need your network of bankers, customers, business partners, employees, family, and friends next time around. Treat them well and respectfully and they will be there for you whenever you launch your future business(es).

The only failure is the failure to learn. When it comes to navigating obstacles and setbacks in your financial life, humility, rather than hubris, is your most reliable friend. Things won't go perfectly all the time and you will encounter situations where it feels like life has pulled the rug out from under you. That's why it's so important to maintain your cool, use your head, and chip away at whatever obstacles get in your way, no matter how large or small. Most times a setback is nothing more than an opportunity dressed in disguise.

CHAPTER 9

FINDING A
MILLIONAIRE MENTOR

Remember we talked about the hero's journey in movies? The next time you watch a movie I want you to pay particular attention to another aspect of the story you're watching. Not the moral of the story...we've all been trained to figure that one out. This time we're after something different. First, try to identify the main character or hero of the story. I don't care if you're watching *The Lion King* or *Star Wars*; you'll see that the hero in the story will be learning something new about the world they're in and—if the story's any good—they'll learn something valuable about themselves as well. It's a time-honored storytelling convention that goes back to the time of the West African Griots and beyond.

At some point in the story, the hero meets another character who guides them to whatever it is they're seeking—the pot of gold, the buried treasure, the solution to their custody battle, the way home, and so forth. That person is their mentor. Pay close attention and you'll notice that, like Rafiki in *The Lion King*, the mentor character almost always has an indirect way of teaching what they know. Rafiki tells Simba he can either run from the past or learn from it. He could as easily have said, "Hey Simba, go back and reconquer the Kingdom from Scar," but there's a strong narrative reason for his cryptic instruction. It forces the hero, Simba, to discover the lesson for himself rather than have it handed to him on a silver platter. Similarly in *Star Wars*, wise old Yoda doesn't tell Luke Skywalker, "Grab a lightsaber and start kicking some Dark Side behind!" Instead he instructs him to, "Feel the force!"

In real life, your own mentors won't carry a staff or walk around in floor-length robes, and they certainly won't hand you a potion that will magically solve all your problems. They are there to guide you, not carry you, though they can and often do have a transformative power in your life. They have the ability to help you discover and transform yourself, teach you how to find your way out of trouble, and discover your own version of Pride Rock or The Force.

MENTORS, INCLUDING
MILLIONAIRE MENTORS, ARE FOR REAL

My millionaire mentors came into my life mostly through family interactions or introductions from someone who thought they saw something special in me. They could sense how hungry I was for new knowledge and that I was willing to listen and learn in order to get it. Over time, as I was able to crystallize my own vision of what I wanted, I became able to consciously target the type of mentors I needed. At one point in your own wealth-building journey, you may find you need a Rafiki, a mentor who injects you with the confidence you need to get over a particular obstacle. That person for me was a man named Al Glover. At other times you may need a Yoda, an astute experienced business man or woman who can teach you to see the bigger picture. My "Yoda," as you'll soon see, was a doctor named John Schwartz. My mentors ignited my intellect and changed my life and career forever. Just as there are dozens of mentor types in movies and literature, there are a myriad of business, finance, and personal mentor types for your particular moments of inflection and need. It will take you time to recognize who is the right person to offer you the guidance you need, though in all likelihood you already know some of your future mentors. They tend to "hide" in plain sight.

HOW TO IDENTIFY A MENTOR

My first question in deciding whether a person can be a mentor to me is a simple one: "Can I learn from this person?" I don't care if they're younger or older than I, nor should you in your own life. Learning frequently comes from people we least expect and age is no guarantor of wisdom. Being old is not the same as being wise. I find it curious that we're usually not even aware of what exactly we're learning—or that a learning moment is taking place—when a transfer of knowledge occurs. Most times, we only realize it later, in retrospect. That's why I advise you to be open-minded at all times in order to increase your chances of surrounding yourself with the best people for you. And remember, listening is learning; talking is not.

My next question to myself about a potential mentor is this: "Is this person an expert in or well-known for having accomplished something I'm interested in doing?" Sure there are many people outside our fields of interest who have much to teach us, but I think it's important when trying to build wealth that we remain as focused as possible on the specific type of mentorship that will get us to our goals. For example, is this person skilled in real estate, or tax issues, or bond buying? Maybe you want to open your own business; in that case, you'll want to seek out mentors with a strong background in opening and operating a business, preferably in your area and in the industry that interests you.

Once you've moved past these initial questions, ask yourself if the person you're thinking about exhibits the Millionaire Mindset we've discussed. Flashiness is often a sign of recklessness and self-promotion, and although self-promotion isn't necessarily bad per se, you should keep in mind that flashiness does not mean someone is knowledgeable, capable, or wealthy. It means they're flashy.

I like to say that if you surround yourself with three millionaires you will become the fourth. Of course, there's no exact science to this idea except that we are all undoubtedly influenced by our surroundings. It's important for us to realize how strong a role we can have in creating those surroundings for ourselves, which includes who we choose to spend time with. Think about it: I know I'm not going to magically lower my golf score by hanging around with golfers who are more skilled than I am, but I'll damn sure be able to pick up some helpful tips, or find a tactic I can mimic. I can observe how a proper swing or putting stroke is executed. I can listen to others discuss strategy. And if I'm lucky, one of them might even deign to watch me and offer a tip or two. Mentors are always on the lookout for mentees.

What trips up a lot of folks is an incorrect assumption about how mentorship works. In my experience, none of my twelve millionaire mentors (and, yes, I keep count) ever picked up the phone, texted, or sent me an email with an investment idea. Zero out of twelve. Unfortunately, some people expect that, *Now that he's my mentor, he's going to call me, and he's going to tell me what I need to do.* I'm here to tell you that he or she is unlikely to do anything of the sort. It ain't gonna happen if you've chosen your mentors well, that is. Mentoring is about helping people who help themselves. It is not about doing the work for you. Never forget that it's a two-way relationship with your mentor, and the payoff for them is your success. Someone giving you a hot investment tip that you then throw your money at is not mentoring; it's horse trading at best. Perhaps the clearest way to understand the relationship is through the old adage about teaching a person to fish so they can feed themselves for life rather than giving them a fish so they can eat for a day. What's being exchanged between you and your mentor are wisdom and tactics, not facts and figures. Here's another bubble I can burst for you, hopefully before it's ever inflated: your mentors have lives and businesses of their own, and even in retirement they tend to be busy people. They aren't hanging around the phone waiting for you to call. No sir. At times you'll even struggle to get them on the phone to answer your questions.

Every mentor is different and once you learn the particular teaching style of each of your mentors, you'll begin to truly reap the benefits of their assistance. Some mentors are people of few words. I've had some that are people of few *syllables*. A couple who've barely said, "Boo." I think that type of reticence comes from my mentors' desire not to answer my questions but rather to teach me how to think about the problems I encounter in my investing life, which, when you boil it down, is really what you want. To learn to fish. To know the right kind of bait, when to be patient, when to reel the line in, and so forth. Plus a strong mentor recognizes that you have something unique to offer the world and he or she will do what they can to help you to develop your special talent and use it to achieve success. Mentors learn from their protégés as well.

You won't agree with everything your mentor recommends or says about you, but you will need to fundamentally trust them, listen carefully to what they tell you (take notes even), and at least try to do what they recommend even if—or especially if—it goes against everything you've always thought. A little bit of humility goes a long way. Too often people get so busy wanting to disagree with their mentors and show what they know themselves instead of listening and reasoning, "You know what? That guy knows a few things I don't, and he may be able to save me a lot of time, money, and frustration. Let me try it his way, and then later I can try it my way." If you disagree with your mentor, I suggest you say nothing at first. Instead, process how you think you should proceed and then do what you think is right.

THE MENTOR/MENTEE RELATIONSHIP

As you grow successful in achieving your goals, you will almost certainly outgrow some or all of your mentors as well. The same person who helped you get your chain of laundromats bought and financed may not be the person you want to advise you about how to scale your business nationwide. There's nothing wrong with this sort of growth; truthfully, it's an important milestone in your development as an investor.

No matter what stage you're at in your evolution as a wealth builder, you'll need to understand what goes into being a good mentee as well. Sadly, many people want to be mentored but they don't yet acknowledge the work required as a mentee to get what's needed out of their mentors. One of my favorite illustrations of the mentor-mentee relationship is in a movie (well, a movie with about nine sequels) called *The Karate Kid*. In those films, Mr. Miyagi was a sort of oracle, which is exactly what your mentor should be to you. A person for you to float ideas by, or ask questions of. A person who can connect you to people you might not otherwise know or be able to reach. But above all, a person who can help you *when and if* you help yourself. That's job number one for you as a mentee. You need to do the work: make the preliminary calls, do the research, develop your ideas into cohesive strategies, and so on. Being mentored is the process of someone understanding *your* hard work and hard-earned capital and helping you to direct your energies toward a more successful outcome.

So how exactly *should* you work with your mentor? Here are a few critical behavioral rules to observe:

1. Never ask your mentor for money, a loan, or investment capital. They'll lose respect for you and they may assume (even if they won't tell you) that you're trying to shortcut the process and don't want to do the tough work required for success. After all, it's likely that most if not all of your millionaire mentors saved and invested their money to start and grow their businesses. They understand money is a tool not a gift. If you have an idea that moves them and convinces them they'll see a huge return on investment, you won't have to ask because they'll volunteer to invest in it.

2. Get your courage up. It's normal to feel afraid or intimidated by your mentor but now is the time for bravery. Do your research and be prepared to be challenged. Remember, you're not trying to become your mentor; you're working to improve the best version of yourself.

3. Don't expect your mentor to bail you out if you get into hot water. Instead, draw up an exit strategy on your own and run it by your mentor for validation and/or adjustment before you make your problem-solving decision.

4. Be prepared to follow your mentor's advice. Remember, you're not taking a poll. You're seeking wise counsel. Value that counsel and

follow it unless you're absolutely sure it won't work for you. Even then, consider a course of action in which you first try what your mentor is suggesting and hold onto your own idea as a Plan B.

5. Report back regularly to your mentor on your progress or lack thereof. They'll want to know that you're listening to their advice and putting forth the necessary effort. They'll need to see how well you adjust to your circumstances in order to best guide you, and they can't do that constructively without knowing what your scorecard looks like.

I want to share the stories of three of my millionaire mentors and the ways in which they were pivotal to my development as an entrepreneur. Their names are Chuck James III, Dr. John Schwarz, and Tim Weldon. The difference that a millionaire mentor can make to your wealth building and life journeys, as you'll see, is incalculable.

Chuck James became a mentor to me back in my late twenties. Chuck's family started a legendary produce business in 1883 that is one of West Virginia's oldest and most successful African American enterprises. They represent what is often called "old Black money." Chuck's great-grandfather C.H. James started the business in 1883 and then handed it down the line until it reached my mentor C.H. James III two generations later.

I met Chuck and his sons when I was out hitting golf balls one day at the driving range. He took a quick liking to me which soon led to dinners, family get-togethers, and a closer relationship. It helped that we were both "Alphas"; Chuck pledged Alpha Phi Alpha when he attended Morehouse Men's College and Wharton School of Business, continuing a James family tradition.

Chuck was the first person ever to take me to a country club, in this case the Annandale Country Club in Pasadena, California. Man, was I completely wowed, not only by the beauty of the environment but by the kinds of people you could meet with access to a private country club like that and the way things worked. When I first arrived in the locker room, Chuck peeked at my brown polo loafers and said, "Cedric, your shoes can use a little shine. Leave them next to my locker and my guy will take care of them." I was blown away.

Through that connection I eventually met and played golf with John Cushman, of Cushman & Wakefield Real Estate fame. I played golf with the CEO of Sunkist beverages. I can't say for sure if Chuck was the only Black member of the Annandale Country Club back then but let's just say he and I were unlikely to be blending into the foreground anytime soon. I was working at the time as a senior consultant at Deloitte and it was Chuck who first asked me, rather prophetically as it turned out, "Ever thought about going into business for yourself, Cedric? You should consider entrepreneurship."

I had tried a few things before on my own while I was in college and shortly after graduation but I never really got far along with them. Nevertheless, Chuck persisted with his encouragement. Years later, when I decided to take the plunge, leave my consulting job at Ernst & Young, and join that entrepreneurial partnership with the German businessmen, Chuck gave me a piece of advice about my partnership agreement that was so simple it was almost banal, and yet it turned out to be totally profound. He said, "When you make these kinds of agreements, make sure to hire a capable lawyer to review them."

At the time I foolishly believed that my MBA and my business law education were knowledge enough for me to be able to negotiate my own contracts. "Yo, I got this," I used to tell myself. I didn't want to spend the $5,000 necessary to hire an attorney because at the time five grand was a lot of money to me. Five grand for something I could do myself? Well, it turned out that my ego and I were wrong, and Chuck was absolutely right; I needed a lawyer. Luckily, I finally relented and did what Chuck recommended. I'd bet dollars to donuts that the Grand Canyon isn't deep enough to hold all the people in the history of business who either didn't know or ignored that particular piece of advice and suffered the ensuing, often devastating consequences. Think about it: a contract is a legal document the same way that a blueprint is an architectural document, right? Wouldn't you consult an architect to review a blueprint? Of course you would, the same way you'd ask a dentist to look at an X-ray of your teeth. That is their specific area of expertise. That doesn't mean you don't know a thing or two about architecture or dental hygiene, but these guys are experts. In matters of architecture and dentistry—and contracts—we need experts, not amateurs. Nothing could be more obvious.

But for some reason when it comes to business deals, most folks don't bother to have an attorney review their contracts because attorneys are expensive and they almost always find something wrong with your deals, which means you have to pay them even more to fix them. It's a ridiculous paradox when you boil it down; people avoid using lawyers in their business deals because the lawyers do exactly what they're supposed to do, which is protect the person that hired them...you! As comical as that may sound there's nothing funny at all about what can happen if you don't hire an attorney to look your deals over before you sign them. A friendly attorney who you've chosen and vetted can prevent conflicts down the road between you and the parties with whom you've contracted, especially after the so-called "honeymoon" period of a deal is over. Contrast that with an unfriendly attorney who's leading a lawsuit by your partners against you when a deal goes sour because you thought you'd agreed to something that legally you hadn't and now you may be liable for repayment plus damages (not to mention the other party's attorney's fees). Or maybe you thought, as I foolishly used to think, *Yo, I got this.*

There's another point about lawyer review that bears mentioning here. We all like to think we're good negotiators, and in many cases, we are, though most people aren't good at negotiating for themselves. Not *by* themselves...*for* themselves. We have a tendency not to ask for enough because we want to be "nice" or appear friendly. We may have self-esteem issues that get in the way of us properly valuing ourselves in the marketplace. The first time you set up any type of deal, a lawyer can help you to understand what's reasonable to ask for and what type of contingencies to plan for. Items like, "Can I buy my partners out someday, or them me, and if so at what price?" "Should I ask for a three-way split in ownership because there are three of us, or can I negotiate to be considered more than an equal partner?" "Is this a fair deal given industry standards?"

As it turned out I did have a major issue with my German business partners and because I'd hired an attorney to review my contract, I was able to call him for advice. I ended up never signing the agreement, thankfully, because it would have shackled me with a noncompete clause in the agreement that would've prevented me from starting the businesses I own today—a business that has become the primary income source for my personal asset accumulation. The wrong move on my part back then could have entirely derailed my journey to Destination Millionaire and kept me from ever gaining the experience and knowledge I'm sharing in this book. Had it not been for my mentor Chuck James, I might have found myself in a world of hurt. With one simple phrase, he taught me a lesson I've carried with me ever since.

In another life we can all go to law school and pass the bar exam. But for this Earthly go-round, having a lawyer review all our business deals should just be looked at as cheap tuition. And like tuition, it should be considered mandatory.

DR. JOHN SCHWARTZ

Another of my mentors, Dr. John Schwartz, was an unfailingly nice man who used to work out at the same World's Gym as I back in the day. He had a personal trainer there named Donald who knew of my interest in business and who graciously introduced us. I was quickly struck by Dr. Schwartz's business acumen and background and so I asked him if we could maybe meet for breakfast at his favorite restaurant in downtown Pasadena. I thought I could learn a lot about business from a guy like that. Instead, I unexpectedly learned something even more lasting and valuable.

Dr. Schwartz was a psychiatrist in private practice who created CME, a company that provided continuing medical education. He also founded and oversaw *Psychiatric Times* magazine, also under the CME banner. At its height, CME grew to hosting close to 160 psychiatry conferences and seminars across the globe. In 1999, Dr. Schwartz sold these businesses for $111 million and moved on to greener pastures. In spite of his success, however, there had been no smooth sailing for him at first. In a subsequent interview with *Psychiatric News,* Dr. Schwartz confessed that, "For the first seven or eight years, almost all of my income except for the bare amount I needed to feed my family and myself went into subsidizing CME. It took a while to get it right, but we finally learned what we were doing and happily turned it around."

He opened up to me almost immediately and I learned that in addition to all that business success he'd also gone through a nasty divorce and nearly lost everything. So, he'd seen the world from way up and from way down. He learned to rely upon all the millionaire traits we discussed in Chapter 5 until he came to personally embody them. As our friendship deepened, we began to meet more regularly, and one day Dr. Schwartz invited me to breakfast at his house. It was a gorgeous mansion on the south side of Pasadena, in a neighborhood filled with beautiful tree-lined streets and historic houses.

During one of our customary chats about business, I learned through observation that an English Muffin is properly opened by carefully perforating the circumference of the muffin with a fork, rather than slicing it open with a knife as I'd always done. Hey, who knew? I'm not sure I'd attribute that circumnavigating fork maneuver exclusively to membership in wealthy society, though it did make me feel mildly out of place. Years later, when my then-wife and I were invited to Dr. Schwartz's opulent wedding at a private social club on the Cal Tech campus called The Athenaeum, I also learned, in the nick of time, that you don't bring gifts to a rich person's wedding. By that I mean I was able to make a furtive dash from the ceremony entrance back to our car to deposit the crystal picture frame I'd intended to hand to the bride and groom at some point. Phew... embarrassment averted.

Sound trivial? It depends on how you look at it. I mention these non-business moments because I think it's important to always be on the lookout for cultural assets along your wealth-building journey. Culture is a form of capital too, and the sooner you realize you're now in the capital accumulation and retention business, the better. Please don't pay too much attention to the English Muffin thing as I later went back and saw that it says "fork split" right there on the packaging (nice one, Cedric). But do pay attention to the wedding because you'll begin to see that social engagements, such as weddings, tennis and golf outings, Bar and Bat-Mitzvahs, Communions, and so forth are where business is conducted and business knowledge communicated, often as vigorously as it is in offices and boardrooms.

John Schwartz was also the first person who "predicted" that I would become a millionaire. I looked up to him, and as important as his show of faith was to me, his value as a mentor was equally rooted in the brave example he set. Dr. Schwartz had nearly been forced to declare bankruptcy in his own psychiatry practice, a setback he discussed with me candidly and often. I found it inspiring to listen to someone speak so openly of his failure, especially in light of how successful he later became. Failure was a story most people tended to keep quiet. Here was a man who treated it as a building block instead of an obstacle. Huge difference.

If you think about it, failure isn't exactly what stops people. It's really the *fear* of failure that prevents us from taking risks we should, or from giving up when we shouldn't. Fear of failure is a powerful emotion. Years ago, when a person took the driver's license test in California, the state examiner used to hand them a note before the test began, which read, "Relax! Millions of people have already passed this test." The purpose of that piece of paper was to keep them from allowing the fear of failure to overwhelm them. Of course, many still failed, though most regrouped afterward, reviewed their mistakes, tried again, and passed the test.

The same is true in business, folks, and it's a message we should all take to heart. People like John Schwartz—who nearly lost it all but found a way to recover—are living proof that grit and courage will pay off. He's also proof, to me as his mentee, that a mentor who believes in you can make all the difference. His "clairvoyance" about me becoming a millionaire someday was only what he hoped would be a self-fulfilling prophecy. Yet it lit a fire in me and sparked my self-confidence because it meant that John, a successful millionaire, had seen something in me. For that alone I'm profoundly grateful. Ever since then I've developed a simple formula for self-confidence which is this: whatever enhances it, use it. Whatever doesn't, disregard it. The world is full of people and circumstances that will be happy to tear you down. So, take care to use only the things that build your confidence. That doesn't mean you should be tin-eared or oblivious to constructive criticism or self-improvement. But whatever helps you to believe in yourself is worth hanging onto and repeating to yourself as often as necessary. The road to Destination Millionaire is often a lonely one. You have to be your own biggest cheerleader at all times, no matter how your deals are going. Self-confidence is essential to wealth building because without it you risk not even trying, and if you don't try, you can't possibly succeed. John Schwartz showed me that in both word and deed.

TIM WELDON

I had a neighbor in Oakland, an African American guy named Tim Weldon. Tim would zip around in his Porsche convertible looking like the happiest man alive. And who could blame him? He owned his office building in downtown Oakland, plus a successful government contracting business. But what you really need to know about Tim is: this cat was dead serious about his money and building wealth. When I met Tim, he was phasing out his business because he was extremely well-invested in real estate and the stock market. His primary residence in Oakland and his vacation home in Naples, Florida, were both paid off in full and his money was making money for him. Tim's wife also had it going on; she retired from the federal government after thirty years and continued to earn 80 percent of her ending salary. Tim was transitioning to retirement back then and we'd sometimes spend time together going to dinner, hanging out, playing golf, and talking at our country club (which I joined, thanks to Chuck James having introduced me to the benefits of country club life). What I unexpectedly came to love about him was what a hard-ass he was! He was raised without a father in his life, in Baltimore. He went to Morgan State University, a historically Black university, for his undergraduate work and then on to Cornell for his graduate studies. When I say he was a hard-ass what I mean is he didn't waste time with people. There's a biblical admonition that says roughly, "Ye shall not cast pearls to swine." [47] Let's just say that Tim possessed pearl upon pearl of business wisdom and that treasure chest of knowledge came along with a swine detector as sharp as a butcher knife. Try actin' a fool around Tim Weldon and trust me, your acting career would be over in a matter of seconds. What I also found interesting about Tim was that he liked nice cars, exotic vacations, and dressing well. He and his wife always had solid money values and health values. Now in their seventies, they continue to eat right, exercise religiously, look incredible, and make Millionaire Money Moves.

Fortunately, Tim took a liking to me and generously shared his business advice, including one admonition that changed my business forever. I had already established my consulting company, which worked with large commercial companies, generating about $5 million annually, but

---

[47] Matthew 7:6.

Tim suggested I look into doing business with the federal government in addition to the private sector work I was doing. My initial reaction was to say, "But Tim, I hear the pay is low and slow." He assured me it was worthwhile in terms of volume and his advice turned out to be spot-on. Remember what I said earlier about trying out your mentor's suggestion before rejecting it out of hand? Well today, with some $90 million in annual revenue from government contracts in my business, I see how smart I was to have listened. What was in it back then for Tim? Nothing but the pleasure of helping a young, Black, less-experienced businessman find a new path to success.

There are people out there like that who have pure intentions. They're not trying to make any money off you. They're just paying it forward and their payoff is seeing their guidance bear fruit for you, hopefully encouraging you to pay some of that forward and help the next person seeking your advice once you've made it. To this day, Tim still challenges me about how I'm managing my money. He'll say things like, "By now, you should have 'X' million dollars piled away," or, "You'll need 'Y' million dollars before you can call it quits." It's funny how, every time I see him, his numbers for me are always higher than the numbers I set for myself. Maybe he senses that, with my competitive nature, I'll inevitably wind up striving toward his higher number. When a mentee rises to a challenge, the end result is always growth.

Knowledge is a form of capital, fellow capitalists, and there is knowledge and battle-tested wisdom out there in droves for those who are open to learning it. Simply reading this book shows that you're ready to consider someone else's viewpoint so consider this a good start, even if you don't agree with all of what I say. My job is to make you a bit uncomfortable, help you recognize what may be getting in your way, and teach you where to turn for the knowledge that may someday make all the difference in your financial life, whether it comes from me or someone else.

Now that you've read these few examples of how powerfully a mentor can change the course of a wealth-building journey, try these steps to begin finding your own millionaire mentors:

1. Make a list of friends and relatives in your social circle, investors, or people who run their own businesses or manage someone else's. If you don't think they're the right mentor for you, or if they're not open or available to mentoring, ask them if they can refer you to someone else. You'll recall that I met my first mentor, Gus Martin, through my Uncle A.J. As you seek your mentors, remember that a little bit of humility goes a long way, so be humble and show gratitude for whatever they can offer.

2. Attend a charitable gala or Chamber of Commerce meeting or event. Your next millionaire mentor may not be in your immediate social circle. Is there a 100 Black Men chapter in your area? What about graduate chapter sorority or fraternity organizations? Many millionaires play golf or tennis for leisure but also for the networking opportunities they provide. You don't need to take up either sport but you can always look out for charitable golf events and choose to attend one.

3. Sign up for a talk or book signing by a successful entrepreneur, or participate in a conference about wealth, real estate, or business in your community (check your library, your house of worship, and your local community events calendars to find one). Bring a business card or have your electronic business card with your contact information easily accessible on your phone. At

an appropriate moment, briefly introduce yourself and let the entrepreneur know your background, what you do, and what you desire to do. Let them know that you're looking to be mentored, and would it be all right to ask them a few questions at a more convenient time (and have the nature of those questions prepared and ready in case they inquire further). Invite them to coffee, breakfast, or lunch, whatever you can afford because you'll be picking up the check. If you invite someone out, do not allow them to pay the check. Your potential millionaire mentor will recognize this as a sign that you're not ready for the big leagues and it could prevent them from introducing you to their valuable contacts who could help you.

4. Sign up for an online class taught by someone you think could be a good mentor for you. Many online education platforms, such as Masterclass, allow for contact between instructors and their students.

5. Once you begin the mentor-mentee relationship, be patient and consistent. Set a monthly or quarterly reminder to touch base with your mentor. Don't overdo it. If they don't respond to you right away, keep your cool and understand that your mentor may be busy and not have time to meet with you or talk with you every week. Gently keep at it and eventually they will respond. The best way to encourage them to stay in touch is by sharing your progress, sending them a thank-you note for their advice, and letting them know the impact it had because your success is a victory for them as well as you. So, be sure to send them an email or text to quickly thank and update them on your progress. It may even prompt them to reach out and

congratulate you. Mentors love to hear that they were helpful, so it's important that you keep them informed. Pay attention to what your mentor is looking to accomplish in their business and if you have contacts or information that may be of use to them, share it with them. A relationship is a two-way street; you must also find ways to give back. Even if your information is not helpful, your mentor will appreciate your attempt at providing value to them.

Finally, be open, be humble, and be diligent in your search. Before you even realize it your network of millionaire mentors will already have begun to take shape for now and for the future ahead. Look for mentors from all races and backgrounds. Good information has no color. I've had the pleasure of being mentored by many Black, White, Jewish, and Hispanic mentors, among others. Your mentors may have a different ethnic background; the point is that a diverse set of mentors will provide you valuable information from varying perspectives. You can learn from anyone knowledgeable, experienced, and willing to help, regardless of their age, race, or religion.

CHAPTER 10

ONE CAN DO WHAT ANOTHER ONE CAN DO

"I thought, 'If they could do it, so can I.'
Now I want people to say, 'If Robert Smith can do it,
I can do that and more.'"

—ROBERT F. SMITH,
African American billionaire

As I peered through the tiny "Door of No Return" at Elmina Castle on the Cape Coast outside of Accra, Ghana, I could only imagine the terror faced by our African ancestors at the dawn of slavery. They were captured without warning, shackled in dark stone rooms like the one I looked into now, stripped of their dignity and all that was familiar—home, family, belongings, language, and religion—and mercilessly thrust into a life of brutal, demeaning servitude over six thousand nautical miles away. The ten million or so able enough to survive the murderous ocean crossing faced a lifetime of rape, beatings, cruelty, and exploitation of their labor for the sole purpose of creating wealth for their White slave masters. I couldn't actually see the past by standing here, but I could feel its echo resonating inside me.

The level of cruelty our forefathers and mothers endured was almost too much to bear. It was as though they'd become invisible as human beings, people who were husbands, wives, children, and grandparents. Neighbors who laughed and broke bread together, friends who loved, married, and helped each other through difficult times. Families who celebrated the births of children and mourned the loss of elders as a community. All of that stolen, negated, commodified. The sheer savagery of slavery extended into even the tiniest details of everyday life; it required total destruction of life as our ancestors knew it. An all-out obliteration of their thriving societies down to the bone. Human beings on slave ships callously tossed overboard to certain death. Communities and bloodlines destroyed. Dreams of the future eviscerated at gunpoint or the tip of a sword. Unspeakable violations of women and children. Loved ones separated, never to see or hear from each other again. And then, there was the psychological torture, millions upon millions of tormented moments spent waiting—in stone rooms, in ship galleys, on the porches of southern plantations—waiting in terror for a sign from God, praying for an escape route from this incessant, waking nightmare.

As I stared through the opening of that tiny door in Africa, I began to understand the story of our enslavement less as a historical abstraction and more like the living, breathing, terrifying psychological wound it was, a tragic combination of depravity and indifference to suffering, all at our expense. It set me to wonder how many generations of our children across the centuries had been robbed of the chance to express their individual brilliance and potential. Of the innumerable crimes perpetuated in the name of slavery, perhaps that had been the most tragic of all.

One thing history teaches us is that hatred doesn't die the way an organism does; instead, when it loses its outlets and is left untreated, it tends to lie dormant and await new openings through which to emerge once more. In our case that transition was almost immediate. Even our hard-won freedom failed to liberate us from the shackles of a determined oppressor. Only in the updated version, the killing and stealing would be done largely at the point of a pen.

After we finally emerged from 400 years of bondage, in spite of our own blood sacrifice, we found ourselves facing a "new and improved" odyssey to endure. Even though slavery was outlawed throughout the land, and freedom and prosperity were promised to all of its victims, a string of unrealized pledges that began with forty acres and a mule quickly revealed themselves for what they truly were. Mirages. Pipe dreams. Skulduggery. What came to fruition in their places were new forms of persecution like economic slavery, housing slavery, opportunity slavery, and incarceration slavery. In many respects, slavery hadn't truly ended; instead, it evolved into newly deceptive, more "socially palatable" forms. For instance, we would be allowed to work the fields as sharecroppers, as my grandfather and father did, but we'd be earning barely enough to feed our families and not nearly enough for the majority of us to buy land, start a business, or meaningfully catch up to the White population who had so forcefully kept us behind. We would only be permitted to purchase property and live in neighborhoods specifically designed to restrict Blacks to certain areas. And so on and so on.

In the century that followed, this form of ghettoization morphed into the practice of segregation through redlining, which artificially kept housing values low in Black neighborhoods and high in White ones, again making it nearly impossible for us to build wealth. And yet we endured. And yet we triumphed. And yet somehow we learned not only to overcome but also to thrive in spite of the roadblocks intentionally set in our way.

The strides we have made in this country as individuals and as a community are truly astonishing. When you view our accomplishments in the context of the adversity we've faced and in so many ways continue to face, they're downright miraculous. Most of what we've achieved we've had to do ourselves because whenever a door of opportunity would open, it inevitably slammed shut long before many of us could get through it— often while we were still standing in the doorway. We've seen far too many demonstrations of opportunity—token opportunity, if you will—rather than true opportunities to make up for the deficit we started with through no fault of our own.

Our ancestors began their lives here stolen from their homelands, tortured in unspeakably brutal bondage for centuries, and instructed never to trust anyone but their so-called masters. This last element is one which I believe had one of the most lasting, severe, and least-recognized impacts of all. For us to change our financial futures, I believe we need to learn to trust, revere, and help each other again. Think about it. Big business relies on partnerships between banks, investors, and corporations that are mostly controlled by White men. Immigrant communities are famous for pooling their money and resources together to help their fellow immigrant businessmen and women raise enough capital to start and grow their businesses. The Jewish community, for one, has successfully done this for millennia despite the traumas of the Spanish Inquisition and the Holocaust. The only true advantage any of these communities have on us is that, notwithstanding the huge head start of the White Anglo community, they've done a better job figuring out how to build together and trust each other. I feel as though we still struggle with that. No one's any smarter or harder-working than we are, that's for sure. If anything these other cohorts may be more focused on the long-term future of their entire communities, and more trusting of each other.

Trust. It's a powerful sentiment and it's no accident that when we leave money to our heirs we frequently use a financial instrument called a trust. Do you recall my early mentor. Mr. Glover helping me with my phone bill all those years ago? That was all about trust, along with a long-term view of our community and my eventual place in it. For we African Americans it's about helping each other. Not to the exclusion of other ethnicities. What I'm talking about is *inclusion* that begins at home. Remember that quote from Arthur Ashe at the beginning of the section called "Plan?" "Start where you are. Use what you have. Do what you can." We have what it takes. We need to learn how to work better together and have each other's backs when it comes to building our individual and community wealth. Look at some of the amazing examples we have to learn from.

Alonzo Herndon was born a slave in Georgia in 1858. Though his family was emancipated seven years later, he still grew up homeless, illiterate, and destitute. He worked as a sharecropper along with the rest of his family, while on his own time he sold everything from peanuts to axle grease to scratch out a living. Most notably, he began to set aside a portion of his earnings as savings to be invested later on.

Herndon learned to be a barber and opened his first barbershop in 1878, right in the thick of Jim Crow Georgia. As he honed his craft, he began purchasing an interest in existing barbershops and opening more of his own. By 1904 he had three thriving barbershops that he owned outright, plus a solid clientele who included many of the state's leading politicians and businessmen. As Herndon's businesses and earnings grew further, he began purchasing real estate.

In 1905 Herndon bought a failing mutual aid association and created from its ashes the Atlanta Mutual Insurance Association, which eventually became the Atlanta Life Insurance Corporation. Under his stewardship, its assets grew from an estimated $5,000 to a whopping $400,000 seventeen years later, an eightyfold increase. The company expanded to several other states and began reinsuring Black-owned businesses against losses and—when possible—merging faltering companies into Atlantic Life.[48]

What about the amazing success of Robert Reed Church? He worked as a riverboat slave for his father who owned the steamships. You read that correctly. White Daddy was not too keen on recognizing his own Black child. Their boat was commandeered by Rebel soldiers in the war, forcing young Church to work for the Confederacy. After a battle near Memphis, he jumped ship and swam downriver. Eventually he found his dad, who showed affection even though he refused to acknowledge their shared lineage. The younger Church made money in bars and pool halls (where he was nearly killed during a race riot in Memphis) and later bought and refurbished distressed real estate, much of it abandoned after a yellow fever epidemic in 1878. He eventually opened a bank called the Solvent Savings Bank & Trust Company and became the richest and most powerful man in Memphis.

One of the first, if not *the* first self-made Black millionaires in this

---

[48] Alexa Benson Henderson, "Alonzo Herndon." *New Georgia Encyclopedia*, July 14, 2020, https://www.georgiaencyclopedia.org/articles/business-economy/alonzo-herndon -1858-1927.

country was Madam C.J. Walker, a.k.a. Sarah Breedlove. Born in 1867 on a Louisiana plantation where her parents had been enslaved in the antebellum South, Sarah worked the cotton fields of the Mississippi Delta starting at age seven. By fourteen she was married, and at seventeen she gave birth to a daughter named Lelia. Three years later, she became widowed and moved to St. Louis to work alongside her brothers who'd become barbers. As fate would have it, Sarah began suffering from *alopecia areata,* a scalp condition that caused her to lose most of her hair. She tried a number of available remedies, including homemade ones created by a Black entrepreneur named Annie Malone.

A few years past the turn of the century, Sarah moved to Denver to work as a sales agent for Malone, and it was there that she married a newspaperman named Charles Joseph ("C.J.") Walker and founded her own scalp-treatment products business. She changed her name to "Madam" C.J. Walker and began selling her products by crisscrossing door-to-door through the Southern and Southeastern US. Eventually she opened Lelia College in Pittsburgh to train workers in her burgeoning hair-care business. In 1910 she set down new roots in Indianapolis where she built hair and manicure salons, another training school, and even a factory.

Shortly after her arrival in Indianapolis, Madam Walker contributed $1,000 to the building fund of the local "colored" YMCA. It was the first of many philanthropical gestures she made, which were soon followed by political contributions to anti-lynching organizations, among many others. Madam Walker became a millionaire starting from the bottom, and left a magnificent and exemplary legacy of giving in her wake.

One of the most remarkable stories in our history belongs to Mary Ellen Pleasant. She was born in the early-nineteenth century, long before Emancipation. Whether or not she was born into slavery is not clear though it's known that she grew up without an education, working as a domestic in New England and eventually as a tailor's apprentice. Her most important work, though, was on the Underground Railroad, where she helped to liberate and shelter untold numbers of fleeing slaves. Pleasant married a man named James Smith who left her an estate worth tens of thousands of dollars when he died a few years after they were married.

Do you recall at the beginning of the book I asked what you would do if by some chance you did come into money unexpectedly? Well, here's what Mary Ellen Pleasant did.

She continued her liberation work and eventually made her way to New Orleans where she learned to cook. When the California Gold Rush took flight in the mid-1800s, Pleasant saw a unique opportunity for herself to travel to the West Coast and cook for all the Black prospectors there. Not only was she able to demand top dollar for her services, she later got a job as a live-in domestic with a wealthy family. She cleverly invested her money based on conversations she overheard from the wealthy men she would serve in the home where she worked. Outside her day job, she continued helping fellow African Americans by connecting them to legal resources, finding them employment, assisting them in setting up businesses, and facilitating travel to safer, non-slaveholding states. At the same time, Pleasant opened and invested in her own businesses, including a livery stable, a dairy farm, and a money-lending operation. Eventually she co-founded the Bank of California and became the principal financier of the Abolitionist John Brown's insurrection at Harper's Ferry (donating more than $800,000 in today's dollars to the cause). By 1875, together with a business partner named Thomas Bell, Pleasant had amassed a fortune in excess of $30 million—the equivalent of almost $700 million in today's dollars!

As impressive as these stories are, I think we can be equally inspired by a far humbler rags-to-riches story. It's the story of a man named Earl Crawley, and it's a story that continues into the present day.

Earl Crawley worked for over forty years as a parking attendant in Baltimore.[49] As of 2021, he's comfortably retired, with his house paid off and a huge stock portfolio that he continues to reinvest. His story too, is a remarkable one though perhaps not in the way you might expect. No movie star tipped him a thousand bucks. Nobody gave him Bitcoin on his birthday. Nobody offered him a higher-paying job. Instead, Earl worked from the bottom up, saving and investing his income carefully and consistently, knowing he only had one path to financial freedom. His first investment was $25 in a mutual fund. He continued investing $25 a month (an average of about a dollar a day in savings) for the next fifteen years. Never much of a reader due to dyslexia, Earl took Arthur Ashe's advice to heart and simply used what he had and did what he could. Since the parking lot where he worked was in a financial district, he began asking investment-related questions of some of the people who came to park their cars. He then started investing what he could in the stock market, blue-chip companies he'd heard of like John Deere and IBM. He diligently reinvested all the dividends they paid in order to compound his profits as his stock portfolio slowly expanded and increased in value over time. Since his salary never exceeded $12 an hour, he also worked side jobs to put his three children through private parochial school. As of this writing, he's sitting on upward of $1 million—*a million dollars*—with his house paid off, a thriving stock portfolio, no debt to speak of, and all his expenses paid by the dividends

---

[49] "How Earl Crawley Saved Up $500,000 While Making $12/Hour," *The Minority Mindset*, February 16, 2018, https://theminoritymindset.com/blog/wealth-12-hour-earl-crawley/.

his stock investments earn. All those assets work for a man named Earl Crawley instead of him having to work for them.

So, if societal or governmental changes are what's necessary for us to thrive, then how do we explain someone like Mary Ellen Pleasant or Earl Crawley prospering like they did? How do we explain Alonzo Herndon amassing a personal fortune at the turn of the nineteenth century or Robert Reed Church, who assembled a banking fortune in that same era? In a country still structured against Black advancement as ours is today, how could someone like Robert F. Smith (estimated net worth as of 2021: $6 billion), have become a billionaire? Or David Steward, the founder of World Wide Technology (estimated net worth as of 2021: $3.7 billion). One could easily argue that times have changed; after all, we've had a Black president, a Black Vice President, Black legislators, and Black judges at all levels of government. The short and easy answer is that there are exceptions to every rule. After all, you can't keep an entire population down, right? While this may be somewhat true, I think it drastically misses the point. The lineage from Alonzo Herndon, Robert Reed Church, and Mary Ellen Pleasant to Robert Smith, Jay-Z, Oprah, Tyler Perry, Earl Crawley, and a host of today's millionaires and billionaires in our community goes far beyond their shared race or some kind of lucky break. The common path to wealth for these enterprising Black people was the same when they were coming up as it is today: securities, real estate, entrepreneurship, and alternative investments. What they had in common wasn't exceptionalism; it was all the traits of the Millionaire Mindset you read about in Chapter 5: Desire, Faith, Courage, Grit, Consistency, Patience, Emotional Control, and so on. How else can we explain their ability to amass the money they needed to start their businesses, purchase real estate, or build their lasting legacies? Imagine the intensity of racism many of them endured. These determined souls began by leveraging the income they received working as domestics, field workers, or artists, and they lived below their means so that they could save as much money as possible to fund their futures. They all made significant sacrifices in order to build the capital needed to fund their businesses given the limited financial resources available to them. They literally had to save their pennies with nearly all of their money allocated toward the sole purpose of achieving Destination Millionaire, starting from the absolute bottom. Even worse for our earliest economic trailblazers like Alonzo Herndon, Robert Reed Church, and Mary Ellen Pleasant, they had to secretly stash money away for their businesses because money could so easily be taken away from African Americans with little explanation or recourse. On top of that, they had to do all their sales and marketing on their own. Back then there was no internet or social media to spread the word about a business venture, or products, or service offerings. There was no Amazon to sell products across state lines or internationally. There was no nationwide market research to identify where demand for your product would be highest. Instead, these Black financial pioneers traveled far and wide to open up operations in different states in order to expand their brands and their wealth. In spite of all the challenges they faced, they found a way to thrive and even pay it forward. They created training programs to uplift others in our community. They taught other Black folks how to budget, build their own businesses, and become financially independent. They saw to it that their personal rising tide lifted up their fellow African Americans' boats as well.

Despite the hopeless circumstances of slavery, extreme racism, discrimination, and oppression, our ancestors found ways to build wealth. From the ashes of chattel slavery they became owners of restaurants, land, clubs, lending institutions, manufacturing companies, and software companies.

They proved that brutal conditions and disadvantaged circumstances cannot and will not stop a person from achieving what they insist on having. The world around us can make things more difficult, impede progress, or lessen the magnitude of our success, but circumstances on their own cannot and will not stop us from achieving Destination Millionaire and beyond. Our millionaires and billionaires have proven over and over that the churning currents of success run richly through our blood.

What then is the difference between these incredible Black success stories and you? Far, far less than you think. They all started from the bottom or at most from modest beginnings. They all experienced life challenges and major setbacks in their journeys. Alonzo Herndon and Robert Reed Church were born into slavery. Mary Ellen Pleasant's mother disappeared when she was a child. Oprah was born into poverty. Shawn Carter grew up in the Marcy Housing Projects of Bed-Stuy before anyone ever called him Jay-Z. Tyler Perry was homeless. Robert F. Smith was the child of school teachers. Yet what they all had in common was a determination to achieve their goals and a willingness to transform their money values and wealth-building behaviors in order to do so. They all developed the Millionaire Mindset, adopted millionaire values, and made Millionaire Money Moves. That blueprint hasn't changed nor will it change. These multi-millionaires and billionaires are proof that nothing can stop you when you refuse to quit. They are proof that the sky and your mindset are your only limits when you decide to fight through adversity, learn from it, and prevail. "The System" or "The Man" can never win against a Black man or Black woman with the right mindset and the right money values who's executing a carefully planned wealth-building system.

We are achieving Destination Millionaire and beyond even in today's tumultuous times.

My own journey has been twenty-four years in the making. Like most of us, I had to start from the bottom. Although I was able to officially declare Destination Millionaire after seven years of focus and effort, it has taken me a full twenty-two years to achieve my endgame goal and position myself to live life on my terms and to pursue my dream of inspiring others to do the same. In the previous chapters, I've shared several of the significant setbacks I've faced along the way: the near collapse of my business, prolonged vacancies in my investment properties, and my own divorce, to name but a few. Trust me, they are a small sample of the numerous and unpredictable hurdles I've run into in my quest to build wealth and reach my endgame. I've endured days and weeks and months in which I wanted to quit so badly I could think of nothing else. It got so tough at one point that If I could have escaped my situation and moved on in life as someone else's employee, I would've gladly taken the job. Despite all the planning and sacrifices I'd made, there were so many times I thought I would never get to my destination. My financial obligations were so severe I wanted to give up. But I couldn't because I knew the only way I could ever dig myself out would be through the significant earning potential of my business.

Among the things that sustained me through my worst moments of despair was a secret I discovered on my own. I found that, if I changed my surroundings, I could change what was going on inside of me. If I looked far and wide for inspiration, I could find enough of it to carry me through until my external circumstances changed for the better. I began to understand that there was never a problem that didn't have enough of a solution to at least keep me going forward. Bit by bit, I found sustenance in positive-themed books, in my mentors, and in the tales of those who came before me and succeeded. I found it in the new friends I made who shared similar dreams, challenges, and determination. I learned that not only does misery loves company—optimism does too.

You can do it. You owe it to yourself and the world.

I know what it feels like to have a vision and desire for wealth—a thriving business and a luxurious lifestyle—and to lack the capital and resources to make those dreams a reality. I know how disheartening it feels to watch others living their best life while you're struggling. It's really not about the money, the cars, the clothes, the houses, and the vacations. What I think we truly desire and envy is the peaceful freedom to live our lives the way we desire to live them and the opportunity to contribute our talent and creativity to the world. Are you a talented cake maker who never had the money or the courage to start your own bakery? Maybe you're a clothing designer good enough for the top fashion houses of New York and Paris. Maybe you're an app developer using your creativity to enrich someone else instead of yourself. Whatever your unreleased talents, you owe it to yourself to liberate them and put them toward your own wealth journey. You have what it takes. Our ancestors' blood runs through your veins.

Today I'm living my financial dream and spending my time as I had planned all those years ago, doing the things that excite and inspire me the most. My hope is to encourage you to live your best life on your terms and to contribute to making the world a better place. I am living proof that living life on your terms and achieving Destination Millionaire and beyond starting from the bottom is achievable.

I'd like to see more Black people live their lives to the fullest and offer the world their creative ideas, talents, and legacies. I understand that many of you have a job and a career that may feel like all you can handle. You may have kids who you have to send to college and who need things (and more things!). You have rent, mortgages, car payments, credit card debts, and other expenses. Those are the circumstances of your life; however, they are not an economic prison sentence. I want you to develop the Millionaire Mindset, Millionaire Values and Behaviors, and make Millionaire Money Moves in order to build wealth and still be able to "do you." Refuse to accept the status quo of living your one and only life to fulfill the dreams and purposes of some other millionaire. Start by creating a five-year, ten-year, fifteen-year or twenty-year M$M Master Plan and flip the script in your favor.

Yes, despite significant economic progress over the past decades, the statistics clearly demonstrate that Black Americans are still experiencing far worse economic conditions as a whole than Whites or other racial and ethnic groups. We're not where we ought to be, though thank God we're not where we used to be either.

Our world has been deprived of too many of the gifts and talents that reside within African Americans. Life's circumstances are preventing too many Black men and women from showcasing their tremendous genius, aptitude, and dreams because of racism, discrimination, and oppression. Yet as much as we may look outward, all too often our mindset, money values, and behaviors, and money moves are what's really keeping us in bondage. My message is a simple one: don't let the power of racism, discrimination, and oppression suppress your talents, gifts, and dreams. Don't allow a lack of faith, confidence, or courage to get in your way. Don't permit a lack of access to capital, business relationships, and opportunities stop you from getting to Destination Millionaire and beyond. Always remember that you too can make it happen even if you're starting from the bottom like so many others. You are not alone.

One of my all-time favorite movie scenes happens toward the climax of a film called, *The Edge*, starring Anthony Hopkins and Alec Baldwin.

It's the story of two rivals, a billionaire tycoon (played by Hopkins) and a photographer (Baldwin), unexpectedly stuck together in the wilderness at the mercy of a gigantic and vicious bear. After several attempts to evade the bear, Hopkins's character comes to the conclusion that their only chance of survival is to build wooden spears and summon the immense courage needed to confront and kill the bear. But it's clear Baldwin's character doesn't believe they can do it. In order to convince him to go along with the plan, Hopkins's character forces Baldwin's character to say over and over, louder and louder, "I'm gonna kill the bear," until he's screaming it at the top of his lungs. Hopkins's character then changes the chant, again at full volume, to "What one man can do, another can do!" It's a remarkable scene, even in a movie, because it shows how the power of persuading yourself that something is achievable can break open the doors to a possibility you never even imagined existed. I get goosebumps every time I see this scene because I imagine how it would feel being stuck in the wilderness with your life on the line having to face the very thing you're afraid of that's been haunting you, knowing that your peace and freedom is dependent upon your doing what seems to be impossible. In moments like this the only thing that can give you hope is knowing that if one man or woman has done it, it's conceivable that you can do it too. In many ways that bear scene is a metaphor for our community's financial situation today. For too long in the life of every Black person in America, there's been a gigantic, vicious bear called racism, discrimination, and oppression stripping us of our peace and freedom, trying to keep us down and destroy our dreams of economic and social prosperity. The question has always been this: what are we going to do about it? We can keep hoping the bear goes home, or has a change of heart, or we can choose to stand up to it and fight it the way an African warrior would—courageously, strategically, relentlessly, and by using the foundations for success built for us by our ancestors. I'm reminded of a phrase uttered by the US Open tennis champion Naomi Osaka right before she played in the finals. When asked what she thought of her chances of winning, she said, "I would like to thank my ancestors because, every time I remember their blood runs through my veins, I am reminded that I cannot lose."

Let's begin to trust and believe that we cannot lose. Achieving Destination Millionaire and beyond is well within our abilities and our heritage. You have what it takes. You are the descendant of the strongest African warriors who survived the treacherous journey to this country, and that same bloodline is alive and churning within you. Tap into it. Tap into the same critical elements of success—faith, desire, courage, emotional control, grit, confidence, consistency, patience—that our ancestors did to survive and prosper. Change your outcomes by transforming your money values and behaviors until you too achieve Destination Millionaire and beyond. And whenever you get weary, as we all do along our journey, remember the words of Robert F. Smith and know that what one can do, another can do.

It's only a matter of time.

CHAPTER 11

WHAT ARE YOU GONNA DO ABOUT IT ON MONDAY MORNING?

The late comedian and activist Dick Gregory used to always say, "We've got a big job and not much time." He knew well that change—be it societal or personal—comes the instant you take the first step, that moment you finally push aside your doubts and fears and tell yourself, *I am going to make this happen no matter what, and no matter how long it takes.* This is true of your financial future. The moment you get started is the moment you will be well on your way.

It's time to tie all of the concepts discussed in the book together and put them into action. Use this checklist, and if ever you need a refresher, refer back to the chapters and sections that support each step.

Always remember that one can do what another one can. That "one" is you, my friend. Good luck and Godspeed.

THE MILLIONAIRE MONEY MOVES ROADMAP

Action Item	Task	Chapter Reference	Done
Create Your M$M Playbook			
Step 1.	**Determine Your Current Net Worth** • Calculate and document your current net worth (the sum of your assets minus the sum of your liabilities).	Chapter 3	
Step 2.	**Determine Your Wealth Aspirations** • Determine and write down your "what," your "why," and your "where." Paint a clear vision of your endgame.	Chapter 4	
Step 3.	**Identify the Right Path(s) for You** • Explore how you will get to Destination Millionaire, by investing in securities, real estate, entrepreneurship, alternative investments, or a combination of all four paths.	Chapter 4	
Step 4.	**Prepare for Your Journey** • Begin the Millionaire Mindset and millionaire values transformation process. • Assemble your M$M Money Team (an accountant, a lawyer, millionaire mentors, and a circle of friends driven by the same desire to reach Destination Millionaire and beyond).	Chapter 6 Chapters 5, 6, 9	
Step 5.	**Depart for Destination Millionaire** (Make Millionaire Money Moves) **Plan** • Document your starting point (start date, age, net worth, Freedom Fund account balances, income for life sources and income amounts, debt level). • Define and document your desired endgame (endgame date, age, net worth, Freedom Fund account balance goal, income for life sources and amounts, debt level).	Chapter 7.1 Chapter 7.1	

• Determine your path[s] to Destination Millionaire and beyond [securities, real estate, entrepreneurship, and/or alternative investments].	Chapter 7.1	
• Create a budget (M$M Power Budget).	Chapter 7.1	
• Chart your five-to-ten-year net worth growth plan.	Chapter 7.1	
• Establish your five-to-ten-year M$M Master Plan. Update your M$M Master Plan monthly, quarterly, and annually.	Chapter 7.1	
• Evaluate and revise your M$M Master Plan every five years.	Chapter 7.1	
Earn		
• Determine how and when you will create additional income streams [and by what amounts] for your M&M Master Plan through your main hustle [job promotion, overtime, career change, etc.], side hustle, and investment hustle [stock dividends, alternative investment income, rental income, or business income].	Chapter 7.1	
• Add your detailed Earn plan to your M&M Master Plan.	Chapter 7.2	
Save		
• Create a Setback savings account, and save 3 percent of your income in it.	Chapter 7.2	
• Open a M$M Freedom Fund investment account, and save 22 percent of your income in it [401(k), IRA, after-tax investment account, etc.].	Chapter 7.3	
• Make savings deposits automatic.	Chapter 7.3	
• Earn more and pay less until you can save and invest 30 percent of your income.	Chapter 7.3	
• Add your Save plan to your M$M Master Plan.	Chapter 7.3	
Pay		
• Establish a 45 percent ceiling on what you pay to others in order to have more money to save and invest.	Chapter 7.4	

		• Optimize how much you pay by minimizing how much of your income you pay out to others.	Chapter 7.4
		• Create a fast and efficient debt pay-down plan using the snowball or avalanche approach.	Chapter 7.4
		• Add your Pay plan to your M$M Master Plan.	Chapter 7.4
		Consume	
		• Calculate how much of your income you currently consume, and create a plan to monitor and limit consumption spending to 15 percent of your income.	Chapter 7.5
		• Add your Consume plan to your M$M Master Plan.	Chapter 7.5
		Invest	
		• Earmark 22–27 percent of your income to fund your investments in securities (401(k), IRA, after-tax investments, etc.), entrepreneurship, real estate, and alternative investments.	Chapter 7.6
		• Add your Invest plan to your M$M Master Plan.	Chapter 7.6
		Reward	
		• Put away 5 percent of your income to fund your Reward account.	Chapter 7.7
		• Design a personal incentives list tied to milestones in your M$M Master Plan (to be updated after the first five years).	Chapter 7.7
		• Add your Reward plan to your M$M Master Plan.	Chapter 7.7
		Give	
		• Give 10 percent to your faith-based organization, favorite charity, political affiliates, or friends and family. If you can't afford 10 percent, give what you can, even if it's your time.	Chapter 7.8
		• Add your Give plan to your M$M Master Plan.	Chapter 7.8
		Execute	
		• Execute your M$M Master Plan.	Chapter 7.9

Step 6.	• Continue making Millionaire Money Moves until you achieve Destination Millionaire and beyond!		

ACKNOWLEDGEMENTS

To Michael Solomon, my ghostwriter, you were well worth the wait. Thank you for your patience and for turning my 1,000 page written thoughts into a masterpiece. You masterfully captured the essence of my message.

I'd also like to thank the following people who were instrumental in helping with this book:

My big brother John Nash Jr. for always telling me the truth even when I don't want to hear it.

Dawn Bell for putting up with having to listen to all my arguments and ideas, and always reminding me to keep my solutions simple and relatable.

Kathleen Jacobs for doing everything for me with style and grace.

Rick Wheeler for being my sounding board and a dear friend.

Ken Arthur for your spreadsheet and web support.

The late Carl Wallace, for introducing me to Mr. Bruce and for the countless hours in your office talking about my dreams and aspirations during my college years.

Gus Martin, Al Glover, the late Gilbert D. Bruce, Robert Taylor, Robert Morgan, Tim Weldon, Dr. John Schwartz, Frank Tucker, Chuck James III, Major Riddick and Rob Heisel for being my millionaire mentors who helped me become the successful businessman I am and who continue to shape my mindset and money values.

John Short and Sheila McBride, for giving me my first major business contract, which kicked off this awesome journey. I cannot thank you enough.

Prosper & Roberta Osei-Wusu my Ghanaian best friends who critically read my book and kept me inspired.

Vance McGhee and Baxter Barber for being available to answer any questions that I had about mortgage lending rules.

Lew Baker, my company 401(k) advisor for being a good friend, reviewer of this work, and steadfast listener to my passionate rants about how our community needs to learn how to build wealth.

Ted Petito my company CFO who's always been supportive and does whatever I need to have done.

June Findlay, my personal lawyer and dear friend who's always had my back.

Patricia Byrd and Ian Partman who have debated with me for years about this book, helped sharpen my arguments, and always made sure that I considered the folks in our community who were dealt a more challenging hand.

David Gardner, co-founder of *The Motley Fool* for being an incredible friend and committed supporter of making black wealth accessible.

Angela Yee, for being so nice, so easy to work with, and a great spokesperson for our community about wealth building.

Larry Quinlan my dear friend and personal financial enthusiast who kept me sharp and connected.

Nathan Thomas my graphic artist who rendered my graphic models and as a white guy is always truly down for equality and the cause.

Kenneth Carter one of my protégés who has argued with and challenged me to the point of reshaping my thinking on issues of financial inequality.

Paul O'Sullivan my frat brother and long-standing friend who allowed me to use our college day's stories in this book.

Rhonda Stinson Nash for raising such wonderful human beings, which allowed me the space and time to do this work.

Gwen Nash for your random thoughts and prayer text messages.

Shenee Gibbons for your inspiration and for several buckets of Red Vines licorice to keep me energized.

Vennard Wright, I cannot thank you enough, for being a great client, connector, and little brother.

James Hill for being a solid influencer, social media mentor, and promoter.

Jey Price and Brianna Yarbrough for creating and building my social media presence for the book.

Derek Chase, my photographer, for making me look ten years younger.

Nick Nelson, "The Brandprenuer" for being my brand ambassador and sounding board.

Smith Publicity and Pubvendo for pouring your hearts into my passion and helping me expand my vision and reach.

Finally yet importantly, to those whose helping hand had a significant impact on my journey and I have failed to mention, please accept my heartfelt apology and thank you for being there for me.